MODERNISM, FEMINISM, AND JEWISHNESS

Modernism, Feminism, and Jewishness explores the aesthetic and political roles performed by Jewish characters in women's fiction between the World Wars. Focusing mainly on British modernism, it argues that female authors enlist a multifaceted vision of Jewishness to help them shape fictions that are thematically daring and formally experimental. Maren Linett analyzes the meanings and motifs that Djuna Barnes, Jean Rhys, Dorothy Richardson, Sylvia Townsend Warner, and Virginia Woolf associate with Jewishness. The writers' simultaneous identification with and distancing from Jews produced complex portrayals in which Jews serve at times as models for the authors' art, and at times as foils against which their writing is defined. By examining the political and literary power of semitic discourse for these key women authors, Linett fills a significant gap in the account of the cultural and literary forces that shaped modernism.

MAREN TOVA LINETT is Assistant Professor of English at Purdue University.

MODERNISM, FEMINISM, AND JEWISHNESS

MAREN TOVA LINETT

CAMBRIDGE UNIVERSITY PRESS
Cambridge, New York, Melbourne, Madrid, Cape Town, Singapore, São Paulo, Delhi

Cambridge University Press
The Edinburgh Building, Cambridge CB2 8RU, UK

Published in the United States of America by Cambridge University Press, New York

www.cambridge.org
Information on this title: www.cambridge.org/9780521880978

© Maren Tova Linett 2007

This publication is in copyright. Subject to statutory exception
and to the provisions of relevant collective licensing agreements,
no reproduction of any part may take place without
the written permission of Cambridge University Press.

First published 2007

Printed in the United Kingdom at the University Press, Cambridge

A catalogue record for this publication is available from the British Library

ISBN 978-0-521-88097-8 hardback

Cambridge University Press has no responsibility for the persistence or
accuracy of URLs for external or third-party internet websites referred to
in this publication, and does not guarantee that any content on such
websites is, or will remain, accurate or appropriate.

For Dominic and Ruth

Contents

Acknowledgments	*page viii*
List of abbreviations	x
Introduction: imagined Jews and the shape of feminist modernism	1
1 "Strip each statement of its money motive": Jews and the ideal of disinterested art in Warner, Rhys, and Woolf	32
2 Transformations of supersessionism in Woolf and Richardson	60
3 Adding bathrooms, fomenting revolutions: modernity and Jewishness in Woolf and Warner	80
4 The race must go on: gender, Jewishness, and racial continuity in Barnes and Richardson	111
5 The "No time region": time, trauma, and Jewishness in Barnes and Rhys	140
6 Metatextual Jewishness: shaping feminist modernism	173
Notes	190
Works cited	216
Index	227

Acknowledgments

In its first incarnation this study benefited from the excellent guidance of my teachers at the University of Michigan. George Bornstein, Todd Endelman, Jonathan Freedman, Anita Norich, Suzanne Raitt, and John Whittier-Ferguson generously shared their extensive knowledge. Suzanne Raitt provided a stimulating introduction to women's modernism. The rigor of Anita Norich's thinking and teaching served as a model for me as I moved from teaching assistant to scholar and professor. And John Whittier-Ferguson continues to inspire my academic work with his nuanced scholarship and dedicated mentoring. While at Michigan I was fortunate to work with Bryan Cheyette, who was visiting for a semester; his groundbreaking work forms a foundation for my own. I am also grateful for the friendship and academic support of Seunghee Ha, John Ramsburgh, and Elizabeth Yellen.

At St. Cloud State University, Judy Dorn, Debra Gold, Chris Gordon, Steve Klepetar, Jeff Mullins, and Suzanne Ross provided much-appreciated advice and encouragement as the project changed shape. At Purdue I am grateful to Emily Allen, Kristina Bross, John Duvall, Minrose Gwin, Margaret Rowe, Aparajita Sagar, and Jennifer William for moral and practical support and for incisive readings. Emily Allen and Jennifer William in particular have given much time and energy to read the manuscript and offer helpful advice. I would also like to thank Amy Feinstein and Miranda Hickman for their friendship, valuable comments on my work, and enthusiasm for things modernist.

At Michigan my dissertation work was supported by grants from the Mellon Foundation, the Rackham Graduate School, the Department of English, and the Marshall Weinberg Prize for Excellence in Judaic Studies. My later work on Jean Rhys's manuscripts, especially material for chapter 5, was enabled by research at the Department of Special Collections, McFarlin Library, University of Tulsa. I am grateful to St. Cloud State University for the funds to carry out that research, and for an additional summer Faculty Research Grant. Finally, I was able to rework my dissertation into this very different book thanks in large part to a junior research leave from the Department of English at Purdue and a Purdue Research Foundation Grant. I am grateful for all these forms of support. I am also indebted to A. Delignat for his kind help with the cover image by Simon Segal. Finally, I want to thank the wonderful team of editors at Cambridge University Press: Joanna Breeze, Ray Ryan, Maartje Scheltens, and my copyeditor Libby Willis.

Some of this material has been published elsewhere. Parts of chapters 2 and 4 appeared in "'The Wrong Material': Gender and Jewishness in Dorothy Richardson's *Pilgrimage*," *The Journal of Modern Literature* 23.2 (Winter 1999–2000), 191–208. Material from chapters 1 and 2 appeared in "The Jew in the Bath: Imperiled Imagination in Woolf's *The Years*," *Modern Fiction Studies* 48.2 (Summer 2002), 341–361. And part of the argument of chapter 5 appeared as "'New Words, New Everything': Fragmentation and Trauma in Jean Rhys," *Twentieth Century Literature* 51.4 (Winter, 2005), 437–466.

My family has been consistently supportive of my academic work, and I would like to thank them here. My father David Linett and his spouse Penny Linett have conveyed their pride and support at all stages of this work. My brother Peter Linett, his spouse Cheryl Slover-Linett, and their amazing daughters Amelia and Sophie have enthusiastically shared my trials and successes. Peter and Cheryl have also read sections of this book and offered insightful comments. My mother Deena Linett has been unstinting in her encouragement, energy, and time; she, too, has read portions of this book as it unfolded over the years, and given valuable feedback. I am deeply grateful for her support. Finally, I want to thank Dominic Naughton for his devotion to our family and for believing not only that I could complete this project, but that it would be worthwhile. I dedicate this book to him, and to our daughter Ruth, who makes everything sparkle.

Abbreviations

References to these sources will be given parenthetically in the text.

BTA	Woolf, Virginia. *Between the Acts*. New York: Harcourt Brace & Company, 1969.
Diary	Woolf, Virginia. *The Diary of Virginia Woolf*. Ed. Anne Olivier Bell. 5 vols. New York: Harcourt Brace Jovanovich, 1977.
GM, M	Rhys, Jean. *Good Morning, Midnight*. New York: W. W. Norton, 2000.
Letters	Woolf, Virginia. *The Letters of Virginia Woolf*. Ed. Nigel Nicolson and Joanne Trautmann. 7 vols. New York: Harcourt Brace Jovanovich, 1978.
N	Barnes, Djuna. *Nightwood*. New York: New Directions, 1961.
Pargiters	Woolf, Virginia. *The Pargiters*. The Virginia Woolf Manuscripts from the Henry W. and Albert A. Berg Collections of the New York Public Library, Woodbridge, CT, 1993.
P	Richardson, Dorothy. *Pilgrimage*. 4 vols: J. M. Dent & Sons, 1967.
Room	Woolf, Virginia. *A Room of One's Own*. 1929. New York: Harcourt Brace Jovanovich, 1981.
SWS	Warner, Sylvia Townsend. *Summer Will Show*. London: Virago Press, 1994.
TG	Woolf, Virginia. *Three Guineas*. New York: Harcourt Brace & Company, 1966.
V	Rhys, Jean. *Voyage in the Dark*. New York: W. W. Norton, 1982.

W	Richardson, Dorothy. *Windows on Modernism: Selected Letters of Dorothy Richardson*. Ed. Gloria Fromm. Athens, GA: University of Georgia Press, 1995.
Years	Woolf, Virginia. *The Years*. New York: Harcourt Brace & Company, 1965.

Introduction: imagined Jews and the shape of feminist modernism

In Virginia Woolf's *The Years* (1937), Eleanor Pargiter describes her philanthropic work with a poor Jewish family, the Levys. She tells her younger sister Milly that "'Mrs. Levy had her rent ready, for a wonder.... Lily helps her. Lily's got a job at a tailor's in Shoreditch. She came in all covered with pearls and things. They do love finery, Jews'" (*Years* 31). Eleanor's description trades in mild turn-of-the-century stereotypes: the Jewish daughter works for a tailor; she dutifully contributes to the rent; and she ostentatiously displays what little wealth she has. But the stereotypes are uninteresting compared with Milly's response to her sister's narrative. "'Jews?' said Milly. She seemed to consider the taste of the Jews; and then to dismiss it." With this response Woolf's text leaves the mundane level of stereotype and presents a compelling moment of half-expressed meaning. Milly knows the Levys are Jews; she has heard about them before. But she nevertheless responds to Eleanor's generalization by repeating the word "Jews" interrogatively. Considering "the taste of the Jews" may literally mean considering Jews' taste in "finery." But Milly also seems to be considering the taste of the word or category "Jews." The text hints here that there is something more to consider than Eleanor's vacuous generalization: some intrinsic quality of Jewness, its *essence* in the sense of an extract, a concentrated form of a scent or flavor.[1] This suggestion that Jewishness has a unique "taste" can be viewed as a blueprint for modernist representations of Jewishness. Modernist authors employ stereotypes, but they use them as ingredients within a more diffuse and mysterious Jewishness, a Jewishness that then serves as a device for shaping their fictions on both thematic and metatextual levels.

The Jews of this study are fictional not only in the sense that they live only within works of the imagination, but also because their Jewishness is a result of the authors' vexed imaginings of what Jews are or could be. The title of this introduction gestures toward this doubly fictional status of literary Jews, with a nod to Alain Finkielkraut, whose *The Imaginary Jew* (1983) explores the disjunction between post- and pre-Holocaust Jewish identities.[2] Finkielkraut maintains that contemporary understandings of prewar European Jewry are so suffused with nostalgia as to cast real doubt upon the links postwar Jews feel to their imaginings of prewar Jewish life. Although the representations of Jewishness I focus on in this study are themselves prewar (or more accurately interwar), they, too, are steeped in an atmosphere of otherness. The characters I consider are not ordinary, or simply stereotyped, European Jews, but instead are saturated with meaning. They are exotic or romantic or eerily powerful; they are weighted with pathos and laden with history; they have a peculiar "taste."

The word "imagined" as opposed to "imaginary," however, stresses the process by which authors imagine characters as integral parts of their creative projects. They may not understand or intend all of the ways in which the characters will function within their novels, but they intervene in existing antisemitic discourses to position their Jewish characters in ways congruent with both their imaginings of what Jewishness is and their own modernist aims. *Modernism, Feminism, and Jewishness* explores the aesthetic and political work performed by Jewish characters in women's fiction between the World Wars. Focusing mainly on British modernism, it argues that key authors enlist a multifaceted vision of Jewishness to help them shape fictions that are thematically daring and formally experimental. Analyzing the varied meanings and motifs that Djuna Barnes (1892–1982), Jean Rhys (1890–1979), Dorothy Richardson (1873–1957), Sylvia Townsend Warner (1893–1978), and Virginia Woolf (1882–1941) associate with Jewishness, this study explores how the authors use Jewishness to create a modernism they touted as feminist and spiritual in comparison with fiction by their male "materialist" counterparts.[3]

These writers see in their Jewish characters reflections of their own emotional pain and alienation from literary history. But at the same time, most of them accept cultural images of Jews bound up with biological, financial, patriarchal, and material forces – forces they wanted to exclude from their feminist modernism. This simultaneous identification and distancing produced a fascinatingly complex set of portrayals, in which a Jew is sometimes a model for the author's art, and sometimes a foil against which her writing must be defined. Taken together, their representations define the contours of interwar Anglo-American allosemitism.

"Allosemitism" is a term invented by Artur Sandauer and brought into contemporary Jewish studies by the sociologist Zygmunt Bauman.[4] It refuses the binary of philosemitism and antisemitism – phenomena which so often bleed into one another – and emphasizes instead the ways in which Jews are made other regardless of the ostensible level of approval. This othering, of course, is a process independent of the behavior of actual Jews. In a study of antisemitism published in English in 1936, Hugo Valentin pointed out something of which we still need to be reminded:

> The view widely prevalent in Jewish and non-Jewish circles that by acting in this way or that the Jews might have been able to avert anti-Semitism is based on an illusion. For it is not the Jews who are hated, but an imaginary image of them, which is confounded with the reality, and the Jews' actual "faults" play a very unimportant part in the matter.[5]

Such imaginary targets of antipathy are considered by Slavoj Žižek when he applies Lacanian psychoanalysis to ideology, and more specifically to hatred. In his essay "'I Hear You with My Eyes'; or, the Invisible Master," Žižek first compares antisemitism to the castration complex and to the Name of the Father:

> I know that castration is not an actual threat, that it will not really occur, yet I am nonetheless haunted by its prospect. And the same goes for the figure of the "conceptual Jew": it doesn't exist (as part of our experience of social reality), but for that reason I fear him even more – in short, *the very nonexistence of the Jew in reality functions as the main argument for anti-Semitism* . . .
>
> A homology imposes itself here between the "conceptual Jew" and the 'Name of the Father' . . . Is the gap that separates effective Jews from the phantasmatic figure of "conceptual Jew" not of the same nature as the gap that separates the empirical, always deficient person of the father from the Name of the Father, from his symbolic mandate?[6]

But Žižek proceeds to reject the analogy, not because a similar split does not obtain between living and conceptual Jews as between real and imagined threats of castration or the empirical and imagined father, but because "the two splits [between knowledge and belief] are of a fundamentally different nature." In the case of the father, his authority comes from his assumption of "a transcendent symbolic agency" of which he is the visible embodiment. The "conceptual Jew," however, must be invisible, "irradiating a phantomlike, spectral omnipotence." He concludes, "In short, the difference between the Name of the Father and the 'conceptual Jew' is that between symbolic *fiction* and phantasmatic *specter.*"⁷ The antisemite's Jew, then, is more than fictional: he is a phantasm. The Jews of feminist modernism hover in the space between the fictional and the phantasmatic. They are, like other characters, more or less developed, more or less "fully realized" (as Richardson would have it); and yet their effects, their roles in contributing to the narrative a mysterious "taste," often surpass the fictional and intrude into the realm of fantasy. Žižek's discussion reminds us that the otherness of modernism's Jews, though based in comparatively tangible differences of nation, gender, and temporality, also gathers to itself a more inscrutable aura, incommensurate with those differences.

The simplest way the Jews of feminist modernism are othered is along the axis of nationality: very few of them are English. With the exception of Woolf, who leaves us to assume that the Jews in *The Years* and *Between the Acts* (1941) are English (though foreignness clings to them nevertheless), modernist women authors mostly create Jews who are immigrants from Central and Eastern Europe and who therefore justifiably retain an atmosphere of foreignness. But as Bauman argues, allosemitism cannot be reduced to xenophobia or heterophobia:

I propose that the proper generic phenomenon of which the resentfulness of Jews is a part is *proteophobia*, not *heterophobia*; the apprehension and vexation related not to something or someone disquieting through otherness and unfamiliarity, but to something or someone that does not fit the structure of the orderly world, does not fall easily into any of the established categories . . . and in the result blurs the borderlines which ought to be kept watertight.⁸

This sense that Jews blur boundaries permeates modernist literature by both male and female authors. Ezra Pound complains of just this problem in Canto XLV, having firmly associated usury with Jews in the Cantos as well as in his critical writings: "with usura the line grows thick / with usura there is no clear demarcation."⁹ Maud Ellmann suggests that T. S. Eliot's antisemitism, too, is related to his wish for fixity: "The Jews, for Eliot, represent the adulteration of traditions severed from their living speech and native soil." Ellmann argues that "by banishing free-thinking Jews from his utopia, [Eliot] was attempting to banish from himself the forces of displacement."¹⁰ Wyndham Lewis makes clear his similar distaste for slipperiness in a diatribe against what he calls the "time school," a group of writers and thinkers he associates with Jews and Jewishness. In *Time and Western Man* (1927), Lewis writes that he has a "propensity for the exactly-defined . . . and the concrete" and a repugnance for "surging ecstatic featureless chaos."¹¹ When he criticizes James Joyce for being a member of the "time" group – romantic, childlike, overly psychological – he is careful to point out that it is only accidentally that he has written a "time book"; it cannot be ascribed to his racial origins. Nevertheless, "Mr. Joyce is very strictly of the school of Bergson-Einstein, Stein-Proust."[12] Lewis favors literature that he aligns with different racial categories: "I prefer the chaste wisdom of the Chinese or the Greek, to that hot, tawny brand of superlative fanaticism coming from the parched deserts of the Ancient East, with its ineradicable abstractness."[13]

Like Lewis's chaotic Eastern Jews, the Jews of feminist modernism cross more boundaries than those of national identity. They also fail to fit properly into categories of race, class, gender, and even religion. As this study demonstrates, they signal multiple boundary-confusions: poor workers paradoxically suggest greed, young people are burdened with history, the "ancient race" conjures both timelessness and modernity, and Jewish male characters are feminized.

Money, of course, is the element allosemitic discourse most commonly associates with Jews, and modernist fiction is not above linking Jews with financial matters and materiality. The authors studied here, though, do not usually portray wealthy Jews. Rather, they imagine poor Jews who are nevertheless metaphorically associated with money. Unlike Edith Wharton's Simon Rosedale in *The House of Mirth* (1905), whose vast wealth enables him to buy his way into high society, the Jews in the novels I consider tend to live modestly and even struggle financially; the only wealthy character is the offstage Ralph Manresa in Woolf's *Between the Acts*. As chapter 1 demonstrates, however, the issue of money is never far from the surface when Jews are represented. Indeed, even when a Jew is portrayed as unusually disinterested, that portrayal depends for its power on the opposing image of the greedy Jew. So boundaries of class and wealth are confused, not so much because the characters themselves have ambiguous class status, but because the texts metaphorically overlay their representations with suggestions of money interest and greed.

The category of time, usually divided into identifiable pasts, presents, and futures, is blurred by imaginings of Jewishness that simultaneously stress the timelessness of the Wandering Jew, the "ossification" of Judaism, and the allegedly hypermodern characteristics of urban Jews. The discourse that claims that the Jew is both ancient and timeless partakes of Christian and racialist discourses. Jews could connote antiquity because according to a dominant strand of Christianity, which I explore in chapter 2, Jewish history ended when it was "fulfilled" by Christ.[14] Many modernist novels, most obviously *Ulysses* (1922) and *Nightwood* (1936), draw on the image of the Wandering Jew doomed by Jesus to wander the earth until the end of days.[15] This image embodies and sustains the ancientness and timelessness Christianity ascribed to "the Jew." Jonathan Boyarin argues that this temporal positioning was a way for Christian Europe to distance its Jewish other. Because Jews lived inside its imperial centers, Europe could not easily consign them to faraway *places*; it banished them instead to the past.[16]

Moreover, early twentieth-century racial discourse described the progress of Jews and other "lower races" as slowed or stopped. George Stocking describes how race science classified and hierarchized human groups in a theory called "social evolution":

Social evolution was a process by which a multiplicity of human groups developed along lines that moved in general toward the social and cultural forms of western Europe. Along the way different groups had diverged, regressed, stood still, and even died out ... The progress of the "lower races" had been retarded or even stopped, but the general level had always advanced.[17]

The prominence of this version of race science meant that a connection with the past, which Judaism already had for Christian cultures, implied racial unfitness for the modern world. It is as a result of the confluence of these Christian and racialist notions, animating modern semitic discourses, that Jewishness came to represent a static kind of time in which Jews, who were obviously living, were relics nevertheless. And confusing things further, Jews were associated with various aspects of modernity: nervousness, alienation, the city, capitalism and/or communism. These strands of semitic discourse are analyzed by Bauman, Matti Bunzl, Sander L. Gilman, George Mosse, Judith Walkowitz, and others.[18] I examine literary versions of the association with modernity in chapter 3, and consider other aspects of the temporality of Jewishness in chapters 4 and 5.

In addition to time, gender is among the most important of the categories whose borders Jewish characters blur. The Jewish men of feminist modernism are feminine even when they threaten women's autonomy with their sexist attitudes. Their femininity is part of a larger cultural association between Jewish men and femininity that began to flourish in the late nineteenth century, and that Otto Weininger's 1903 *Sex and Character* (*Geschlecht und Charakter*) strongly reinforced. Lewis put this view succinctly in *Hitler* (1931), describing Jews as "[f]eminine, and in many ways unpleasant."[19] It finds expression, too, in Elizabeth Bowen's *The House in Paris* (1935), where the protagonist's mother says of her daughter's Jewish lover, "there is always that touch – Jewish, perhaps – of womanishness about him that a woman would have to ignore and yet deal with the whole time."[20] The association has been traced to at least four roots. Sigmund Freud ascribes a subconscious belief that Jewish men are emasculated (castrated) to fears of circumcision. In his analysis of Little Hans, Freud writes that "[t]he castration complex is the deepest unconscious root of anti-Semitism; for even in the nursery little boys hear that a Jew has something cut off his penis – a piece of his penis, they think – and this gives them the right to despise Jews." He then mentions Weininger, proposing a reason Weininger equates Jews with women: "Being a neurotic, Weininger was completely under the sway of his infantile complexes and from that standpoint what is common to Jews and women is their relation to the castration complex."[21] Sander Gilman relies on this linkage in his influential studies of discourses that portray the Jewish male body as feminine, hysterical, and diseased.[22]

A second explanation is implied by Ritchie Robertson, in an essay on Weininger: he traces the feminization of Jewish men to older images of sensual Jewish women.[23] I gather from this that the association of Jewishness with bodiliness (which I discuss in detail in chapter 4) is a major source of the link to women, since women were already connected to the body while (gentile) men were linked to reason, intellect, or the soul. (Weininger makes this distinction explicitly, describing Jews and women as soulless.)

A third source of this feminization is proposed by Matthew Biberman, who argues that it emerged from the needs of a somewhat deflated model of masculinity when bourgeois capitalism supplanted the chivalric code: "[A]ntisemitism functioned initially as a ceiling for men: it represented a range of stigmatized masculine behavior (e.g., avarice, sexual dominance, cruelty) in a culture that simultaneously enshrined the image of the masculine Christian knight as the pinnacle of manhood." But when "the merchant dislodged the knight . . . the Jew now served as the floor for modern male identity . . . The new vision – the Jew-Sissy – enabled the proper Christian male to acquire a sense of superiority."[24]

And a fourth explanation is offered by Daniel Boyarin, who suggests that there is some basis in reality for the claim that Jewish men of the nineteenth- and early twentieth-century diaspora were more feminine than Christian men. Boyarin ascribes this phenomenon to Talmudic culture, which resisted militaristic models of manliness, valuing instead qualities, such as delicacy and gentleness, which Western Christian cultures associated with women.[25] These four explanations differ in the degree to which they historicize and validate the phenomenon of the feminine Jewish man, but they are not mutually exclusive. Indeed, they trace what are surely intertwined strands of one of the most powerful images of Jews in modern literature.

The feminization of Jewish men, of course, has consequences for the representation of Jewish women. One outcome is their relative absence: as Ann Pellegrini puts it in *Performance Anxieties* (1996), "in the homology Jew-as-woman, the Jewish female body goes missing. All Jews are womanly but no women are Jews."[26] Not surprisingly, there are very few major Jewish women characters in modernism. Molly Bloom is half-Jewish, but until the dubious "womanly" narrative of the final chapter, she is more object than subject in *Ulysses*. Warner's Minna Lemuel, an important character in *Summer Will Show* (1936) (whom I discuss in chapters 1 and 3), is that rare thing, a central character who is both female and Jewish. Pellegrini counters the erasure of the Jewish woman by bringing "the construction of the Jewish female more directly into analysis" in her readings of Freud, Sarah Bernhardt, and Sandra Bernhard.[27] While my discussions of Warner's Minna do not focus on the erasure of Jewish female bodies, they do consider the confluence of her femininity and Jewishness as part of Warner's feminist revision of antisemitic discourse.

The image of the effeminate Jewish man created a strong ambivalent response in the writers considered here. As feminists they (like the diasporic Jewish women Boyarin describes) appreciated feminine qualities in men: gentleness, humility, nurturance, patience, loyalty, and domestic skill (think of Leopold Bloom making breakfast for Molly every morning). Woolf married a nurturing Jewish man; Richardson seriously considered marrying her gentle Jewish suitor Benjamin Grad; Rhys found friendship at a low point in her life with Simon Segal, a compassionate Russian-Jewish painter she met in Paris. All these men are represented, with various degrees of verisimilitude, in fiction. But *ars longa, vita brevis*, and feminine Jewish male *characters* run into one or both of these problems: the writer's misogyny, which, despite her feminism, limits her approval of these qualities in men (this is especially the case with Rhys, and with Richardson in the first part of her career); and/or the writer's antisemitism, which prompts her to align the Jewish male character with other less positive attributes and prevents her from embracing the feminized Jewishness she has constructed. They also run up against biology – no matter how gentle, these characters are men, and moreover, men linked through their Jewishness to what the authors considered the source of Western patriarchy: the "Old Testament" and its patriarchal God. Their authors thus engage in literary versions of feminist antisemitism, which I discuss particularly in chapter 4.

Given the extent to which Jewish characters are bound up with these financial, temporal, and gender issues – and indeed, as critics are beginning to note and as I argue here, bound up with the very project of many writers' modernisms – one might well be surprised to find how limited the history of critical attention to modernism's dealings with Jews has been. As Bryan Cheyette points out in his 1993 study *Constructions of "the Jew" in English Literature and Society*, many prior critical treatments of literary Jews offered ahistorical descriptions of stereotyped Jewish characters, assuming that those stereotypes remained fixed from Chaucer to Joyce. Cheyette, on the other hand, has shown that semitic discourse – his term for the ways a given culture understands and portrays Jews at a particular time – is inherently unstable and ambivalent, structured by contradictions. Only recently, then, have critics learned to approach representations of Jews and Jewishness in more nuanced and historicized ways. This has left much ground to be visited and revisited.

In the past decade there has been renewed interest in representations of Jews in modern English poetry and fiction. Several book-length studies of allosemitism and its role in the creation of modernism have focused on canonical male authors such as Henry James, Pound, Eliot, and Joyce.[28] In addition, *Modernism/Modernity* has published two special sections on "T. S. Eliot and Anti-Semitism: The Ongoing Debate" and sponsored a roundtable on the same topic at the 2004 Modernist Studies Association Conference in Vancouver.

But restricting such studies to canonical male authors stems from – and perpetuates – three key misconceptions about modernist literature. First and fundamentally, it extends the obvious limitations of canonicity itself, narrowing the field of inquiry and implying that only those few authors were innovative, influential, or reflective of cultural biases. Second, focusing only on male authors' use of semitic discourse encourages the assumption that only male modernism depended on such discourse for its self-definition, an error I particularly wish to correct. Third, neglecting to study women authors' representations of Jews bolsters the view that because these authors were feminist, antifascist, and often bisexual or lesbian, their political stances about Jews must be similarly progressive. That is, there is a tacit assumption within modernist criticism, lingering from first- and second-wave feminism, that it was the male authors who were antisemitic and sometimes fascistic (with the celebrated exception of

Joyce), whereas the female authors were "politically correct" across the board.[29] This third misconception remains powerfully at play especially in criticism of Woolf, whose undeniable antisemitism continues to be downplayed by reverential critics. Erin Carlston notes that "Sapphic Modernism in particular is often aligned with a politically progressive 'modernism of the margins'" and points out that "any systematic division of political tendency along gender lines is inadequate" to describe the political valence of "writing by both men and women."[30]

However, as I challenge these problematic assumptions, my goal is not to condemn authors for writing antisemitic scenes or using Jewishness as a foil for their characters' growth. Instead, I am interested in documenting how allosemitism functions for the authors as they craft their literary responses to prior and contemporary "masculine realism" (to use Richardson's phrase). Given scholars' emphasis during the last few decades on issues of race, nation, sexuality, and gender, of marginality and diaspora, of "minor" literature and canon-formation, it is vital to examine the ways Jewishness was instrumental to early twentieth-century imaginings of these sociopolitical categories and processes. By exploring the political and literary power of semitic discourse for key women authors, *Modernism, Feminism, and Jewishness* fills a significant gap in the account of the cultural and literary forces that created modernism. The study demonstrates how central imagined Jewishness was to the literary milieu that produced not only Eliot and Joyce, but also a body of important fiction by women. Precisely because "outsider" Jews reflected for women authors their own tenuous standing in literary circles, their portrayals seem to me particularly interesting, contradictory, and worthy of study.

When Bonnie Kime Scott refers to key women modernists as "the women of 1928," she not only suggests a riposte to Pound's valorization of "the men of 1914" but highlights a salient fact about literary modernism: women's modernism arrived late on the scene.[31] For the most part, modern women novelists published their first major creative works in their thirties, while their male counterparts had begun to define modernist fiction in their twenties. To take three canonical examples: Ernest Hemingway published two collections of stories in his early twenties, and his first novel in 1926, at age twenty-seven. D. H. Lawrence published his first novel, *The White Peacock*, in 1911, at age twenty-six. Joyce published *Chamber Music* in 1907 when he was twenty-five, and would have published *Dubliners* at around the same time but for a seven-year battle with his publishers over its language. By contrast, Warner was thirty-two when she published her first book of poems, *The Espalier*, in 1925 and thirty-three when she published her first novel, *Lolly Willowes*. Rhys was thirty-seven when she published her first collection of stories, *The Left Bank and Other Stories* (1927), and thirty-eight when she published her first novel, *Quartet* (1928). Richardson was forty-two when she published *Pointed Roofs* (1915), the first volume of *Pilgrimage* (1915–1967). And Woolf was thirty-three when she published *The Voyage Out* in 1915. Since Quentin Bell notes that she knew she would be a writer "from the first,"[32] and her father encouraged her intellectual pursuits (though his enforcing of gender roles certainly mixed that message), this delay seems attributable to the forces preventing women from intellectual work that she describes in her essays. The only one of the women modernists I discuss who began publishing in her twenties is Barnes, but one might not wish to date her literary career from 1915 when she published her pamphlet *A Book of Repulsive Women* with Guido Bruno at age twenty-three, especially since Barnes later refused to authorize republication. Although she did write plays for the Provincetown Players in the meantime, she published her first book of serious poems mixed with prose and drawings, *A Book*, when she was thirty-one, and her first novel, *Ryder*, in 1928 when she was thirty-six. This belated entrance onto the literary scene signals an important disparity between male and female writers of the period. Even though Jane Austen, the Brontës, and George Eliot had made women's fiction both respectable and artistic in the nineteenth century, as Woolf discusses in *A Room of One's Own* (1929), women writers were still at a disadvantage in the early twentieth century when it came to writing and publishing serious fiction.

The women writers I discuss in this study all display misgivings about their right to write, an anxiety about being imposters in literary culture. Even Woolf wrote to her brother-in-law Clive Bell that her "boldness" in writing *Melymbrosia*, the early version of *The Voyage Out*, "terrifie[d]" her.[33] She provides the most sustained discussion of her worries about women's literature in *A Room of One's Own*. Although that text is rightly viewed as a feminist manifesto, it often takes a defensive tone, demonstrating that Woolf comes to the topic of women's literature not confidently but with some trepidation. Her discussion of the Manx cat, for example, mocks Freud and the "castration complex" but also highlights how "absurd" women seem when they trespass on the sacred ground of serious literature (*Room* 13). She muses about how women might write if they wrote *as* women, pointing out that the "expected order" of events in fiction, where "a wave heap[s] itself, a crisis com[es] round the next corner," is a masculine literary conceit (*Room* 91). Not only do women have "no tradition behind them, or one so short and partial that it [is] of little help," but even the shape of fiction "has been made by men out of their own needs for their own uses" (*Room* 76, 77). There is no "common sentence ready for her use" (*Room* 76). So when women come to writing, Woolf acknowledges, the effect for readers accustomed to masculine literature is "baffling" (*Room* 91). Most troubling is that, because of the difficulty women have in writing at all, the minds that shine through their texts are rarely "incandescent" (*Room* 57).[34]

Rhys's similar but less self-conscious anxieties about being a woman writer are encapsulated in her belief that the woman writer was seen as a "freak," and that, as Carole Angier puts it, "in England especially, the most persecuted person of all is the *woman writer*."[35] Even as a child, Rhys's relationship with books required bravery and defiance. In her autobiography *Smile Please* (1979), she relates that her nurse, Meta, told her that if she read too much her eyes would "drop out and they will look at you from the page . . . I half believed her and imagined my pupils like heads of black pins and all the rest gone. But I went on reading."[36] She also notes that she envisioned God as a book, an image that only heightened her sense that she herself could have little to do with books – certainly writing them would be beyond her grasp.

Women modernists' uncertainty about their literary authority is underlined by a striking similarity between Rhys's and Warner's stories of how they came to write. Their stories foreground the accidental and the material, in contrast with, for example, Joyce's bold sense of a vocation as he portrays it in *A Portrait of the Artist as a Young Man* (1916). In *Smile Please* Rhys describes her initiation into writing; I quote it at length because of its telling, disingenuous focus on an ugly table. She begins by describing her new room in Fulham:

The first morning I woke up there it seemed to me the furniture was so like that in the room I had just left that moving hardly made any difference. But the table, which had been in the middle and covered with a cloth [in the previous room], was now pushed directly under the window and was bare and very ugly. I had put my brush and comb on it, and a box of powder, but they looked small and unimportant. I must get some flowers or a plant or something, I thought. I can't bear that table.

. . .

After lunch I walked along looking into shop windows . . . I passed a stationer's shop where quill pens were displayed in the window, a lot of them, red, blue, green, yellow. Some of them would be all right in a glass, to cheer up my table, I thought. I went into the shop and bought about a dozen. Then I noticed some black exercise books on the counter. They were not at all like exercise books are now. They were twice the thickness, the stiff black covers were shiny, the spine and the edges were red, and the pages were ruled. I bought several of those, I didn't know why, just because I liked the look of them. I got a box of J nibs, the sort I liked, an ordinary penholder, a bottle of ink and a cheap inkstand. Now that old table won't look so bare, I thought.

It was after supper that night – as usual a glass of milk and some bread and cheese – that it happened. My fingers tingled, and the palms of my hands. I pulled a chair up to the table, opened an exercise book, and wrote This is my Diary. But it wasn't a diary. I remembered everything that had happened to me in the last year and a half. I remembered what he'd said, what I'd felt. I wrote on until late into the night, till I was so tired that I couldn't go on, and I fell into bed and slept.

Next morning I remembered at once, and my only thought was to go on with the writing.[37]

In this narrative Rhys pretends – perhaps even to herself – that she bought the exercise books and pens merely for decoration. The tingling in her hands represents her deflated version of what more confident writers might have called inspiration. She writes "This is my Diary" because she lacks the assurance necessary to embark on a genuine literary project; but she notes in this later autobiography what she could not admit then, that "it wasn't a diary." (The writing she did in these exercise books became *Triple Sec*, the earliest version of *Voyage in the Dark* [1934]). Similarly, in buying the kind of pen nibs she likes, she acts in accordance with a preference that would have been irrelevant for someone buying pens merely to decorate her table.

Like Rhys's story of the origin of her writing career, Warner's briefer narrative stresses the fortuitous and ascribes her first poems to the lure of the material on which she writes. In an interview with *PN Review*, Warner discusses writing her first poems:

When did I begin to write? I was led away by paper. I'm always led away by blank paper. We had a great many photographs in our work [editing *Tudor Church Music*], black and white photographs of manuscripts, and there were always some throw-aways. And the white was the most beautiful smooth white photographic paper and nobody wanted it, and I wanted it, and having collected it by degrees I thought, "I must do something about all this handsome paper – I think I'll write a poem." So I started writing poems on this handsome paper.
. . .
I never thought of being a professional writer. I never thought of being a professional anything, to tell the truth. I just slopped along like Mrs. Warconisher's English Lady, you know, doing one thing at one time and another at another.[38]

Much as Rhys buys pens and exercise books to fill the empty space of her table, Warner begins to write poems to fill the empty pages of the beautiful paper she has brought home from her work as a musicologist. And just as Rhys betrays more familiarity with writing than she acknowledges when she describes the pen nibs as "the sort I liked," Warner admits wanting the paper when nobody else did. Her use of the word "slopped" shows a diffidence about serious writing analogous to Rhys's when she writes "This is my Diary" on the first draft of her novel. According to Warner's biographer, Claire Harman, Warner felt a guilty pleasure in her writing: "Among the things she brought home with her were dozens of smooth, blank rotographs which would otherwise have been thrown away as wastepaper. On these she wrote poems – about one a week in 1922 – with a delicious sense of indulging a secret vice."[39]

Unlike Rhys and Warner, Richardson does not provide a pithy narrative about her journey into writing; on the contrary, she documents that journey over the thirteen novel-chapters of *Pilgrimage*. But the beginnings of her writing career were similarly hesitant and haphazard. Although she was a close friend (and briefly lover) of H. G. Wells from her early twenties, it did not seem to occur to Richardson that she, too, could be a novelist until she was in her late thirties. At thirty-three she began writing book reviews for her friend Charles Daniel's monthly magazine.[40] About a year later, in 1907 or 1908, while in Vaud, Switzerland, she was reading the *Saturday Review* and found many of "middles" (brief articles on social or literary topics) disappointing. Gloria Fromm describes her response: "In protest, on a winter's night while still in Chateau d'Oex, she herself wrote one of these miscellaneous articles . . . and sent it to the *Saturday Review* the next morning, neglecting to include a return address and nearly forgetting the whole thing."[41] The "middle" was published, and she continued to write sketches for the *Saturday Review* until 1912.[42] Like Barnes and Woolf, Richardson began her professional career in journalism, but even this was for her a careless, or we might say carefree, enterprise. When she finally began working on a novel, at age thirty-eight, she did accede to a grander conception of her talent, and by the time she finished *Pointed Roofs*, "she knew [it] was only the first part of a whole already conceived as *Pilgrimage*."[43] In that long series of novels, Richardson dramatizes her protagonist's slow realization that she might write: "there was a woman, not this thinking self who talked with men in their own language, but one whose words could be spoken only from the heart's knowledge, waiting to be born in her" (*P* IV, 230). Miriam Henderson begins her literary career as a translator, and even this role catapults her into both delight and guilt. Encouraged by her Jewish suitor, Michael Shatov, to translate Russian stories into English, Miriam begins the work, marveling at the sentences she has made. Like the tingling hands that override Rhys's conscious intentions, Miriam's sentences come to her of their own volition:

How had she thought of them? She had not thought of them. She had been closely following something, and they had come, quietly, in the midst of engrossment . . . It was a curious marvel, a revelation irrevocably put down, reflecting a certain sort of character . . . more oneself than anything that could be done socially, together with others, and yet not oneself at all, but something mysterious, drawn uncalculatingly from some fund of common consent, part of a separate impersonal life she had now unconsciously confessed herself as sharing. (*P* III, 132)

Even though her work is a translation, and the sentences are not entirely hers, Miriam feels as though they express her "irrevocably" and yet draw her out of herself and into a "fund of common consent." But, like Warner, she feels a strong sense of guilt about this work:

But when at last suddenly in the middle of a busy morning, she began turning into rounded English words the thorny German text, she eluded [Michael's] inquiries and hid the book and all signs of her work even from herself. Writing she forgot, and did not see the pages. The moment she saw them, there was a sort of half-shame in their exposure, even to the light of day. And always in transcribing them a sense of guilt . . . It was in some way from the work itself that this strange gnawing accusation came, and as strangely, each time she had fairly begun, there came, driving out the sense of guilt, an overwhelming urgency; as if she were running a race. (*P* III, 140)

This guilt seems to stem in part from her sense that she is dissecting the original, from fear that her own language will disfigure the beauty she finds in Leonid Andreyev's stories, which she is reading in a German translation. But it also comes from a sense of transgression in doing such delightful work, from her sense that she has no right to a writing life:

With each fresh attack on the text, the sense of guilt grew stronger; falling upon her the moment, having read the page of German, she set to work to apply the discoveries she had made. It was as if these discoveries were the winning, through some inborn trick of intelligence not her own by right of any process of application or of discipline, of an unfair advantage. She sought within her for a memory that might explain the acquisition of the right of escape into this life, within, outside, securely away from, the life of every day. (*P* III, 141–142)

Like Warner and Rhys, Richardson's autobiographical protagonist focuses on the materiality of her project, emphasizing the table, the lamp, and the pages themselves. She gains a sense of comfort from thinking that "[n]othing would matter now that the paper-scattered lamplit circle was established as the centre of life" (*P* III, 134). One morning she fears that the magic might have dissipated, but she finds to her relief that "[t]he spell of the ink-stained table had survived the night" (*P* III, 135). As the project consumes more of her mental energy, she realizes that "everything in her life existed only for the sake of the increasing bunch of pencilled half-sheets distributed between the leaves of her roomy blotter" (*P* III, 140–141). This focus on the materials of writing differs sharply from Stephen Dedalus's scribbles on a matchbook in *A Portrait of the Artist as a Young Man*. Stephen *hears* his villanelle in his head – the writing is a mere mnemonic. For Miriam's writing, on the contrary, like Warner's and Rhys's, the material matters as a sort of anchor, holding the writer steady in the exhilarating but guilt-inducing sea of the writing life.

Barnes seems to be the exception to this trend of guilty hesitation in the face of a literary career. Although I would ascribe her belated publication of her serious work in book form to some of the same psychosocial forces that held up the careers of her fellow women modernists, she did start publishing earlier than they; if we count the publication of individual poems, she began her career in 1911 and established it in 1914, as the new *Collected Poems* (2005) demonstrates. In Phillip Herring's reading, Barnes's confidence came from the influence and example of her grandmother Zadel Barnes, herself a journalist, critic, poet, suffragist, friend of Lady Wilde (Irish nationalist, poet, and Oscar's mother), and generally powerful woman role model.[44]

Partly in response to their misgivings about their right to write (and in Barnes's case, following the example of her feminist grandmother), the authors I consider here clearly situate their writing in a context of feminist defiance. They compare themselves to their male contemporaries, implicitly or explicitly; they write articles about their male peers in which they criticize them on feminist grounds; they theorize "feminine" writing and its differences from "masculine" writing. It is for these reasons that I am calling their work "feminist modernism": although they had mixed reactions to the word "feminist," their efforts to create a women's modernism that would reflect the woman writer's mind, resist masculine narrative styles, and portray fully imagined women characters (something few of their male counterparts were able to do) can undoubtedly be called feminist.

The other side of Woolf's *A Room of One's Own* is clearly her embrace of writing *as* a woman, though as a woman whose mind will *become* "incandescent" through its transcendence of sex. Her stories there of "audaciously trespassing" on the Oxbridge campus serve as analogues for women's audacious entrance into literature (*Room* 6). When she complains about the ways Arnold Bennett, John Galsworthy, and Wells represent the fictional Mrs. Brown (in "Mr. Bennett and Mrs. Brown" [1924]), it is significant that it is a woman character they fail to see. Woolf is not only criticizing their realist method, but implicitly also their masculinist view that fails to apprehend the woman accurately. In *Room* and her shorter essays, Woolf constructs a narrative in which women come to writing in a way that seems at first unwieldy, but inevitably revalues social and cultural phenomena, contributing to their cultures much more than individual works. In "Women and Fiction" (1929), for example, Woolf writes that "when a woman comes to write a novel, she will find that she is perpetually wishing to alter the established values – to make serious what appears insignificant to a man, and trivial what is to him important."[45] Her famous description of murdering the Angel in the House in "Professions for Women" (1931) sums up her determination to clear the way for women to write, to express womanhood and yet paradoxically escape it by achieving a state of impersonality that only those who are unencumbered by sex-consciousness can achieve.[46]

Unlike Woolf, Rhys avoided explicit theorizing of gender in literature. As Angier says, "abstraction was alien to her."[47] She expressed her feminist stance less directly, in fiction, first by her relentless focus on exploited and miserable women. Angier notes that Rhys's "whole aim as a writer was to cut through the polite and pretty surface of things, and reveal the reality she saw beneath: cruelty, egotism, lack of any decency, sympathy, or imagination."[48] Angier does not describe this aim in feminist terms, but it is the "polite and pretty" idealization of womanhood – especially young, beautiful womanhood – that Rhys "cut[s] through." Besides centering her fictions on marginalized women (as Molly Hite points out in *The Other Side of the Story* [1989]), Rhys has them comment on literature or perception in gendered terms, gradually assembling a feminist argument about male control of representation.

In *Voyage in the Dark*, for example, Anna Morgan and her friend Maudie discuss Zola's *Nana* (1880), which Anna is reading. Maudie says, "'I know; it's about a tart. I think it's disgusting. I bet you a man writing a book about a tart tells a lot of lies one way and another'" (*V* 10). Maudie feels that *Nana* is disgusting not because she is morally high-handed but because she is defensive, since she herself knows how to "swank" (and more) to get men to take care of her financially. Including this comment very early in the novel, Rhys turns our attention to the fact that we are reading a woman's representation of a "tart," and that it will bear little resemblance to portraits by men. By the time she writes her last novel, *Wide Sargasso Sea* (1966), Rhys takes as her subject the different ways men and women perceive events. She demonstrates that the English man (*Jane Eyre*'s Edward Rochester, though he is not named) insists on seeing Antoinette as a player in a script already written by sexism, racism, and imperialism. There is no breaking through that script to allow Antoinette's voice to be heard. Rhys thus implicitly argues for a feminist view of literary representation.

While Woolf analyzes and Rhys dramatizes women's exclusion from representational control, Warner characteristically offers a parable. In a lecture on "Women as Writers" (1959), Warner demonstrates her sense that women's literary authority is precarious by citing *A Room of One's Own* at the outset and then developing a metaphor for women's entrance into literary history: they sneak in through the pantry window.

Suppose, for instance, that there was a palace, which you could only know from the outside. Sometimes you heard music playing within, and the corks popping, and sometimes splendid figures came to an open window and spoke a few words in a solemn chanting voice . . . And then one day you discovered that you could climb into this palace by the pantry window. In the excitement of the moment you wouldn't wait; you wouldn't go home to smooth your hair or borrow your grandmother's garnets or consult the Book of Etiquette. Even at the risk of being turned out by the butler, rebuked by the chaplin [sic], laughed at by the rightful guests, you'd climb in.

In something of the same way, women have entered literature – breathless, unequipped, and with nothing but their wits to trust to. A few minutes ago, or a few centuries ago, they were writing a letter about apoplexy, or a recipe for a custard. Now they are inside the palace, writing with great clearness what they have in mind to say – for that is all they know about it, no one has groomed them for a literary career – writing on the kitchen table, like Emily Brontë, or on the washstand, like Christina Rossetti, writing in the attic, like George Sand, or in the family parlour, protected by a squeaking door from being discovered at it, like Jane Austen, writing away for all they are worth, and seldom blotting a line.[49]

Warner's debt to Woolf in this lecture is evident in her references to recipes and other forms of casual writing, in the writers she describes working in the midst of domestic interruptions, in the aside that "no one has groomed them for a literary career," and in the suggestion that women are "unequipped" to enter literature and so write "breathless[ly]." She also alludes to *Room* in her mention of a rebuking chaplain. Warner thus joins Woolf in pointing out that women writers of the early twentieth century lack a writerly inheritance. Her image of the "pantry window" portrays women's lowly status with regard to literary culture; and she justifies women's breathless entrance by creating a picture of a palace so enticing that, given the chance to climb in, "you wouldn't wait."

Richardson's dense style contrasts with Warner's lighthearted one: her repertoire does not seem to include the parable. But she engaged quite fervently with feminist questions. She had some qualms about the word as it was used in England, noting that "feminist" often meant someone who believed "that the faults of women were the faults of the slave," that women were debased by circumstance, and that they needed thoroughgoing change to become whole and healthy.[50] She herself believed that women have always been whole, that they simply see differently from men (that is, synthetically) and that women's "consciousness has always made its own world . . . It can be neither enslaved nor subjected."[51] With this caveat – that she sometimes distanced herself from the word itself – I call her a feminist without hesitation, for she, along with Woolf, was an outspoken critic of masculinist views of women and male dominance within culture and literature.

A glance at Richardson's articles collected in Scott's anthology *The Gender of Modernism* (1990) demonstrates her literary brand of feminism. Scott includes a review entitled "The Reality of Feminism" (1917) from which the quotations above are taken; an essay in *Vanity Fair* called "Talent and Genius" (1923) that ascribes talent to men, genius to women; two additional *Vanity Fair* pieces called "Women and the Future" (1924) and "Women and the Arts" (1925); and a work of film criticism from the journal *Close-Up* (edited by H. D. [Hilda Doolittle], Bryher [Winifred Ellerman], and Kenneth Macpherson), entitled "Continuous Performance: The Film Gone Male" (1932).

In "Women and the Future," Richardson argues that women are essentially egoists, and that only "completely self-centered consciousness can attain to unselfishness."[52] Men's view of women, failing to grasp this fact, is limited because it is difficult "even for the least prejudiced, to *think* the feminine past, to escape the images that throng the mind from the centuries of masculine expressiveness on the eternal theme: expressiveness that has so rarely reached beyond the portrayal of woman, whether Madonna, Diana, or Helen, in her moments of relationship to the world as it is known to men."[53] In a review of Wells's *In the Days of the Comet* (1906), Richardson criticizes him for his portrayals of women:

> So far he has not achieved the portrayal of a woman, with the one exception of Leadford's mother. His women are all one specimen, carried away from some biological museum of his student days, dressed up in varying trappings, with different shades of hair and proportions of freckles, with neatly tabulated instincts and one vague smile between them all.[54]

In her own novel Richardson works to present Miriam Henderson's consciousness in its fullness, and to show her in relation not to "the world as it is known to men" nor to men themselves, but in relation to her physical environment, her acquaintances, her intimate women friends, her employers, the world of work, and perhaps most important, the city of London. Like Woolf, she stressed the importance of portraying women "not always in their relation to each other, but in relation to reality" (*Room* 114). While Richardson was an essentialist about women's nature, her views about women's synthetic consciousness give rise to a portrait not of a circumscribed spirit but of a capacious and variable mind.

Barnes's feminist stance can be seen clearly in her journalism. As Carolyn Burke describes it, Barnes "frequently interviewed women who did not fit into traditionally feminine categories: her subjects included the labor organizer Mother Jones, the suffragettes who endured force-feeding [Barnes herself underwent force-feeding as part of her research], women boxers, and a policewoman who wrote poetry."[55] But she also expressed that stance implicitly in fiction, focusing, like Richardson, on women characters in relation to a host of people and things, with men among the least important. In *Ladies Almanack* (1928) she satirizes but also celebrates the lesbian community around Natalie Barney. She includes an anecdote about angels giving birth to the first lesbian, the story being "the part about Heaven that has never been told." In it "all the angels . . . gathered together so close that they were not recognizable, one from the other. And not nine months later, [out of an egg hatched] the first Woman born with a Difference."[56] And of course, Barnes centers *Nightwood* on the relationship between Nora Flood and Robin Vote, with Robin's earlier marriage to Felix Volkbein serving as an obstacle to Robin's freedom. In fact, Herring notes that "Barnes wrote Emily Coleman that she had wedded Robin to Felix to rebut the received opinion that lesbians would be heterosexuals if they had men to love."[57] So one reason for Felix's inclusion in the novel (I discuss others in chapters 4 and 5) is to refute the ideological assumption that marriage is the route to women's fulfillment.

Their strong, conscious sense of nonbelonging in the realm of literature was an important source of these writers' interest in Jews, whom they viewed as outsiders to European culture generally, and to literary culture in particular. Woolf makes a striking comparison in this context. Even before she has set out her arguments in *A Room of One's Own* that women writers have been at a disadvantage because of their material circumstances, she compares women to Jews in a discussion of their common lack of the social capital necessary for writing. In her 1920 argument with Desmond MacCarthy ("Affable Hawk") in the pages of the *New Statesman*, she writes that women do still face powerful obstacles to literary work: "But, 'Affable Hawk' argues, a great creative mind would triumph over obstacles such as these. Can he point to a single one of the great geniuses of history who has sprung from a people stinted of education and held in subjection, as for example the Irish or the Jews?" (*Diary* II, 341). Leaving aside the inaccuracy, even silliness, of her challenge, I want to stress her link between women and Jews in the matter of writing: for Woolf, women and Jews (and the Irish) share a major disadvantage when it comes to literary endeavors.

Richardson similarly describes Jews as "unpracticed" in writing. She does not compare women to Jews on this account, however, but distances herself from them, implying that while women are of course native speakers of their own languages, Jews somehow are not. Of a German magazine *Zeitung* she writes that it is "mostly composed of Jewish contributions & the Jews using German very much as Zangwill used English, are the worst offenders. They positively revel in all these trimmings . . . , & contribute thereto their own peculiar, funny & pitiful, solecisms" (*W* 428). Similarly, when she describes an autobiography written by the painter Adrian Allinson, her husband's friend, she says that he is

not only falling headlong into all the pitfalls awaiting the amateur, but also, being half-Jewish, pirouetting, with an only too obvious delight into the solecisms so very very few Jews, (of those divorced from their own tradition & unable to do more than skate along the surface of any other; as distinct from the genuine Hebrew) ever escape. (*W* 473)

I discuss Richardson's distinction between the "genuine Hebrew" and "those divorced from their own tradition" in chapter 4. Here I want simply to note Richardson's insistence that Jews are not at home in European languages, wherever their birthplaces: both the Anglo-Jewish writer Israel Zangwill and Allinson were born in London. Although Richardson disavows a connection with Jews on this count, her work shows an interest in them that moves along the axes of belonging and use of language. Woolf and Richardson, like the other writers considered in this study, identify with Jews because of a sense of their common outsider status and lack of literary authority. Mary Gordon's comment in her introduction to *A Room of One's Own* resonates in this context. She writes, "The shapely sentence: it is another necessary legacy, the lack of which makes every woman writer parvenue" (*Room* x). The women writers I study see Jews and themselves as interlopers in literary culture. Their identification is always limited by the antisemitic assumptions they concurrently accept, but it nevertheless drives their interest in Jewishness as a structural device, a theme, and a motif.

This identification underlies the most basic use of Jewish characters in modernist literature: as mirrors to reflect some characteristic – often alienation – of the non-Jewish characters. Rhys emblematizes this use of a Jew as a reflection of a protagonist's nonbelonging when she has the Jewish painter Serge Rubin in *Good Morning, Midnight* (1939) tell Sasha Jansen that once when he visited England, he bought "'a fine suit . . . I looked quite an Englishman from the neck down'" (*GM, M* 95). Sasha empathizes with this feeling of not quite looking like those around her: every morning she spends "an hour and a half trying to make [herself] look like everybody else" and knows that even "with all this [she doesn't] succeed" (*GM, M* 106). Serge's outsiderhood highlights Sasha's similar alienation.

Rhys expressed her own alienation in terms similar to those she gives Serge and Sasha. In her autobiography she writes, "I would never be part of anything. I would never really belong anywhere, and I knew it, and all my life would be the same, trying to belong, and failing. Always something would go wrong. I am a stranger and I always will be, and after all I didn't really care."[58] The contradiction between "all my life would be the same, trying to belong" and "after all I didn't really care" is echoed in Woolf's famous comment in *Three Guineas* (1938) that she has no country. Woolf depersonalizes the feeling of strangeness when she writes that "as a woman I have no country. As a woman I want no country. As a woman my country is the whole world" (*TG* 109). But while women's exclusion is potential salvation as well as disability in *Three Guineas*, Woolf's assertion that she wants no country registers more a defiant acceptance of reality than a decisive embrace.

Male modernists such as Hemingway and Joyce certainly also used Jews to figure their feelings of social marginalization and exile. But they did not consider themselves outsiders to *literary culture*; they did not feel they lacked a tradition in which to write or literary fathers with whom to struggle. Because women modernists connected their outsiderhood specifically to being women writers, their identification with Jews took on particular resonance. Beginning with this simple identification with Jews as outsiders, they expanded their imaginative involvement with literary Jews – in ways I describe in the following chapters – until their Jewish characters helped to shape myriad aspects of feminist modernism. Jews thus became integral to their aesthetic and political projects.

Indeed, it is not surprising that Jews should play a prominent role in interwar fiction by both men and women. In the years leading up to the Holocaust, antisemitism and semitic discourse generally reached their height. British antisemitism was certainly less violent than continental antisemitism, and it differed from continental forms in its conception of race. Race thinking in Central Europe was infused with the biological determinism we have come to associate with Nazism. British people, on the other hand, tended to use the term "race" loosely, often synonymously with "nation"; and although most saw Jews as a separate race, they also tended to believe that Jews could be assimilated into British society, whereas continental race science usually categorized Jews as unassimilable.[59] The belief that "England can assimilate anything" (P III, 167), as Miriam Henderson puts it in *Pilgrimage*, was a hallmark of British race thinking.

This did not, of course, prevent British culture from exploiting allosemitism.[60] During the period from the 1890s through the Second World War, Jews were often in the news as players in British and Zionist politics and as victims of antisemitic eruptions. Benjamin Disraeli, the most influential Jewish figure of nineteenth-century Britain, died in 1881, the year before Woolf and Joyce were born. His flamboyant identifications with his Jewish heritage did much to bring a racialized Jewishness into public discourse. The Liberal antisemitism that surfaced in opposition to Disraeli "led easily into the progressive, anti-imperialist anti-Semitism of the Boer War period."[61] Indeed, in 1900–1901 the Boer War divided the Liberal Party, with some who opposed the war expressing antisemitic objections.[62] From 1895 to 1898 the Dreyfus Affair in France had received wide coverage in the British press. Meanwhile, immigrants poured into Britain between the 1880s and the First World War, resulting in an influx of 120,000–150,000 East European Jews.[63] The number of new immigrants decreased in 1905, when antialien feeling resulted in the Aliens Act, which made it far more difficult for poor Eastern European Jews to enter Britain.[64]

In 1913 news of the trial of Mendel Beiliss of Kiev, who was accused of murdering a young boy for ritual purposes, was reported in British newspapers. *The Times* published several articles in which the correspondent described the trial as a crucial event in modern political history. "It is daily becoming clearer that under the forms of law a momentous political struggle is being fought out. This is *not* the Beiliss case. It is possibly a final fight for existence on the part of the innermost powers of reaction against all modern forces in Russia."[65] When Joyce has Leopold Bloom consider the "evidences for and against ritual murder," he may have been thinking of the Beiliss case, though the novel's setting in 1904 prevents any specific reference.[66]

British writers would have been aware, too, of two issues which during the First World War and in the next few years brought antisemitic discourse to a high pitch in British politics and the mainstream press: conscription and Bolshevism. The 1916 Conscription Act had exempted Russian immigrants, who, having escaped persecution in Russia, would have been unlikely to want to serve in the British Army on the same side as the Tsar. This exemption caused resentment that led to the East London Aliens Conference in 1917, at which conference participants described Jews as unpatriotic cowards. The Conscription Act was subsequently extended to cover remaining aliens from "friendly" nations. These aliens, most of whom were Russian Jews, were given three weeks to apply to return to Russia or stay in Britain and enlist.[67]

Also in 1917, as Sharman Kadish demonstrates, the Russian Revolution prompted a widespread fear of Bolshevism that was projected onto Jews. Jews were said to be the authors of Bolshevism, plotting the ruin of the great Russian nation and later of all Europe. Bolshevism and Jews were linked by government officials and mainstream newspapers like *The Morning Post* and *The Times*. From 1918 Britain was assisting the White Army in Russia and denying the evidence of its pogroms against Jews. When Prime Minister David Lloyd George planned to open trade negotiations with the Soviets, *The Times*, opposed to such recognition of the Bolsheviks, printed "The Jewish Peril" – an article about the newly translated *Protocols of the Elders of Zion* – in 1920. The article speculated on the authenticity of the document, but leaned toward accepting its truth because it seemed to propose a blueprint for what was happening in Russia. The *Protocols* sparked a spate of antisemitic articles and diatribes in most quarters of the British press. The furor over this particular issue in the mainstream press died down in 1921 when *The Times* published an exposé of the forgery, but right-wing groups and publications continued to use anticommunism to incite hatred of Jews.[68]

British antisemites reconciled the idea that Jews were Bolsheviks with the concurrent belief that Jews were big bankers in control of the European financial markets by assuming that Jews favored Bolshevism in search of their own profit. One *Times* article explained that the Bolsheviks were "adventurers of German-Jewish blood and in German pay."[69] Allegedly, the bureaucracy necessary for a Communist state would provide opportunities for exploitation.[70] This contradiction is embodied in the very application of the *Protocols*, which outlined a plan for Jewish domination, to the 1917 Revolution.

Debates over Zionism also ran through British culture, bringing the question of the "nationality" of Jews to public attention.[71] British support for Zionism was sparked by various concerns, including the potential benefits of a friendly presence in the Middle East, a general sympathy for nationalist causes, and what many saw as British philosemitism. Kadish argues, however, that the 1917 Balfour Declaration, which promised Palestine to the Jews, was an attempt to turn Jews away from Bolshevism (by giving them a healthier national cause to support) and to further Britain's war aims. She claims that the British government believed not only that Jews were leading Bolshevik Russia, but also that these Jewish Bolsheviks would be inclined to support Zionism. Moreover, important Britons believed that Jews were extremely powerful in the United States. They thought, therefore, that expressing support for Zionism would keep Russia in the war and increase support from the United States for the Allied cause.[72] Whatever the multifaceted ideological motives for the Balfour Declaration, the decision to support Zionism intersected with various other strands of British political life. And as Zionism became an important topic in British politics, Jews remained conspicuous in the public eye.

In the cultural realm Jews and Judaism were the subjects of many books, book reviews, and articles. To take the *Times Literary Supplement* as an example: between 1918 and 1939 the *TLS* published roughly 200 short book notes and longer review articles about Jewish topics, with the number of longer articles (as well as the total number of articles) increasing as the time period proceeded. There are notices about published lectures originally given in the United States on the topics of Jewish religion, history, and political and social status. Several reviews about Zionism and Jewish history – including a review of a collection of articles on Zionism by Albert Einstein[73] – consider whether Zionism or assimilation will best help the Jewish people to thrive. Some consider Jewish life in Palestine and other parts of the Empire, such as South

Africa. These articles are not without antisemitic barbs; for example, one article in 1927 blames antisemitism in part on Jews' "aloofness" and reluctance to share their cultural "gifts" with Christian Europeans.[74] But for the most part these articles are fairly dispassionate, even at times academic, considerations of aspects of Jewish religion and history.

In the 1930s articles about antisemitism, Nazism, and "the Jewish Question" begin to appear more frequently. References to events in Germany as early as 1933 often take a knowing tone, lacking elaboration and assuming an audience aware of antisemitic persecutions. For example, a review of a book on Jewish life in the Babylonian period begins with the comment that "[w]hen this book was published there was no particular reason for Jewry to fear that one of the unhappy periods with which it deals was about to be repeated"; there is no mention of Germany and no return to this subject.[75] An article about the role of Jews in the struggle for minority rights adopts a similar tone, ending with the assertion that the facts it has been discussing are "worthy of being borne in mind to-day when Germany seems to be moving in this respect in a retrograde direction."[76] In March 1939 there is a large-headlined article about the new, unexpurgated translation of *Mein Kampf*. The reviewer is less critical than one might expect, observing that "it would not be surprising if this publication increased sympathy for those ideas of Herr Hitler which do not immediately threaten our own interests in the world." This is because

there is much more in these 576 pages than a handbook of aggressive foreign policy. There is an amateurish, neo-Darwinian theory of history; a highly emotional exposition of the theory of the racial State, more appealing in some aspects than the vision of the Communist State; a treatise on education, and, above all, a running flow of comment on all the baffling social problems which vex the man in the streets of Western Europe.

The author decides that "however detestable Herr Hitler's methods, however brutal the passions he aroused in his followers, his own early experiences have given him a sharp eye for the diagnosis of present discontents." He does acknowledge, though, that Hitler's "hatred of Jewish blood, thought, and traditions is the very essence of his attitude."[77] Immediately below this review of *Mein Kampf* is an article entitled "In Defence of the Jews," a review of Wyndham Lewis's 1939 book *The Jews – Are They Human?*[78] The irony of using Lewis's lukewarm and belated defense as a counterpoint to Hitler would not have been lost on modernist writers.

Within Britain the 1930s saw the rise of a right-wing contingent led by Oswald Mosley's British Union of Fascists that insisted that Jews were a subversive element in societies across Europe. In the early 1930s, Todd Endelman records, antisemites "plastered thousands of small labels decrying Jewish world domination on vending machines, mailboxes, lamp posts, and the walls of shops and public buildings in London and other large cities."[79] The BUF conducted raids of the East End of London between 1935 and 1937, smashing shop windows, desecrating synagogues, and beating up Jews on the streets. As Endelman writes:

In one attack in October 1936 . . . a week after a Fascist procession through the East End was stopped by an anti-Fascist front of about 100,000 people ("the Battle of Cable Street"), Blackshirts retaliated by smashing the windows of twenty-nine Jewish shops in Mile End Road and sixteen Jewish shops in a row in Green Street. In one instance, they threw a man and a little girl through a shop window while the crowd chanted "Down with the Yids."[80]

The reference to the huge antifascist front gives a sense that while the BUF commanded mainly radical right-wing support, it made its voice heard throughout London, sparking intense controversy among British Jews and non-Jews as it wreaked havoc on the East End Jewish community.

Not only did these events in urban centers trouble the domestic political and social scene, but the British press also covered events in Germany comprehensively after the Nazis took power in 1933. According to Andrew Sharf, the tone of the reports was generally sympathetic to German Jews, but when the question of refugees came up, so, too, did antialien sentiment. From 1933 to 1936, then again in 1938, controversy about refugees filled the newspapers. The articles displayed a limited sympathy: the British disapproved of the way Nazis were treating Jews, but they had no room for the refugees in Britain.[81] The government also used its concerns about Arab uprisings to limit severely the number of Jews allowed to enter Palestine; it did not change this policy at any time during the Second World War, in spite of reports about the death camps. As a result of these various controversies and the strength of social antisemitism, no one who read British newspapers in the years between the wars could miss the centrality of Jews to the British (and European) sociopolitical scene. Portraying the Jew as capitalist and communist, destitute refugee and enemy of the state, representative of antiquity and of modernity, social and political discourses continually filled in the outlines of the "conceptual Jew."

Modernism, Feminism, and Jewishness is organized around five discrete thematic strands with which Jewishness is entangled in feminist modernism.

Each chapter considers two or three writers and traces the relationship of Jewishness in their work to the chapter's theme. Because Jewishness is tied so tightly to thematic and formal aspects of the novels, my analyses range fairly widely, proposing readings that are separable from the inquiry into Jewishness and offering fresh interpretations of varied motifs. The study seeks not to extricate Jewishness from its enmeshment in the issues that each chapter highlights, but instead to consider its intricate embeddedness in the layered meanings that structure each novel.

To this end, I discuss authors and their works in multiple chapters, circling back to analyze texts in new contexts. This structure reflects the multifaceted nature of antisemitic discourse: I treat varied aspects of a given representation at different points in the book. It also, I hope, enables readers to reencounter the novels from different vantage points and demonstrates the proposition that Jewishness served modernism as a powerful tool, shaping the texts from all sides.

In this task my thinking has been shaped by several overlapping fields of inquiry. Feminist studies forms the largest backdrop for this work, both by setting the terms of the underlying questions (What is feminist modernism? How should we understand women's literary history and its relation to the canon? Through what categories were early twentieth-century women able to define themselves and their work?) and by conducting the specific debates in which I intervene.[82] Queer theory has influenced my thinking about gender performance, enabling me to see the ways in which Jewishness and racial identity generally are gendered and sexualized. It has helped me to see the power that relationships between women have within the fictions and the odd textual maneuverings that result from lesbian panic. And it has made clear the extent to which feminist modernism coincides with lesbian modernism.[83] Most basically, my work participates in conversations within Jewish studies, especially "the new Jewish cultural studies" (as Daniel and Jonathan Boyarin call it in the subtitle of their 1997 collection) which focuses on the machinations of semitic discourse in cultural expression and the intersections of Jewishness with race science, psychoanalysis, and identity categories such as gender, sexuality, and class.[84] The turn of the twenty-first century, as Bunzl puts it, is a "moment that grants theorizations about Jewishness a place in ongoing discussions about race, ethnicity, nationness, diaspora, memory, religion, gender, and sexuality"; this study takes advantage of that moment to theorize the place of Jewishness within the broader concerns of feminist modernism.[85]

The following chapter begins unraveling the tangle that is modernist Jewishness by analyzing the reverberations of the longstanding association between Jews and money in the work of Warner, Rhys, and Woolf. Each author used this association to explore and critique a literary culture increasingly obsessed with profit. Several critics have studied the unstable relations between modernist writers and expanded mass culture. This chapter offers an account of one means by which three important feminist modernists reacted to the commodified literary culture and considered its implications. Portraying a Jewish storyteller in *Summer Will Show* and a Jewish painter in *Good Morning, Midnight*, Warner and Rhys revise antisemitic stereotypes to reflect on the place of art in social spheres debilitated by the profit motive. With very different political results, in *The Years* Woolf creates a poor Jewish factory worker who represents the threat of contamination by financial need. Through their Jewish characters these authors worry over the prospects of disinterested art.

Chapter 2 turns to a religious component of modernist Jewishness. It shows that when Richardson and Woolf set out to forge a feminist literary consciousness that would eschew egotism yet value the experiences of individual minds, they drew on the rhetoric of supersession: the theological notion that Christianity superseded Judaism. This rhetoric enabled them to position their work as superior to "masculine" writing, in that they associated their spiritual, feminist art with Christian "advancement" over a Judaism linked to materiality and masculinity. As I demonstrate in chapter 1, Woolf's *The Years* represents Jewishness as money interest; in this chapter I locate related images in *Three Guineas*, which reconsiders the problem of money interest and proposes a solution steeped in Christianized rhetoric. I then explore the ways in which Richardson's *Pilgrimage* identifies Judaism with patriarchal bias and "the letter," Christianity with feminism and "the spirit," and its own artistic approach with the "Christian" elements. While racial rather than religious categories dominated interwar thinking about Jews, this chapter demonstrates that religious discourse maintained its power to influence literary representations.

Chapter 3 explores two literary manifestations of the early twentieth-century cultural association between Jews and modernity. In *Between the Acts* Woolf views modernity in oppositional terms: as a political and economic force that on the one hand unifies people into masses (mass consumers as well as mobs, parties, and militant nations) and on the other hand fragments continuity and community. *Between the Acts* explores the dangers of both aspects of modernity, but it is in the critique of modernity's ruptures that Woolf enlists her otherwise minor Jewish character. For Warner, who joined the Communist Party in 1935, modernity held the potential for socialist revolution. In *Summer Will Show* she employs Jewish aspects of the 1848 revolutions in France to express her commitment to revolution while criticizing its likely excesses. Warner uses Jewishness for what could be called liberal humanist ends: to underscore the value of art even within revolutionary societies.

Chapter 4 turns to the intersection of gender and race that constructs literary Jewishness by considering the paradoxical genderings of Jewish male characters in Barnes's *Nightwood* and Richardson's *Pilgrimage*. They are presented as too feminine, but also as too patriarchal, threatening to entrap women by the force of biology which they represent and promote. Given the Janus-faced nature of antisemitic discourses, these contradictory claims are unsurprising. This chapter, however, traces some of the ways in which the opposing depictions actually dovetail. By advocating racial continuity, the Jewish men accept for themselves the very role they impose upon women: they allow themselves to be used as tools of a biologically framed social agenda. Ultimately, both women protagonists escape that force, engaging in lesbian romance rather than surrendering to Jewish men. These novels set the lesbian against the Jew in a way that upsets any complacent sense that the politics of feminist modernism are consistently progressive.

Chapter 5 extends the inquiry into the varied connections between Jewishness and time, demonstrating that Barnes and Rhys use Jewishness to explore the phenomenology of timelessness. In their presentation of characters whose identities have been fragmented by trauma, Barnes's *Nightwood* and Rhys's *Voyage in the Dark* and *Good Morning, Midnight* contribute insightful portrayals to the literature on the psychological effects of traumatic experience. Barnes and Rhys link Jews to timelessness for several reasons, among them their sense that Jewish history bears a thematic and psychological resemblance to their personal traumatic histories. Here the prototypical use of an imagined Jew to reflect a character's emotional state takes on additional complexity: it is not just that "the Jew" is alienated like the novels' protagonists, but that he is similarly outside of history, exiled, like the traumatized characters, from the ordinary sense of personal continuity. The liminal status of Jews with regard to the categories of history, race, nation, and gender contributes to their usefulness as reflections of or counterweights to the liminal temporal existence of traumatized psyches.

Not only do the writers I consider use Jewish characters for thematic purposes, but they also manipulate the meanings that Jewishness has accrued in their work to help define their particular versions of modernism.

Chapter 6 briefly revisits the work of each author before turning to Richardson and Woolf, highlighting each writer's metafictional uses of Jewishness as a model, foil, or scapegoat for some aspect of her artistic approach. By focusing on these metatextual processes, the final chapter confirms the book's largest claim: that feminist modernism relies on Jewishness as a means to shape its own identity.

I

"Strip each statement of its money motive": Jews and the ideal of disinterested art in Warner, Rhys, and Woolf

When the historian J. A. Hobson caricatured Jews as *"homo economicus"* in his 1891 study *Problems of Poverty*, he provided a pithy label for the ubiquitous stereotype of the obsessively wealth-seeking Jew.[1] Many eighteenth- and nineteenth-century authors, such as Maria Edgeworth, Charles Dickens, and Anthony Trollope, drew upon this stereotype to explore and protest the increasing commercialization of their cultures. Anglo-American modernist authors, on the other hand, with the notable exception of Edith Wharton, tended to eschew the literary progeny of Shylock, the greedy Jewish financiers and swindlers through whom the earlier authors voiced their disgust with the excesses of industrial capitalism. (This is not to say, as will become clear, that the prototype of Shylock was irrelevant to their characterizations.[2]) Their reluctance was due perhaps not so much to their understanding that the stereotype was spurious or unethical, but to their concern that as a stock figure it suggested the Victorian and Edwardian realism against which they defined themselves.

However, the alleged financial power of Jews did come close to home for early twentieth-century writers because it had become linked with the accusation that Jews controlled publishing houses and the press. William Brustein notes that "[a]s the nineteenth century unfolded, economic anti-Semites would . . . charge that Jews inordinately controlled the major means of production."[3] Hobson helped to make this claim respectable in his coverage of the Boer War, where he "attacked the extensive Jewish influence within the British and Johannesburg press, which had served to arouse the British masses to support Britain's imperialistic policy in South Africa."[4] This association between Jews and print culture seems to have resonated with modernist writers, who, of course, were forced to submit to the power of editors and publishers in a market increasingly aimed at popular rather than serious artistic appeal.[5] By the interwar period, there were also increasing numbers of Jews visible in artistic circles, writing and painting as well as publishing and reviewing literature and the arts.[6] Apparently prompted by these associations between Jews and the world of art, several important modernist novelists portrayed not Jewish businessmen or financiers,[7] but Jewish artists or creative types – characters who, though they are crucially disavowed, nevertheless stand in some ways for the authors themselves.

Ernest Hemingway's Robert Cohn in *The Sun Also Rises* (1926), for example, has literary pretensions and an interest in cathedrals as representations of "'something or other,'" as Jake Barnes half-recalls.[8] Although Jake and the other characters feel little but disdain for him, he is actually so similar to Jake, as Walter Benn Michaels points out, that the novel must work obsessively to differentiate them.[9] Since Jake is one of Hemingway's alter-egos, Cohn is related more closely to Hemingway himself than the author would have liked to acknowledge. D. H. Lawrence's soulless painter and sculptor Loerke serves similarly as a telling opposite for Lawrence's persona Rupert Birkin in *Women in Love* (1920). He has artistic talent, but he approaches art from a standpoint diametrically opposed to Lawrence's own. His presence allows Lawrence to stage a debate between competing aesthetic theories. Loerke believes, somewhat contradictorily, that art "should interpret industry" because "machinery and the acts of labour are extremely, maddeningly beautiful" and that art is purely formal, having "no relation to anything outside that work of art."[10] Ursula Brangwen, on the other hand, believes that art does bear relation to the world. She insists on recognizing a painting of a horse as an artifact made by a particular psyche when she says, "'But why does he have this idea of a horse? ... I know it is his idea. I know it is a picture of himself, really'" – a comment which enrages Loerke. Ursula sensibly points out that "'the world of art is only the truth about the real world, that's all.'"[11] This debate is disingenuous because Loerke, the proponent of the formalist approach, is described as ratlike and cold, a "gnawing little negation" who sexually exploits girls and young women and beats them to make them sit still for his portraits.[12] Significantly, Birkin and Gerald Crich decide he must be Jewish just a couple of pages before he spouts his inhumane theory.

James Joyce, far more sympathetic to Jews than Lawrence, creates in *Ulysses* (1922) a Jewish Everyman in whom commingle the artist and scientist, and with whom Stephen Dedalus needs to commune before he can surpass his narrow, egotistical aesthetic assumptions. Leopold Bloom is another self-portrait of Joyce, a more mature version than Stephen, as early critics such as Wyndham Lewis understood (and in Lewis's case, lamented).[13] His presence enables Joyce to set a human being who comfortably accepts materiality against one who (as we see in Stephen) cannot yet integrate the body and the spirit. All these characters serve the novels in which they appear not only by playing their particular roles in the plot, but also by providing a stage on which the authors play out and present the results of their artistic questions and theories. The prevalence in modernism of Jewish artist figures as opposed to financiers does not mean, of course, that modernists were less antisemitic than their earlier counterparts. Cohn is feminized in a world where masculinist values are paramount; Loerke verges on the satanic. But modernists do use Jews self-consciously to interrogate their own identities as artists and the literary culture in which they struggle to succeed.

This culture was increasingly based in mass-market publications and advertising, and often seemed to squeeze out, or to preclude, serious, "high-art" literature. Modernist writers had various responses to such a culture, from pessimistic withdrawal to enthusiastic attempts to maneuver within it and harness its energies for their work.[14] But most seem to have been concerned that literary and cultural standards were being lowered by the market forces that drove publication. As Mark Morrison puts it, many writers expressed "what has become a familiar set of concerns: culture controlled by corporations; public debate constricted by advertisers' prejudices; profit and the 'bottom line' sacrificing the original, the creative, to the tried and true, to the 'lowest common denominator'; copy that requires little thought and panders to readers' taste for the sensational, uncritical, and merely entertaining."[15] Several critics have studied the complex and unstable relations between modernist writers and expanded mass culture, making substantial contributions to the history of modernist culture and correcting sweeping condemnations of modernists as coterie snobs.[16] What I hope to contribute here to the newly complicated picture is an account of one *means* by which three important feminist modernists reacted to their commodified literary culture and thought through its implications. In this chapter I trace ways in which Sylvia Townsend Warner, Jean Rhys, and Virginia Woolf revisited the stereotype of the greedy Jew as they wondered and worried about the possibility of disinterested art within a literary culture obsessed with profit.

One difference between these authors' use of artistic Jewish characters (or, in Woolf's case, of a Jew who *prevents* artistic expression) and that of

Hemingway, Lawrence, and Joyce is that in the women's fictions we find Jews providing a focus for economic and social critiques of the artistic milieu, while their male counterparts seem to use their Jewish artists to mull over more personal or abstractly aesthetic concerns.[17] In the women's fictions Jews help the authors to express a longing for a disinterested sphere within which they might write. In Hemingway's and Lawrence's fictions, they serve more clearly as foils against which the artists can define their fictional alter-egos – as humane as well as brilliant (Lawrence) or hard-boiled as well as capable of deep feeling (Hemingway). And in Joyce's *Ulysses* Bloom serves as a sort of inverse of a foil: a model for the integration Stephen needs to achieve before he can use his presumably far greater talents.

We might attribute this difference between these representative men and women writers to the greater power of men within the world of publishing. Because the women authors felt they had a much smaller and shorter literary tradition to draw upon, because so few women held positions of power in the press or in publishing houses, women (as I discuss in the introduction) felt themselves at odds with the world in which they needed to succeed. Their anxiety about their relative exclusion from this sphere – their lack of control over the means of production – is manifest in their use of Jews to figure the financial aspects of literary culture. It is not that their male colleagues were not anxious about money, of course. Lawrence was very poor when he was writing *Women in Love*, and Joyce was famously insolvent. But the women's greater exclusion from publishing power may have prompted them to create figures through whom they could explore the power and dangers of the literary profession.

Perhaps it is also the case that the women writers felt more shame at entering the writerly market than their male contemporaries. In his study of American literary antisemitism, Jonathan Freedman extends Catherine Gallagher's claim that women writers, in Freedman's words, found that "entering the booming sphere of letters was a profoundly transgressive act":[18]

For to prosper in this marketplace was psychically tantamount to selling one's self on the open market or opening oneself up to the endlessly proliferating play of language – a play that generates economic value out of nothing in the same way a usurer generates value from money, not labor. In either case, material success is streaked with shameful similarities to prostitution or usury.[19]

Freedman demonstrates that several nineteenth-century writers portrayed Jewish characters as means of responding to just this problem. They used

Jews to express their shame (as well as their pride, Freedman argues) at being able to make money from writing. Indeed, as we will see, Woolf described writing for pay in these very terms, using images of prostitutes and Jews as a way of both articulating and disavowing her shame.

The three writers I consider here launch their inquiries into the financial aspects of artistic culture not by creating Jewish art dealers, publishers, or patrons; instead, Warner and Rhys create Jewish artists – a storyteller in Warner's *Summer Will Show* (1936), a painter in Rhys's *Good Morning, Midnight* (1939) – and Woolf creates a poor worker in a tallow factory in *The Years* (1937). But these characters are embedded in social contexts that their authors make clear are debilitated by the profit motive. Warner critiques bourgeois interpersonal relations as contaminated by economic modes of thought that make every social relation one of indebtedness for some abstract good received (*SWS* 291). Rhys demonstrates throughout *Good Morning, Midnight* and her other novels how the exchange of money defines not only personal relations but self-image, especially for women. And Woolf laments in *Three Guineas* (1938) how difficult it is to "strip each statement" one hears or reads "of its money motive" (*TG* 96). These three writers use the strong literary and cultural link between Jews and money to respond to these concerns, treating issues of political, personal, and artistic integrity with disparate political results.

Warner's *Summer Will Show* employs a sympathetic Jewish character to criticize bourgeois social relations and the commodification of art within that philistine culture. Warner worked on the novel from 1932 to 1936, joining the Communist Party in 1935 in the midst of its composition. Her critique of middle-class views of love and art is informed by, though not reducible to, her Communist sympathies. However, the novel also questions a Communism so dogmatic that it would become as harmful to art as the bourgeois culture it attempts to remake. To embed in her novel these critiques of both bourgeois commodity-culture and Communist single-mindedness, Warner creates a bohemian Jewish storyteller, Minna Lemuel, to whom notions of disinterested art gather. Warner revisits the stereotype of the greedy Jew and revises it, both to reject antisemitism and to stage her inquiry into the possibility of a sphere where financial interests make way for human and aesthetic value. I discuss the ways Jewishness is integral to Warner's critique of narrowly economic Communism in chapter 3. Here I focus on the ways the ideal of disinterested art is figured by a Jewish woman who flourishes, for a time, outside the strictures of the European bourgeoisie.

In *Summer Will Show* the upper middle-class Englishwoman Sophia Willoughby goes to Paris after her two children have died, seeking her estranged husband. She wants not to reunite with him permanently, but to seduce him or, failing that, bargain with him, to try to replace her children. She abandons this plan when she falls in love with her husband's mistress, the Jewish Minna Lemuel. The women's relationship is framed by the February and June revolutions of 1848; Minna is, as far as we know, killed at the June barricades, and we last see Sophia in Minna's flat, reading the newly printed *Communist Manifesto*.

Warner begins her meditation on disinterested art when Sophia first encounters Minna, using Sophia's stereotypical expectations of Minna to create an analogy between greed for money and lust for power over an audience. When Sophia arrives at Minna's crowded apartment, looking for her husband Frederick, she listens to Minna's compelling tale of the pogrom that killed her parents when she was a child. Before that disaster, Minna explains, some Jewish families had moved to her village because another pogrom had destroyed theirs. Minna tells her audience that she "'lorded it over the newcome children, and discovered the sweets of tyranny'" (*SWS* 126).

And you must still savour them, thought Sophia, seeing that mournful dark glance flicker slowly over the listeners, as though numbering so many well-tied money-bags. Our ears are your ducats. You are exactly like a Jewish shop-keeper, the Jew who kept the antique shop at Maycene, staring, gloating round his shelves, with a joy in possession so absorbing that it was almost a kind of innocence. In a moment you should rub your hands, the shopkeeper's gesture. (*SWS* 127)

This passage introduces Sophia's "casual antisemitism"[20] and playfully revises the stereotype on which she relies by shifting the object of greed: instead of money, Minna covets the attention of an audience. By relating greed to the art of storytelling, the text begins to explore the political implications of artistic power. It thereby establishes the overlapping oppositions of disinterestedness/interested endeavors and art/propaganda. These oppositions are integral to crucial questions of the 1930s: what roles could artists play in revolutionary struggles, and what obligations to the political world should they accept? Like her left-wing British contemporaries, Warner wrestled with these questions in her writing throughout most of the decade.[21]

Sophia's image of Minna as the artistic counterpart of a greedy shopkeeper raises these questions and begins the text's use of Jewishness as a way to explore them. Because Jews are linked to interestedness and greed by a long history of cultural and literary stereotypes, Warner can use Minna to meditate on *dis*interestedness, particularly disinterested art. But she does not merely use Minna as a field of play for this inquiry; she allows her an active role in her own representation. As Minna looks around at her audience, she seems preternaturally sensitive to Sophia's unspoken response:

At that moment the slowly flickering glance touched her, and rested. It showed no curiosity, only a kind of pondering attention. Then, as though in compliance, Minna's large supple hands gently caressed themselves together in the very gesture of her thought. Sophia started slightly. The glance, mournfully numbering, moved on. But answering Sophia's infinitesimal start of surprise there had been a smile – small, meek, and satisfied, the smile of a dutiful child. (*SWS* 127)

Minna's uncanny performance of this stereotyped Jewishness mocks the terms through which Sophia understands her. She simultaneously plays *into* Sophia's caricatured picture of Jews, plays *with* her expectations, satisfied by her "start of surprise," and plays *up to* her like a "dutiful child." Her staged Jewishness exhibits what Terry Castle calls the novel's "theatrical, even phantasmagorical air."[22] Minna's enactment of her role as "the Jewess" stresses to readers the constructedness of the meanings that have accrued to that label, preparing us for the text's use of Minna to represent disinterestedness – just the opposite of Sophia's stereotype.

While Warner relies on the image of greed as a background for her Jewish character, she insists on her revision of that image: the novel makes clear that Minna's only interest is a delight in her own artistic power. In the final episodes of part II, the narrative establishes that it is Sophia, not Minna, who is stimulated by the prospect of controlling money. In those passages Sophia stops at her agent's and collects "twenty-five good golden English pounds".

"I love money," she told herself, walking obliviously past shop-windows. "There, perhaps, the true unexplored passion of my life awaits me." And remembering how Byron had written,
   So for a good old-gentlemanly vice
   I think I must take up with avarice
she took pleasure in imagining herself back again at Blandamer, sitting by the library fire, reading *Don Juan*, and letting her thoughts stray with the turning of a page to rent-roll and consolidated bonds. (*SWS* 196)

Then Sophia meets one of Minna's friends, a Jewish composer who is reduced to playing guitar on the cold streets, and learns that Minna is starving: she can earn nothing as a storyteller because "there is no time now for art," and she has given away what she did have to her poorer friends. Outraged by this news, Sophia seeks out Minna to give her the money she is carrying.

In this scene Warner returns to the stereotype by invoking its most famous representative, Shylock, only to reject it again:

At the weight of the chamois-leather bag, coming so warm from Sophia's muff, Minna's eyebrows flicked upward.
"Gold," she said, and counted the pieces. "Twenty-five English pounds. Well?"
Under her play-acting of Shylock she was trembling violently, as people tremble with famine, with excitement, with intolerable strain of anxiety.
"Well, Sophia?" (*SWS* 212)

When Sophia explains her intentions, Minna replies that she will "'take the money and be grateful'" – but she immediately deposits it all into a collection box marked "For the Polish Patriots" (*SWS* 213). Minna's unselfishness cements the women's relationship: Sophia feels "released" and can echo Minna's cry "'Vive la liberté!'" sincerely. "Somehow, by that action, so inexplicable, unreasonable, and showy, Minna had revealed a new world; and it was as though from the floor of the Luxembourg Palace Sophia had seen a fountain spring up . . . , glittering and incorruptible, with the first splash washing off all her care and careful indifference to joy." The women walk off together, their faces "carelessly joyful" (*SWS* 214).

It is Minna's "inexplicable" and even "showy" generosity that creates the possibility for joy and love. The imagined fountain not only conjures the sexual relationship that Sophia and Minna will enjoy, but also an ideal space of "incorruptible" integrity.[23] The novel later links Minna's generosity explicitly to Judaic ethics. "'When I was a child in my father's house,'" Minna says, "'I learned some Hebrew, and one of the things I learned was, that in our Hebrew language there was no word for charity. The word I must use, my father said, was Justice.'" Rather than a supererogatory gesture, giving money as Minna does "to the poor and to the sick, to artists and beggars and frauds" is viewed in Jewish tradition as no more than just (*SWS* 361).

Warner emphasizes Minna's generosity and poverty in order to place her outside the self-interested culture from which Sophia is beginning to be freed. But the problem of Sophia's wealth remains. Sophia worries that revealing it will undermine their happiness by removing them both from this space of freedom: "How was she to intimate to Minna that the twenty-five pounds devoted to the Patriots of Poland was not the ending of her resources? On that triumphant outcry of 'I have beggared you now!' it would have been tactless to mention the margin between herself and beggary" (*SWS* 226). But Sophia wonders how Minna could be unaware of her wealth:

> Yet Minna . . . could scarcely have been Frederick's mistress and yet suppose that twenty-five pounds was all that stood between Mrs. Frederick Willoughby and indigence. Besides, she was a Jewess, one of a race who can divine gold even in the rock; she should be able to divine it in a bank too. Ridiculous, thought Sophia, still turning and twiddling the problem; ridiculous that one should feel obliged to break it gently to her that one is blessed with comfortable means. Of all people, she should digest such information most naturally; for she is a Jewess, with a proper esteem for money, and she is an artist, with no hoity-toity scruples about taking it. (*SWS* 226–227)

That Minna does not seem to realize how easy it will be for Sophia to get more cash again refutes Sophia's unthinking antisemitism, and Sophia's nagging worry about letting Minna know she has money belies her conviction that as a "Jewess" Minna would properly "esteem" that money. These obvious contradictions extend Warner's linkage of Minna's *indifference* to money to her Jewishness and artistry.[24] In the end, Minna's innocence makes Sophia decide not to risk explaining her financial situation. Instead, she decides to pawn some of her jewelry: "The money resulting from a visit to the Mont de Piété would be, in some mystical way, cleansed from the sin of original wealth; it would not offend Minna, or flaw the illusion of poverty on which, she supposed, everything depended" (*SWS* 228). Their relationship depends on poverty because Warner is methodically, in the midst of her lively and engaging narrative, building a case against the bourgeois commodification of love and art.

She advances this case by making Sophia's illusory poverty a reality. A resentful Frederick, having lost his mistress to his wife, decides to cut off Sophia's access to her money. First, he responds to her request to send her luggage by delivering it without her jewels or valuables, pretending he is keeping them safe from Minna's friends, whom he calls "revolutionary bobtail" (*SWS* 242). Two days later, when Sophia visits her great-aunt's house where Frederick is now staying, Frederick asserts his power, enforcing the double standard that allows him a mistress from any class but refuses Sophia any place among bohemians, Jews, and revolutionaries. " 'Minna Lemuel is not a fit person for you to associate with' "

(*SWS* 263). Outraged by his hypocrisy, Sophia hits him with "the whole force of her fist." But he has the upper hand:

"[U]ntil you mend your manners you can whistle for your jewels and your scent-bottles, and everything else you like to think yours. Not a penny do you get from me. It's mine, do you understand? By the law, it's mine. When you married me it became mine . . . I've written to the bank already and given orders that your signature is not to be honoured." (*SWS* 264–265)

Through this plot device Warner both reminds readers of the inequity of nineteenth-century marriage laws and completes Sophia's estrangement from her customary wealth and power. She thus delivers her more fully into Minna's hands, to be freed from the strictures she once knew as privilege.

Minna is not only poor, but crucially female, bohemian, Jewish, exiled, and bisexual. If only because she is expelled from them, Minna can hardly have much stake in the categories of identity that have until now policed Sophia's life: gender, class, Englishness, compulsory heterosexuality. Before she came to Paris, Sophia already understood the social limitations placed on a "respectable" woman; now she can see her previous life as entirely based in an economy of obligations.

Sophia had been brought up in a world policed by oughts. One ought to venerate age, one ought to admire the beautiful. One ought to love ugly Mary Thompson because she was so clean, God because he was so good . . . , Mamma because she was so kind, Frederick because he was her husband. One ought to devote oneself to one's children because, if well brought up, they would be a comfort in one's old age. Behind every love or respect stood a monitorial reason, and one's emotions were the expression of a bargaining between demand and supply, a sort of political economy. (*SWS* 290–1)

This passage, in which Sophia reflects on her own past values, is the focal point of the portrait of bourgeois European culture that Warner has been creating. This world is not just *based* on "oughts" but "policed" by them, suggesting that one could hardly escape from this economy even if one's inclinations were to bestow love or respect for idiosyncratic reasons. But an inclination to love without a "monitorial reason" would be highly unlikely, given that "one's emotions were the expression" of this bargain, and nothing more. That is, for someone trapped in a culture that commodifies not only art but love, emotion is constrained and predetermined by a simple cost-benefit analysis.

But as the passage goes on to assert, now that Sophia is living in revolutionary Paris with Minna, outside the culture of emotion-surveillance, she has learned how to love unreasonably, without the greed implied by the economy of "demand and supply":

> At a stroke, Minna had freed her from all this. Unbeautiful and middle-aged, unprincipled and not intellectual, vain, unreposeful, and with a complexion that could look greasy, she offered her one flower, liberty. One could love her freely, unadmonished and unblackmailed by any merits of body or mind. She made no more demands upon one's moral approval than a cat, she was not even a good mouser. One could love her for the only sufficient reason that one chose to. (*SWS* 291)

Minna has come to represent emotion that is free from economic and gender constraints – free, indeed even from constraints compelled by "moral approval." The word "unblackmailed" implies by contrast the persuasive power of propaganda, and here the critique of *interested* art that begins when Sophia compares Minna's need for an audience to greed for money comes full circle. In fact, in the paragraph that follows, the narrative returns to the subject of Minna's "artfulness": "Like the work of art, her artfulness was for art's sake . . . Calculating with unscrupled cunning upon the effect she might have, her calculations stopped short there[;] she was unconcerned as to whether the effect of the effect would advantage her or no" (*SWS* 291).

Warner has turned the stereotype of the greedy Jew thoroughly inside-out, aligning Minna with disinterested love and, perhaps paradoxically, genuine artfulness. Because its interest is limited to its own effectiveness, the kind of art Minna stands for can neither become propaganda nor be adulterated by the profit motive. It remains free, therefore, both from Communist insistence that art serve the cause and from the bourgeois assumption that art should bear financial fruit. In this idealized realm of emotion and art free from money interest, Sophia is able to speak and listen in a way she never has before: "From the time when they left the Luxembourg Palace she had breathed this intoxication of being mentally at ease, free to speak without constraint, listen without reservation" (*SWS* 239). But because this state of affairs, Warner is well aware, *is* an ideal, Minna dies (we have to assume) in the fighting during the June Days. She dies as a result of a final act of generosity: she welcomes, as he leaps over the barricades, Sophia's colonial nephew Caspar, now enlisted in the *Gardes Mobiles*. Caspar stabs her in the chest with his bayonet.

It is perhaps appropriate that Minna's death is never made certain because Sophia cannot find her body.[25] Her final bodilessness reinforces not only the erasure of Jewish women within the misogynist and anti-semitic discourse of feminized Jewish men, but the impossibility of that which she represents. Working against both Communist and capitalist dogmas, Warner has employed a disinterested Jewish woman artist to counter the stereotype of the greedy Jewish male financier (and perhaps the male Jewish artists of Hemingway and Lawrence as well). Warner's sympathies are clear, her politics admirable. Yet because her portrayal of a generous Jew depends on the opposing caricature, the image of the greedy Jew lingers, in spite of her efforts, as the mirror, the opposing ghost, of her rewriting. The stereotype being revised shows through the resulting revision, creating a palimpsestic effect that is hard to ignore. This conjuring of the greedy Jew through the disinterested one can have contradictory political effects: it can reinforce the conjunction in readers' minds between "Jew" and "greed," and it can simultaneously demonstrate the arbitrary nature of the link between "the Jew" and any metaphoric tenor. In various forms this contradiction runs through all the novels I discuss in this study; and one thing it shows clearly is the tenacity of the meanings that had accrued to "the Jew" by the interwar period, arbitrary as they were and are.

The pattern through which Warner revisits and rejects the stereotype of the greedy Jew as part of a comment upon the commodification of art in her society is strikingly similar to that in Jean Rhys's *Good Morning, Midnight*. The 1939 novel chronicles Sasha Jansen's immersion in a world of commodified personal and social relations during a trip to Paris in 1937. It meditates on the extent to which European society rests on the circulation of money and goods, and to which human beings, women especially, are defined by how successfully they can procure and brandish (often wear) these goods. Even successful accumulation of commodities, of course, cannot bring satisfaction, since no sooner has one triumphed over or through a commercial exchange, than one must attempt the next. Rhys analyzes and mocks this process when she has Sasha worry for days about having her hair dyed the perfect "blonde cendré," only to forget about it in the taxi on the way back from the salon. She is satisfied and peaceful for the time it takes her to eat lunch in the Luxembourg Gardens (used here, as in *Summer Will Show*, as a site of calm and possibility); but then she begins planning to buy a hat and dress, to "get on with the transformation act" (*GM, M* 62–63).

In addition to being entangled in the incessant desire created by commodity capitalism, Sasha is trapped in her traumatized psyche, where all the gods are dead and the world has been reduced to an "enormous machine" made up of "innumerable" flexible steel arms that end in either lights or mascara-laden eyes (*GM, M* 187). As this image implies, one is constantly seeing and being seen in this novel; but this visual interplay rarely leads to any sort of human connection. Instead, it leads to a sense of raw and painful exposure. On the first page of the novel, for example, Sasha remembers an incident from the night before, in which she began to cry in front of two strangers in a bar. The woman reacted by shaming her further, saying, "'I understand. All the same . . . Sometimes I'm just as unhappy as you are. But that's not to say that I let everybody see it'" (*GM, M* 10). That she will cry in public becomes one of Sasha's constant worries, adding to her fear of being watched and her intense desire to blend in, to look respectable. The feeling of exposure climaxes at the end of the novel when Sasha accepts the cruel-eyed man next door, whom she has labeled a *commis voyageur* (traveling salesman), into her bed. As Catherine Vaughan points out, the traveling salesman incarnates the very circulation of money and goods that has both enticed and (necessarily) failed Sasha throughout the novel.[26] This ending links the themes of commodification and exposure in a disturbing portrait of a woman who says "yes – yes – yes" to the repetition and insatiability of commodity culture.

In such a world it is hard to imagine a disinterested sphere or a safe space. But there is one space in the novel that does seem removed from the relations of exchange and exposure that dominate the rest of Sasha's world: the artist's studio belonging to Serge Rubin, a Jewish artist she meets through her Ukrainian acquaintance, Nicolas Delmar. Although when she sees him she immediately decides he has "that mocking look of the Jew, the look that can be so hateful, that can be so attractive, that can be so sad" (*GM, M* 91), Serge's studio turns out to be a place where Sasha feels singularly accepted, not mocked. This is partly due to their shared understanding of those within the dominant culture: like Sasha, Serge believes such people have "cruel eyes" and know exactly to whom it is safe to be cruel (*GM, M* 32, 97–98). It is also due to their shared status as outsiders who, as I describe in the introduction, cannot manage to look quite like those around them. Rhys creates in Serge a sympathetic counterpart to Sasha, while also using him to introduce and comment on the ideal of disinterested art.

To do this, and to make clear that she aims to counter the stereotype of the greedy Jew, Rhys establishes Serge's generosity and indifference to money. Sasha narrates an incident in which Serge demonstrates both that indifference and a disinclination to shame her by responding to her rudeness. Serge has given her a tiny cup of port rather than the large brandy she desires.

> I have an irresistible longing for a long, strong drink . . .
> I say in a loud, aggressive voice: "Go out and get a bottle of brandy," take money out of my bag and offer it to him.
> This is where he starts getting hold of me, Serge. He doesn't accept the money or refuse it – he ignores it. He blots out what I have said and the way I said it. He ignores it as if it had never been, and I know that, for him, it has never been. He is thinking of something else. (*GM, M* 94)

It is a mark of Serge's compassion that he ignores her rude behavior "as if it had never been"; but it is also symbolic that what he ignores is an offer of money. As Vaughan argues, Serge seems to be outside the realm of commodity culture, "neither a consumer nor a seller."[27]

In this context Serge's inability or refusal to have sexual relations with the mulatto woman he describes having met in London takes on a different tinge. He describes this woman as utterly depressed, never leaving the house unless after dark, alienated from her husband, and an object of obvious derision for the people in the building. She has fallen down, drunk and crying, outside his door, and he has let her in and tried to comfort her. Serge assumes, demonstrating a condescending, sexist attitude, that "'what she wanted was that I should make love to her and that it was the only thing that would do her any good. But, alas, I couldn't'" (*GM, M* 97). Some critics see this scene as evidence of his misogyny; others fail to see the condescension in his assumption that the woman needed sex, and some even criticize him for not providing it;[28] Linda Camarasana argues that this story suggests that Serge is homosexual, that Rhys is drawing upon associations between Jews, artists, effeminacy, and homosexuality.[29] It seems to me that Camarasana's is a plausible reading, though it does not remove the patronizing tone of Serge's assumption. But in the context of Serge operating outside the realm of exchange that governs nearly every other relation in the novel, his inability ("I couldn't") to have sex with the woman resonates differently: although Serge thinks she wants him to "make love to her," he has no desire for someone in such misery, someone "at the end of everything," someone who had "turned into stone" (*GM, M* 95–96). To take what he thought she was offering, when she had so little, would be to take advantage of her unhappiness. His refraining from making this brief relationship sexual is in a way analogous to his ignoring the rude way Sasha offered him money: it maintains the dignity of the other, such as it may be. It refuses to exploit.

The possibility that Serge remains outside exploitative relations is bolstered by the attitude to money he demonstrates when Sasha decides to buy one of his paintings. He had gone out to see a friend, while Delmar showed Sasha the paintings. When he has to discuss the price of the painting upon his return, he becomes uncomfortable:

"I want very much to buy one of your pictures – this one."
It is an old Jew with a red nose, playing the banjo.
"The price of that is six hundred francs," he says. "If you think it's too much we'll arrange some other price."
All his charm and ease of manner have gone. He looks anxious and surly. (*GM,M* 100)

Significantly, it is when he believes that Sasha cannot pay him at all that his "charm and ease" return.

I say awkwardly, "I don't think it at all too much. But I haven't got the money . . ."
Before I can get any further, he bursts into a shout of laughter. "What did I tell you?" he says to Delmar.
"But have it, take it, all the same. I like you. I'll give it to you as a present."
"No, no. All I meant was that I can't pay you now."
"Oh, that's all right. You can send me the money from London. I'll tell you what you can do for me – you can find some other idiots who'll buy my pictures."
When he says this, he smiles at me so gently, so disarmingly. The touch of the human hand . . . I'd forgotten what it was like, the touch of the human hand.
"I'm serious. I mean that. Take the picture and send me the money when you can." (*GM, M* 100)

Serge regains his gentle manner as soon as he finds himself finished with the business transaction and back in the realm of nonfinancial interpersonal relations. But the rest of the novel has taken pains to demonstrate that such "human" relations are extremely rare, if not impossible. This is why Sasha has forgotten what the "touch of the human hand" is like: not because no one has touched her, but because people have touched her with hands made metaphorically of steel, like the hand in her dream that points the way to the International Exhibition (*GM, M* 13) and like the arms of the machine she imagines at the end of the novel. Rhys has marked the gentle Jewish Serge as outside the strictures not only of nation and gender, as I discuss more fully in chapter 5, but also of the *modus operandi* of a consumer culture that reduces all relations to exchanges of money.

Sasha, though, is thoroughly immured in that culture, and she persists in making a plan to pay him. They arrange to meet, but as Vaughan notes, it is Delmar who arrives to take the money; Serge does not show up. He does, however, write to Sasha later, telling her that Delmar has handed over the money, thanking her, and apologizing for not keeping their appointment. His note stresses their human relation over their business relation. For one thing, the transaction is finished, but he makes a point of writing to thank her; in addition, Serge offers to change the painting for any other: "He says that if I don't like the bonhomme, if I find him too sad, he will change him for one of the landscapes or for anything else I want and that he will try to get to the Gare du Nord to say au revoir to me (I bet he won't), and he is my friend, Serge Rubin" (*GM, M* 109). This note caps Rhys's portrait of an antistereotypical Jew – generous and kind – who stands out from the rest of the characters in the novel by distancing himself as much as possible from commercialism in both art and human relations.

In Serge's studio Sasha also escapes, temporarily, from the feelings of exposure that stalk her throughout the rest of the narrative. Serge accepts her tears when she suddenly begins to cry, responding differently from all the other characters. Reading this scene, we remember the woman in the bar who criticized an embarrassed Sasha for letting "everybody see" her feelings (*GM, M* 10). In Serge's studio Delmar responds more compassionately but still with discomfort: " 'Oh, madame, oh, madame,' Delmar says, 'why do you cry?' " (*GM, M* 93). But Serge soothes the shame she feels at being "such a fool": " 'But cry,' le peintre says. 'Cry if you want to. Why shouldn't you cry? You're with friends' " (*GM, M* 93). With this ability to tolerate her tears, Serge shows more compassion toward Sasha than she shows herself, given that she mocks her own emotional states throughout the novel. Serge next softens Sasha's feelings of exposure when he rejects her comparison with the "mulatto" woman he describes as being " 'at the end of everything.' " When Sasha hears that the woman cried and asked for a drink, she says, " 'Exactly like me' . . . 'I cried, and I asked for a drink.' 'No, no,' he says. Not like you at all' " (*GM, M* 95). This reassurance helps Sasha listen to the story without the raw self-consciousness that often interferes with her ability to imagine others' experiences.

Moreover, when Serge ignores her offer of money for brandy, he is refusing to *see* her bad behavior; unlike the people who stare at her in bars and unlike the world-as-machine with eyes on each flexible arm, Serge does not visually probe her. On the contrary, he puts on a mask and dances for her. "He holds the mask over his face and dances. 'To make you laugh,' he says. He dances very well. His thin, nervous body looks strange, surmounted by the hideous mask" (*GM, M* 92). Serge willingly becomes a spectacle, shielding Sasha from becoming one herself.[30] As she watches him dance, listening to the Martiniquean music on the gramophone, she has a peaceful fantasy of lying in a hammock near the sea. She feels safe for a rare moment. And after he has left, Delmar arranges Serge's paintings around the walls of the studio, creating another spectacle for her. "I am surrounded by the pictures. It is astonishing how vivid they are in this dim light . . . Now the room expands and the iron band around my heart loosens. The miracle has happened. I am happy" (*GM, M* 99).

Serge's studio – outside of commercial exchange, safe from exposure – is an idealized space. Looking at Serge's paintings, Sasha goes "off into a vague dream. Perhaps one day I'll live again round the corner in a room as empty as this. Nothing in it but a bed and a looking-glass. Getting the stove lit at about two in the afternoon – the cold and the stove fighting each other. Lying near the stove in complete peace . . . " (*GM, M* 99). Sasha wishes she could find herself in such an empty, perfect space. But even within her fantasy, Sasha, perhaps unconsciously, acknowledges the impossibility of this ideal, for it has within it a looking-glass, that tool of women's objectification and constant threat to Sasha, who says earlier that her life is composed in part of "looking-glasses I look nice in, looking-glasses I don't" (*GM, M* 46). This detail echoes the nagging fact behind Serge's attempt to remove himself from the world of commodified art: he needs money, and he gets it by selling his paintings. When Sasha meets Delmar to pay for the painting, he tells her that two years ago, Serge was living in filth:

'La crasse, madame . . . I said to him: 'You can't go on living like this.' "Je m'en fous," he said . . . However, I talked to him and in the end he managed to get the money to give this exhibition. And his pictures were bought. Yes, they were bought . . . And then he did move. He went to this beautiful, respectable room where you saw him.' (*GM, M* 103)

As much as Serge would like to resist the fact, art is unavoidably attached to money. He cannot live outside commodity culture.

It is clear that Rhys does not imagine that a disinterested artistic sphere actually exists, but that she is using the ideal to critique a consumerist culture that turns art into a commodity as unsatisfying as a new hat. It is because of the longstanding link between Jews and money that Serge makes such an effective site for this critique. Rhys has rejected the stereotype, while relying on it to play out a longing for a disinterested realm in which art objects are gifts rather than merchandise. As in *Summer Will Show*, the generous Jew in *Good Morning, Midnight* depends on readers' familiarity with its opposite. The image of the greedy Jew is not entirely erased by the text's insistence on Serge's generosity; it is overwritten, leaving the previous outlines visible.

Whereas Rhys and Warner set out to revise and refute the stereotypical Jew's entanglement with money, that entanglement could be said to haunt the textual unconscious of a scene in *The Years*, which Woolf conceived in 1932 and published in 1937. *The Years* focuses on social relations – it began as *The Pargiters*, an "essay novel" that included expositions of various social issues portrayed in alternating fictional chapters. It depicts the ways the modern public world invades privacy, denying the characters coherent meditations, interrupting conversations, truncating insights. There is value in the external reality the novel focuses on instead: "This one, however, releases such a torrent of fact as I did not know I had in me . . . Of course this is external: but there's a good deal of gold – more than I'd thought – in externality" (*Diary* IV, 133). But the focus on facts rather than the internal worlds of *To the Lighthouse* (1927) and *The Waves* (1931) precludes the meditative tone that dominates the earlier novels and lends a certain superficiality to the characters' thoughts. The novel self-consciously thematizes this lack of depth by emphasizing the interruptions that keep the characters from engaging in more profound musings.

In portraying a failed attempt at communication and artistic communion, the scene I discuss in this chapter is representative. In the "Present Day" chapter of *The Years*, Sara Pargiter sits in her "sordid" flat discussing poetry with her young cousin North Pargiter. The two cousins seem to occupy an ideal space of artistic harmony, a space outside what they call the "procession" of professional, patriarchal society. As if to validate his sense (and ours as we read this novel) that such moments are all too rare, North begins to recite Andrew Marvell's poem "The Garden," in which the speaker laments that "busie Companies of Men" intrude upon innocence and quiet. But his recitation – and the cousins' communion – breaks down under the pressure of a Jew's presence in the adjacent bathroom.

But as he reached the end of the second verse –
 Society is all but rude –
 To this delicious solitude . . .
he heard a sound. Was it in the poem or outside of it, he wondered? Inside, he

thought, and was about to go on, when she raised her hand. He stopped. He heard heavy footsteps outside the door. Was someone coming in? Her eyes were on the door.

"The Jew," she murmured.

"The Jew?" he said. They listened. He could hear quite distinctly now. Somebody was turning on taps; somebody was having a bath in the room opposite.

"The Jew having a bath," she said.

"The Jew having a bath?" he repeated.

"And tomorrow there'll be a line of grease round the bath," she said.

"Damn the Jew!" he exclaimed. The thought of a line of grease from a strange man's body on the bath next door disgusted him.

"Go on – " said Sara: "Society is all but rude," she repeated the last lines, "to this delicious solitude."

"No," he said. (*Years* 339–340)

The sounds of the Jewish neighbor bathing seem to North to have invaded even the poem ("was it in the poem or outside of it?"). The grease of the "strange man's body" invades the cousins' privacy and thwarts their communication, so that North must repeat Sara's words in an effort to understand her meaning. Their thoughts are deflated along with the poem when the thin walls fail to protect them from the sounds of the Jew as he dirties the communal bathtub.

When North is too disgusted to continue the poem, Sara explains how burdened she has felt by Abrahamson's presence. She tells North that when she first saw the grease on the bathtub, she thought she had better find a job. That morning, we learn, she "rushed out in a rage," stood on a bridge, and watched the workers passing by beneath:

"And there were people passing; the strutting; the tiptoeing; the pasty; the ferret-eyed; the bowler-hatted, servile innumerable army of workers. And I said, 'Must I join your conspiracy? Stain the hand, the unstained hand,' – he could see her hand gleam as she waved it in the half-light of the sitting-room, ' – and sign on, and serve a master; all because of a Jew in my bath, all because of a Jew?' " (*Years* 341)

This scene leaves the causal link between "a Jew in [Sara's] bath" and her feeling that she must "sign on, and serve a master" unclear, prompting immediate interpretive and political questions: how does Abrahamson's Jewishness relate to Sara's fear that she must "stain the hand" by entering the professional world? And further, how does Jewishness propel the scene's present-time plot, in which the abandoned poem seems to represent the defeat of imagination? Critics' inquiry into these questions has been precluded by faith that Woolf, married to the Jewish Leonard for more than twenty years by the time she writes *The Years*, could not possibly use a Jew to represent the clearly negative forces against which Sara struggles.[31] The scene, they suppose, must be ironic; Woolf must intend for us to read Sara's aversion to Abrahamson against its grain. However, inquiry into this scene and its drafts reveals that what threatens to entrap Sara Pargiter is the world of financial interest which precludes imaginative freedom. This world is represented throughout the draft versions of the scene, as well as in its published version, by a Jew.

To argue that Woolf rejected her early social antisemitism, critics often quote the first part of her 1930 letter to Ethel Smyth, in which she admitted it was snobbish to let Leonard's Jewishness dampen her enthusiasm for their marriage. But even in that confession – in the part rarely quoted – Woolf reproduced stereotypes of Jews whose "vitality" includes accumulating capital:

How I hated marrying a Jew – how I hated their nasal voices, and their oriental jewellery, and their noses and their wattles – what a snob I was: for they have immense vitality, and I think I like that quality best of all. They cant die – they exist on a handful of rice and a thimble of water – their flesh dries on their bones but still they pullulate, copulate, and amass (a Mrs Pinto, fabulously wealthy came in) millions of money. (*Letters* IV, 195–196)[32]

Similarly, within *The Years*, even Eleanor, who is shown to be sympathetic to Jews by her relations with the poor Levy family, associates them with displays of wealth. Although Eleanor "did not like talking about 'the poor' as if they were people in a book," she nevertheless tells her sister (as I note in the introduction), that they " 'do love finery – Jews' " (*Years* 31).

Just as having Jewish "best friends" does not absolve one from charges of antisemitism, Woolf's antipathies need not have been overcome in 1912 when she married Leonard.[33] In fact, her letters make clear that her marriage did not eradicate her prejudices. In 1932 she wrote, again to Smyth, about a gathering with Leonard's family: "talk, talk, talk, and all save perhaps 2 hours and 10 minutes utter waste. When the 10 Jews sat around me silently at my mother in law's tears gathered behind my eyes, at the futility of life: imagine eating birthday cake with silent Jews at 11 pm" (*Letters* V, 23). The significance of this letter is not that Woolf found the gathering boring, but that after all those years she could not or would not stop seeing the Woolfs merely as a collection of Jews rather than as her husband's particular family. As Hermione Lee points out, moreover, Woolf typically exaggerated the number of people present at these gatherings: "Whenever she referred to the big ceremonial family gatherings the Woolfs went in for, she would always (especially in letters to Vanessa or Vita or Ethel) multiply their numbers, as a joke about how Jews do multiply (and 'pullulate' and 'copulate' and 'amass')."[34]

That both letters just quoted are to Smyth and that Lee mentions three recipients in particular suggest Woolf's sharp awareness of audience: she must have assumed that Smyth (and Vanessa Bell and Vita Sackville-West) would appreciate the antisemitic jibes. Rather than mitigating Woolf's culpability, her willingness to use antisemitism to engage her reader shows how little she understood, or minded, the stakes of her own antisemitism. The next year she wrote to Quentin Bell that she wanted to skip a party for a woman engaged to a Rothschild: "I've no clothes and can't be bothered to rush out and buy gloves, hat, and shoes, all for a Jew" (*Letters* V, 258). The diction and cadence of the phrase "all for a Jew" recall us to Sara's refrain in *The Years*, " 'all because of a Jew in my bath, all because of a Jew.' " Given letters such as these, and the many disdainful references to Jews in the diaries, it is not feasible to use biographical data to insist that Woolf must have disavowed Sara's repugnance for Abrahamson.

But the biographical argument is not the only possible defense against the *prima facie* antisemitism of the scene. Jane Marcus, in her important study of Woolf's oeuvre, reads this scene as a "sacred drama," where Sara, in solidarity with Jews and workers, decides that she must join a redemptive and democratic "conspiracy," which will "work toward a better world." Marcus links this conspiracy to the "society of outsiders" described in *Three Guineas*, offering an optimistic way to understand Sara's narrative.[35] But to "sign on" is to do quite the opposite of what Woolf's "Outsiders' Society" advocates. Marcus's positive vision of the "conspiracy" cannot account for Sara's description of the procession of workers as "servile," her lament that she has to " 'sign on and serve a master,' " or her "rage" at feeling pressured to join them. In fact, Sara's moment on the bridge resembles a scene imagined by the narrator of *Three Guineas*, a scene that helps to validate Sara's protest. When the narrator is discussing the "Act which unbarred the professions" to women, she imagines "the educated man's daughter [standing] on a bridge" and asking herself what she should do with the unfamiliar coin in her hand. "The moon even, scarred as it is in fact with forgotten craters, seemed to her a white sixpence, a chaste sixpence, an altar upon which she vowed never to side with the servile, the signers-on" (*TG* 16). With its return to the image of the bridge and its use of the terms "servile" and "signers-on," this scene confirms that Woolf endorses Sara's predicament. It is not to achieve solidarity with Jews or workers that Sara feels pressured to "sign on," but to escape from her Jewish neighbor. North understands that her words "meant that she was poor; that she must earn her living" (*Years* 342).

At least at the time she is describing to North, Sara wanted to move out of the flat where she had to share the bathroom with Abrahamson, but could do so only by earning more money. So she tried to elicit sympathy from the man at the newspaper office: "'But the Jew's in my bath,' I said – 'the Jew ... the Jew ...'" (*Years* 342). Since Sara is still living in this flat and sharing the bathroom with Abrahamson, *The Years* suggests that she decided against accepting the job. In "The Loudspeaker and the Human Voice," Margaret Comstock argues that since Sara has not moved out of the flat, we can infer that she has confronted her antisemitism, and now exhibits solidarity with her working-class Jewish neighbor.[36] Because the novel abandons the topic without further explanation, this reading may seem possible. However, if we look not only at this scene but also at Sara's character in the novel as a whole, we find another explanation for her continued presence in the flat. Sara is characterized by her refusal to think or act along socially prescribed lines.[37] She does not marry, but neither does she devote her life to a parent, as her cousin Eleanor does. She alone of the characters resists endorsing the war effort in the air-raid scene (*Years* 285–286). She is describing to North a time when she felt pressured to "sign on" to the world of workers, but by remaining in the flat, she demonstrates her triumph over the mental slavery that the newspaper job would have entailed. In *Three Guineas*, after all, Woolf describes journalists as "slaves," insisting that to write for money is to prostitute the mind (*TG* 99).

The drafts of this scene in *The Years* support this interpretation: we see Sara – called Elvira in the early versions – decide it would be even worse to corrupt her sense of truth by writing for pay than to live next to Abrahamson. She wonders how she could possibly "put [the truth] into 2,000 words. No, I shall say, I had rather share my bath with Abrahamson ... For all I know he's a good fellow" (*Pargiters* 8:12). Comstock is right, then, that at least in the early draft Sara (Elvira) has moved past the *acute* phase of her disgust by the time she talks to North (George); but her conclusion that Sara stays in the flat as a gesture of solidarity is unconvincing. It seems instead that refusing to write for pay *even though* it would allow her to escape from Abrahamson only demonstrates Sara's integrity: even with this temptation, she declines a place in the social hierarchy.

More recently, David Bradshaw has argued that Woolf "take[s] care to positively identify with Jews and to provide a precise historical context for

Sara's smear on Abrahamson which leaves the reader in no doubt as to the heinousness of her outburst."[38] The historical context to which Bradshaw refers is the rise of British fascism. He makes his most compelling claim when he points out that on the way to Sara's flat, North notices the symbol of the British Union of Fascists chalked on all the doors and windows along the "long vista" in the East End.[39] For Woolf to include that symbol just before North's visit to Sara, Bradshaw suggests, indicates her linkage of Sara's antisemitism to violent fascist antisemitism. As important a detail as the chalk symbols are, Bradshaw's claim depends on Woolf recognizing the continuum between drawing-room antisemitism like Sara's, and the type of brutal, harassing antisemitism embraced by Oswald Mosley's Blackshirts. But it is not at all clear that Woolf acknowledged this continuum; on the contrary, that she did *not* see the two types of antisemitism as closely related is demonstrated by the fact that she tried to publish her antisemitic story "The Duchess and the Jeweller" in 1938,[40] and that throughout the decade she regularly used Leonard's family as the butt of her antisemitic jabs and jokes.

Furthermore, if Woolf wanted us to see Sara *as* fascist, as Bradshaw claims, she could not very well have Sara espouse the belief that it is harmful to "sign on" to a place in the social hierarchy. The chalked symbols do show Woolf's awareness of the danger Jews faced from the BUF in the East End where Sara lives; but they do not mean she understood her complicity or Sara's in the antisemitism of fascism. We can see from this scene, instead, how easily "polite" antisemitism could coexist with antifascism in the 1930s. What seems obvious from our post-Holocaust vantage point – "the appalling closeness of Sara's anti-Jewish invective to the rabble-rousing rhetoric of Mosley and his followers"[41] – was not necessarily apparent (perhaps especially to English people of Woolf's social background) in the years before the Shoah. If we bear in mind the distinct implications of various types of antisemitism in the 1930s, we may view the chalk circles as a bit of realistic detail that demonstrates little about how Woolf intended us to read Sara's comments. Instead, they provide a context for Sara's living space: she is poor, and she lives among Jews who work in the garment trade and therefore amid potential anti-Jewish violence, which Woolf would certainly condemn. The novel does not, though, seem to link Sara's views about Jews to Mosley's.

But the largest gap in Bradshaw's argument, and in any argument that insists that Woolf abhorred Sara's antisemitism, is that it does not account for the importance and validity, in Woolf's view, of the problem

Sara faces and blames on her Jewish neighbor. Sara's worries about staining her hand by joining the professions are exactly congruent with Woolf's anxieties about intellectual freedom in *Three Guineas*. If Woolf wanted readers to reject Sara's scapegoating of Abrahamson, she would have to undermine Sara's whole passionate point. But instead, she herself emphatically validates this point both in *The Years* and in *Three Guineas*.

This returns us to the questions posed earlier: what does Jewishness have to do with the pressure Sara feels to corrupt her vision by entering the world of journalism? How is it linked to the themes, encapsulated by the interrupted Marvell poem, of solitude invaded, privacy broken, and communion destroyed? Reading *The Years* and its draft versions alongside *Three Guineas* reveals Woolf's recurring fear that imaginative autonomy might be unrecoverable, squeezed out by a homogenizing consumerist culture. The drafts of the scene demonstrate how suitable the figure of the Jew seemed to Woolf for representing this danger to the imagination. From her initial drafts in 1934 through her final revisions, Woolf saw fit to associate Jewishness with the threat of intellectual slavery.

In both *The Years* and *Three Guineas*, Woolf expresses her worry that modernity – the rise of fascism, militarism, consumerism, all those forces that attempt to press disparate minds into identical molds – would stamp out freedom of thought, encroach on the privacy of the mind. *Three Guineas* meditates on the possibility for disinterestedness, for freedom from ties that bind the imagination: "By freedom from unreal loyalties is meant that you must rid yourself of pride of nationality in the first place; also of religious pride, college pride, school pride, family pride, sex pride and those unreal loyalties that spring from them" (*TG* 80). Writing professionally, the narrator claims, prevents this disinterestedness, and is, in fact, a sort of mental prostitution (and "to sell a brain is worse than to sell a body") (*TG* 93). This argument explains Sara Pargiter's predicament. Her privacy is being infringed upon and her creativity obstructed by the Jew who shares her bathroom; but if she gets a job to escape him, she falls into a similar trap, still forfeiting her solitude and mental freedom.

Woolf wrote the "Jew in the bath" scene many times over during the summer of 1934. She began one set of drafts on June 4 and worked on it throughout the month, then began a second set on July 1. In the July versions of the scene, George (whose name will become North by 1936) interprets Elvira's quirky phrases for us and wonders about her meanings and motives. This version addresses the interestedness of contemporary society, especially of literary culture, more explicitly than the published scene. Like her later incarnation, Elvira has to "stain the hand" – that is, she must write for money. Here we are in George's head:

> Elvira had gone back to the book that she had dropped. She was flicking over the pages; she was dipping, diving, she was caught within some machine: the blood royal, the unstained hand – he remembered the phrases; they meant, he supposed, that in some vague way that she felt . . . that it is better to give than to take; better to remain outside the patriarchy – that is, the hierarchy of organized society, than to accept membership; better to remain obscure, unpaid, subsisting on a meager allowance. But why better? What was the idea . . . behind such an impulse? Something that was difficult to express, some ancient prejudice or instinct to the effect that human nature degrades itself by taking? that pleasure, happiness lie in what is voluntary? in our day the traitorous are the successful; that it is they who impede progress, put a ring on the natural expanse of the mind. (*Pargiters* 7:6)

The constraints (rings) that those who are successful within the "hierarchy" put around the mind are made literal by the ring that Abrahamson puts around the bathtub. Here, in George's thoughts, is an argument very like the central claim in *Three Guineas*: only by remaining outside "organized society" can one protect one's autonomy. To accept membership – in *Three Guineas* by joining a society (even an antiwar society), here by writing for another – is slavery or prostitution of the mind.

Still, why is this mental prostitution figured by a Jew? According to the drafts, the association is explained by an underlying link between Jews and financial interest:

> "Ought to be a law,["] she observed. ["]Every man one who writes, a lecturer [who] gets himself up to instruct the people should be forced to add, 'the Jews in my bath' in capital letters, The Jews in my bath.["] She meant, he supposed, that the tract she had been skimming She meant that they wrote for money, he supposed. (*Pargiters* 7:8)

All those who own culture, Elvira says, ought to be honest enough to admit that they write for money, that they are themselves "owned." Their sale of the mind is signified by this incessant phrase, "'the Jew[']s in my bath.'"

This passage is repeated in the drafts. A few pages earlier is another version:

> "~~If I were Lord Chancellor~~, she remarked, I should make it
> ~~It ought to be a law~~, she remarked:
> ~~Every lecturer, every preacher every~~
> The Jews in my bath . . .

The Jews in his bath tub, she observed;
but he doesn't have the common honesty to say so.
She meant that the article she was skimming was written for money, he supposed. (*Pargiters* 7:5)

Here the "he" who is not honest enough to admit his affiliations is the writer of the article Sara is skimming. In the July drafts of this scene, then, Woolf uses a Jew to represent the money interest that in *Three Guineas* prostitutes the mind of the writer. Whereas in *The Years* Abrahamson represents an abstracted invasion into Sara's private space, vaguely connected with the world of professional writing by driving Sara toward the "servile innumerable army of workers," here Jews represent a direct involvement with money, a commercialism that shows in greater detail why it is so difficult to preserve private judgment.

In *Three Guineas* the narrator asks her interlocutor: "Do you pursue the same rather extravagant policy there – glance at three daily papers and three weekly papers if you want to know the facts about pictures, plays, music and books, because those who write about art are in the pay of an editor, who is in the pay of a board, which has a policy to pursue . . . ?" (*TG* 96). Being "in the pay of" someone else was crucial in *The Pargiters*, where Elvira suggests that the more successful one is, the more one must play into this system of intellectual harlotry: "Big wigs, all took pay; they had Jews in their baths" (*Pargiters* 7:9). The Jew in the bath of "big wigs" represents the same mental prostitution that is described more straightforwardly in *Three Guineas*.[42]

Taken together, *The Pargiters* and *Three Guineas* connect the ideas of prostitution, corruption, Jews, and money interest until they describe what ails British culture. George accepts Elvira's metaphor of "the Jew" and wonders how to create an expansive, free culture: "The Jew was in all their baths as she put it. The problem, how to get rid of the line of grease, how to live . . . decently, expansively" (*Pargiters* 7:10).[43] George and Elvira use the figure of the Jew to represent both an invasion into the private home and the corruption of the public world. The image of the line of grease signals a fear of contamination, even abjection. As Leena Kore Schröder has argued, and as I discuss further in chapter 6, Woolf used Jewishness as a shorthand for the threat of viscosity: "[I]n a grim logic, it is the figure of the conceptual Jew in Virginia Woolf's work who embodies the abjection of the 'clean and proper' self."[44] And as Schröder points out in her discussion of "The Duchess and the Jeweller," money is a key "agent" of abjection, "keeping the world of the aristocrat and that of the Jew implicated one in the other."[45] Here, too, Woolf draws upon images of greasiness or sliminess to figure the money interest that threatens Sara's integrity and forces her to rub shoulders with the likes of Abrahamson.

In fact, in the earliest versions of the scene, written in June 1934, Elvira is more overtly disgusted with her Jewish neighbor and has not, as she may have in *The Years*, moved past the most acute stage of her reaction. Here it is she rather than George/North who exclaims, "'Oh damn the Jew!'" And the "grease" of the later versions is called instead "slime." "'[H]e'll use all the hot water, but that's not what I mind. [I]ts leaving a track of slime around the edge of the bath'" (*Pargiters* 6:112). Here Abrahamson causes a breakdown of communication and creativity even more directly: "Water was running. As it ran, the play, the play they were creating together, which Elvira had been making, wore thin, collapsed" (*Pargiters* 6:113). This version of the scene goes beyond associating "the Jew" with intellectual and cultural slavery; it denies any purpose to literature and culture at all, if that which Abrahamson represents is going to compromise them: "'If Abrahamson is going to have a bath, whats the good of reading The Tempest?'" (*Pargiters* 6:113). This line expresses clear despair about the impotence of imaginative art. "The Jew," standing for overwhelming financial pressures and thereby for mental slavery and prostitution, is poised to destroy the possibility of disinterested art and undermine intellectual freedom, which *Three Guineas* deems our most valuable human goods.

Three Guineas, with its utopian proposals that women might remove themselves from this dangerously corrupt culture, suggests that Woolf did retain some hope that mental freedom could be protected. In *The Years* she states and demonstrates the problem: not only in this scene but through all the instances of thwarted thought she details various forces (sexual predation and repression, gender strictures, professional pride, militarism, and capitalist tyranny) that suppress imagination. In *Three Guineas* she tries to imagine solutions. She does not, of course, link all the threatening forces to Jews; but the one that most directly menaces Woolf's own art *is* figured by a Jew, that readily available and durable symbol for entanglement with money. If there is an irony in the scene in *The Years*, it is that the most crucial mechanism that protected Woolf from the mental prostitution involved in her own profession was the Hogarth Press, which her Jewish husband Leonard established so that she could keep her hand "unstained," not having to kowtow to other editors and publishers.

Woolf's relative removal from the world of profit-seeking publishing did not mean that she was unconcerned with money. As her diaries show, she thought about it frequently, noting her sales figures and planning what she would do with the profits from each novel, particularly after sales of *To the Lighthouse*, published in 1927, enabled her to buy a car (*Diary* III, 147).[46] The other side of this concern with profit is clearly the anxiety I have traced, expressed throughout the late 1930s, that she might be corrupted by it. And perhaps, as Freedman argues about Henry James and earlier British writers, Woolf used the constellation of images of Jews, prostitutes, and slaves to express her shame at writing for pay herself. In his astute study *Am I a Snob?* (2003), Sean Latham analyzes Woolf's manipulations of financial and cultural capital. He describes *Orlando* (1928) as demonstrating Woolf's romanticization of those who have enough money to be free from money. Her contradictory celebration of this kind of snobbishness (the rich aristocrat does not deign to think about money because she has so much) parallels Woolf's conflicted responses to earning money from her writing.[47] Her wish to make money and yet be free from its pressures leaves a deep ambivalence in her representations of money and writing, in which she both hungrily imagines all the money she might make from her novels, and passionately denounces the practice of writing for pay. This ambivalence finds expression in the portrait of Abrahamson, the impoverished Jewish factory worker who paradoxically stands for financial interest.

In spite of their reluctance to use the "types" of nineteenth-century fiction, then, the three women modernists this chapter considers continued to associate Jews with money interest. Rhys and Warner worked to revise that link, though the image of the greedy Jew cannot entirely be effaced by representations of generous Jews. But they did seek actively to write over the past with new words, images, and associations. Woolf, on the other hand, covertly relied upon the old image in her feminist search for a disinterested artistic sphere, a sphere in which women could be free from the manipulations she describes so vividly in *A Room of One's Own* (1929). This raises a question I consider further in the next chapter: what does it mean when antisemitism stains the very feminist project we admire?

2

Transformations of supersessionism in Woolf and Richardson

Modernism for Virginia Woolf and Dorothy Richardson meant many of the things it meant for James Joyce: perhaps most importantly, experimental fictions designed to portray the interior rather than the exterior lives of their characters.[1] But their literary projects were also feminist, and explicitly opposed to Joyce's egotistical "titanic failure," as Richardson described it (*W* 68). They defined themselves against male literary traditions and set out to forge a feminist literary consciousness that would eschew egotism yet value and represent the experiences of particular minds. In this effort they drew on rhetoric of surpassing, improving upon, and superseding that enabled them to position their work as superior to prior and contemporary "masculine" writing.

In her foreword to *Pilgrimage* (1915–1967), for example, Richardson describes her dilemma as she set out to write a novel in 1911. The realist novel, represented, she says, by Honoré de Balzac and his "English follower" Arnold Bennett, was already being succeeded by a more highly articulated realism that valued literature insofar as it provided "mirrors of plain glass" rather than mirrors that were "rose-coloured and distorting." Richardson set out to produce a "feminine equivalent" to this contemporary realism (*P* 9). To do this she had to discard "a considerable mass of manuscript" (*P* 10). As she began again, she became aware

> of the gradual falling away of the preoccupations that for a while had dictated the briskly moving script, and of the substitution, for these inspiring preoccupations, of a stranger in the form of contemplated reality having for the first time in her experience its own say, and apparently justifying those who acclaim writing as the surest means of discovering the truth about one's own thoughts and beliefs. (*P* 10)

Richardson also calls her new work a "searching" and "joyous" adventure, a journey upon "a fresh pathway" (*P* 10). She does not claim to be the only explorer of this pathway, but recounts her realization, once she began walking along it, that Joyce, Marcel Proust, and Woolf were walking there as well (actually, Woolf is "mounted upon a magnificently caparisoned charger"). Moreover, Richardson modestly uses the word "equivalent" to compare her work with contemporary "realism." But what she describes is clearly, in her view, an advance. In the passage above, she claims that in her writing "contemplated reality" has "its own say" in the literature of her experience for the first time. To achieve this she discards her former, inadequate attempt, which she implies was too similar to the available models. Her use of the word "substitution" in her description of the preoccupations that drive literature suggests a process whereby the inadequate "old" is replaced with the superior "new." This newness, the first appearance of "contemplated reality," makes clear that Richardson considers her feminist modernism to be a major step forward from the realism of Bennett.

Woolf, of course, also compared herself favorably with Bennett. In "Mr. Bennett and Mrs. Brown" (1924) and "Modern Fiction" (1925) she differentiates herself from him and the realist writers John Galsworthy and H. G. Wells. Woolf, too, takes an explicitly modest stance even as she makes the case that her own approach (and that of select contemporaries) is an advance upon the work of these writers. She begins "Modern Fiction" by acknowledging that literature does not move progressively, but cyclically. "We do not come to write better; all that we can be said to do is to keep moving."[2] She concedes that she and those contemporaries she approves of (at the moment, Joseph Conrad and Thomas Hardy) "only know that certain gratitudes and hostilities inspire us; that certain paths seem to lead to fertile land, others to the dust and the desert."[3] Using the word "path," echoing Richardson's "pathway," Woolf compares her writing to a journey; in fact, like Richardson she implies a journey weighted with spiritual value: a sort of pilgrimage. Like Christian in John Bunyan's *The Pilgrim's Progress* (1678), the writer must not allow herself to be led down paths that lead to "dust and the desert," but must find the road toward spiritual salvation. Indeed, Woolf uses the opposition of spirituality versus materiality in her description of her difference from Bennett, Galsworthy, and Wells: "If we tried to formulate our meaning in one word we should say that these three writers are materialists. It is because they are concerned not with the spirit but with the body that they have disappointed us."[4] In spite of her modesty, then, she depicts her modernism (and now Joyce's) as clearly superior to "materialist" realism, just as the spirit is viewed in Western Christian culture as superior to the body.

The body, in turn, is strongly associated with Jews, whom Paul of Tarsus and successive Christian thinkers described as bodily, unspiritual, and materialistic (I discuss this view at greater length in chapter 4). To distinguish the work of these feminist writers from masculine "materialism," then, the Christian doctrine of supersessionism could provide a convenient discursive tool. Using the theological notion that Christianity superseded Judaism, Woolf and Richardson associate their own feminist art with Christian "advancement," and link features of literary and cultural masculinity and materiality to Judaism. This assertion may seem less odd with regard to Richardson than with regard to Woolf; after all, Richardson was deeply interested in Christianity, while Woolf rejected religion, declaring (only partially tongue in cheek) in 1940 in "A Sketch of the Past" that "certainly and emphatically there is no God."[5] But supersessionism was a powerful cultural, not merely religious, assumption. It circulated (and still circulates) in secular society, contributing its power, for instance, to the racialist notion common in the early twentieth century that Jews were an old and stagnant people.

The doctrine of supersessionism, which held that the "new" covenant replaced the "old," was disavowed by the Catholic Church in the reforms of Vatican II. Before that point, it was a feature of orthodox Christianity, and even now some groups of Christians argue explicitly that supersessionism is an integral part of Christian theology.[6] Indeed, many passages from the Christian foundational writings ("the Gospels"), Acts, and the Pauline epistles demonstrate supersessionist attitudes. These attitudes, in spite of their now heretical character, continue to be widespread at least in American culture today.

An example from my own classrooms may be informative here. Each time I have taught Diane Samuels's play *Kindertransport* (1995), students have defended a supersessionist claim made by one of the characters. In the play a British woman has adopted a German Jewish refugee child. When she finds that the child has not been eating her lunch because it contains ham, the adoptive mother tells the child that she may eat pork now. "[T]he Lord Jesus said that we needn't keep to the old laws any more. They had their day years ago . . . New things have come to put in their place."[7] I explain to my students what supersessionism is and why this remark is an instance of it. In one class a student defended the character's statement by citing the biblical parable of the wedding. In this parable (Matt. 22:1–14), those who are invited to a wedding feast for a king's son do not bother to attend. The king asks his servants to summon the invited guests, but not only do they not come, some of them even kill the servants who have come to escort them to the feast. Finally, the angry king tells his servants to invite anyone they can find on the thoroughfares.[8] Jesus, according to Matthew, compares the king's situation with the kingdom of heaven. One meaning seems clear: if the Jews do not wish to participate in the redemption offered them through Jesus (the king's son), others will take their place in the kingdom of heaven. Rosemary Ruether points out that the parable also includes a punishment of the guests: "The king, in turn, 'was angry, and he sent his troops and destroyed those murderers and burned their city.' . . . Matthew thus tells us that unrepentant Israel is rejected, but also that God will punish it." Ruether describes this parable as "a complete story of the Church's identity over against apostate Israel."[9] This story, accusing Jews of ingratitude and even cold-blooded murder, makes it appear inevitable that Christians should usurp their position as God's children. It both predicts and justifies the replacement of Jews by Christians.

In Matthew this parable follows immediately upon a similar one in which the tenants of a vineyard kill the owner's messengers, and finally, the owner's son. As Ruether confirms, the most obvious way to read this parable is to take the owner as standing for God, the vineyard as Israel, and the tenants as the Jews, who kill the servants, or prophets.[10] The tenants' murder of the owner's son is the final, outrageous confirmation of their disrespect. In Matthew's version that parable concludes, "Therefore I tell you, the kingdom of God will be taken away from you and given to a nation producing the fruits of it" (Matt. 21:43).[11] Together, the two parables threaten Jews with an allegedly well-deserved displacement and replacement by Christians (supersessionism is also called "replacement theology"). It is not surprising, then, that we can find numerous examples of unthinking supersessionist thought in everyday religious conversation: in the assertion that messianic (Christian) Jews are "completed Jews"; in Christians wondering why Jews keep Kosher "anymore"; in the very phrases used to describe the covenants accepted respectively by Jews and Christians: the "Old Testament" and the "New Testament." The mere existence of a "new" covenant would seem to invalidate its predecessor, just as a will or contract dated 2007 supersedes a version of the will or contract dated 2006.

Even a sympathetic Christian, criticizing Christian antisemitism in *The Catholic Register* in 1987, describes Judaism as an incomplete form of Christianity: "When a Hindu or a pagan becomes a Christian, he is converted. When a Jew becomes a Christian, he is completed. This is surely Jesus' point of view too, for He said He came not to destroy the Law and the Prophets but to fulfill them."[12] In fact, if we search for the *Catholic Encyclopedia* on the internet, we find the text of the Encyclopedia from 1908, not marked as itself invalidated by Vatican II. In an article entitled "Christianity," we read the official early twentieth-century Catholic view of the relation of Christianity to other religions. The text asserts that Judaism is the only religion relevant to the origins of Christianity, though Christianity surpasses it: "We have so far seen, in its origin and growth, the essential independence of Christianity of all other religious systems, except that of Judaism, with which, however, its relation was merely that of substance to shadow." The article has elaborated on that relationship earlier, claiming, with similar arrogance, that "Christianity is developed from Judaism in the sense that it embodies the Divine revelation contained in the latter creed, somewhat as a finished painting embodies the original rough sketch."[13] If we fail to notice the 1908 copyright in small print at the bottom of the article, we will invest this article with the imprimatur of the contemporary Catholic Church. In any case, this article demonstrates the Church's official view of Judaism at the time Woolf and Richardson were writing.

The encyclopedia's imagery of substance versus shadow and finished painting versus rough sketch provides good examples of the attitude Christianity has historically taken toward Judaism. As Ruether describes it,

> Christianity confronted Judaism with a demand for a conversionist relation to its own past that abrogated that past, in the sense that that past itself no longer provided a covenant of salvation . . . It declared that in this cornerstone alone there is salvation, while the covenant of Moses provides no cornerstone in itself, but exists only to predict the true cornerstone.[14]

It is for this reason that bodies such as the Christian Scholars Group on Christian–Jewish Relations have had to affirm publicly that Judaism is a living religion, and that God's covenant with the Jews "endures."[15]

As powerful as it is, this supersessionist strain of thought might nevertheless seem to be limited to theological debate, irrelevant to the ways most people think or write about Jews in secular societies. Indeed, those who study the ways Jews were imagined in Christian cultures over the past several hundred years are constantly mindful of the paradigm shift usually dated sometime in the nineteenth century. Around this time, Western animus against Jews moved from anti-Judaism – theological prejudice against Jews as a religious group – to antisemitism – "scientific" prejudice against Jews as a "race." As Sander Gilman puts it, "the discourse concerning the Jew move[d] from a theological to a pseudoscientific paradigm."[16] This shift is crucial for understanding why, for example, Inquisitors of the fifteenth and sixteenth centuries were for the most part satisfied if Jews converted to Christianity, whereas the Nazis were not appeased even if those with Jewish grandparents were devoted Christians – they were racially tainted regardless. Those of us who study early twentieth-century fiction, then, generally focus on racial representations.

But paradigm shifts do not create neatly packaged conceptual stages, in which one strain of thought is sealed off from the influence of earlier strains. Rather, discourses attendant on earlier paradigms linger into later ones – not perhaps making much sense in the new context, but surviving nevertheless. While racial understandings dominate in the modernist period, religious conceptions of Judaism regularly disrupt the hegemony of race science.[17] Or, to think about it in terms of Raymond Williams's concept of the "residual," Christian theological views of Jews leave a residue that is transformed by and incorporated into the dominant discourse of race science.[18] In this chapter I show that this particular theological discourse retained power to shape semi-religious and secular views of Jews and Judaism in the interwar years. Both Woolf and Richardson rely on supersessionist attitudes and discourses to give form and power to their experiments with aesthetic value.

Having linked Jewishness to the ways in which the mind of the artist and her products are degraded by their entanglement with money interest (as I show in the previous chapter), Woolf sets out in *Three Guineas* (1938) to devise an antidote to such a state of affairs. The explicit impetus for *Three Guineas*, however, is an attempt to answer a male correspondent who inquires, "How in your opinion are we to prevent war?" (*TG* 3). It is therefore worth asking why Woolf spends so much time in the polemic lamenting how difficult it is for the artist to approach her art with a mind free from social and financial coercion and how circumstances might be changed to make disinterested art possible. How does the question of disinterestedness in the artistic realm relate to the question of how to prevent war, that most political of questions?

The answer can be found within the argument that was most controversial in Woolf's time and most celebrated in our own: that the realm of art, including the pressures on the mind of the individual artist, is inseparable from the realm of politics, even in its narrow sense. Woolf had been making comparable arguments since at least *A Room of One's Own* (1929), where she describes fiction as "like a spider's web . . . attached to life at all four corners" and suggests that changes in the world pull, stretch, and tear at the web. When the web is deformed by such pressures, it becomes clear that "webs are not spun in midair by incorporeal creatures, but are the work of suffering human beings, and are attached to grossly material things, like health and money and the houses we live in" (*Room* 41–42). In *Three Guineas* Woolf expands this claim, asserting not only that material things affect the artist, but that the state of the artist's mind affects the world: if she is free, she helps to compose free culture; if she is enslaved, she helps to corrupt the larger society. That is, the cultural and personal spheres are inextricable: "the public and the private worlds are inseparably connected; . . . the tyrannies and servilities of the one are the tyrannies and servilities of the other" (*TG* 142). Woolf thereby sets the stage for considering issues of artistic freedom as integral to issues of political freedom.

Woolf's thesis in *Three Guineas* is that English patriarchal society is already inherently fascistic and must free itself from pernicious elements within before it can protect itself from fascism abroad. She describes the English misogynist, telling women their "real places," as a dictator in embryo, and asks,

is not the woman who has to breathe that poison and to fight that insect, secretly and without arms, in her office, fighting the Fascist or the Nazi as surely as those who fight him with arms in the limelight of publicity? . . . Should we not help her to crush him in our own country before we ask her to help us to crush him abroad? (*TG* 53)

This argument seemed to many in her own time to be impossibly abstract, unhelpful in a time of dire need to protect European liberty from the swelling power and reach of the Nazis.[19] It often seems to us, however, to include a brilliant analysis of the ways in which fascism was deeply misogynist and patriarchy necessarily dictatorial. What I want to emphasize here, though, is that the dissolution of boundaries around the personal, artistic, cultural, and political spheres means that the question of how to make disinterested art possible constitutes part of the question of how to protect all other sorts of liberty, the stated goal of the correspondent who asks how to prevent war. Preventing war in *Three Guineas* becomes a means toward protecting liberty as much as protecting liberty helps to prevent war. Woolf evades the direct question of how to prevent war by tackling the more fundamental question of how to protect liberty. And the form of liberty that interests her most is liberty of the imagination, of thought.

This focus raises the stakes of Sara Pargiter's problem in *The Years* (1937). It means that it is not only the individual artist whose integrity is at risk from the power of the "money motive" (*TG* 96), but English culture as a whole. The narrator of *Three Guineas* describes how writing professionally, as Sara was considering, is a sort of mental prostitution. "'But what,' she may ask, 'is meant by "selling your mind without love?"' 'Briefly,' we might reply, 'to write at the command of another person what you do not want to write for the sake of money'" (*TG* 93). Although such a writer is certainly a victim of her poverty, her corruption nevertheless spreads to affect her whole society, turning the victim into a menace: "But when a brain seller has sold her brain, its anaemic, vicious and diseased progeny are let loose upon the world to infect and corrupt and sow the seeds of disease in others" (*TG* 93). The "progeny" of the "brain seller" do more than disrupt a moment of artistic communion as Abrahamson does in *The Years*; they make disinterested culture impossible:

So to ask the daughters of educated men who have to earn their livings by reading and writing to sign your manifesto would be of no value to the cause of disinterested culture and intellectual liberty because directly they had signed it they must be at the desk writing those books, lectures, and articles by which culture is prostituted and intellectual liberty is sold into slavery. (*TG* 92)

In fact, it becomes doubtful that English culture exists at all, since without intellectual liberty, Woolf implies, there is no culture to protect: "Therefore let us define culture for our purposes as the disinterested pursuit of reading and writing the English language. And intellectual liberty may be defined for our purposes as the right to say or write what you think in your own words, and in your own way" (*TG* 91). In order to work toward culture thus defined, Woolf tells her readers, they must "strip each statement of its money motive, of its power motive, of its advertisement motive, of its publicity motive, of its vanity motive" (*TG* 96). Although she has abandoned the figure of the "Jew in the bath" as she moved from *The Years* to *Three Guineas*, Woolf has remained intensely concerned with the ways money interest and other coercive forces result in intellectual and political slavery.

The only time that *Three Guineas* explicitly mentions Jews, in fact, it links them to women as victims of fascist oppression. Here Woolf addresses men who were being targeted by Nazism:

You are feeling in your own person what your mothers felt when they were shut out, when they were shut up, because they were women. Now you are being shut out, you are being shut up, because you are Jews, because you are democrats, because of race, because of religion. It is not a photograph that you look upon any longer; there you go, trapesing along in the procession yourselves. And that makes a difference. The whole iniquity of dictatorship, whether in Oxford or Cambridge, in Whitehall or Downing Street, against Jews or against women, in England or in Germany, in Italy or in Spain is now apparent to you. But now we are fighting together. (*TG* 102–103)

While the tone of the passage is hostile (men had to be oppressed in their own persons before they could understand the "iniquity of dictatorship"), the basic sympathy is nevertheless clear. Dictators, the passage reminds us, shrink people. They reduce humans to one facet – sex, race, religion, ideology – and prevent them from making and remaking themselves as Mrs. Dalloway does when she gathers herself into the diamond shape,[20] as Mrs. Ramsay does when she fades into her "wedge-shaped core of darkness,"[21] or as Woolf herself does when she writes (*Diary* IV, 161). They prescribe whole lives from the outside.

In demonstrating this, *Three Guineas* implicitly critiques Woolf's own use of Abrahamson in *The Years*. In that novel Abrahamson is defined by the grease he leaves around the bathtub. That grease is absurdly external to and separable from his essential humanity, yet the ring of grease becomes a sign of the mind encircled by chains of social and financial pressure. *Three Guineas* acknowledges that Jews are victims of fascism, and must not be confused with its perpetrators. Nevertheless, some of the imagery Woolf uses here conjures, and in fact seems to linger from, the images that Sara Pargiter uses to describe the pressures of the professional world in *The Years*. First, recalling the ring of grease, Woolf uses another circular metaphor to describe the tyranny of "the public world, the professional system," which "forces us to circle, like caterpillars head to tail, round and round the mulberry tree, the sacred tree, of property" (*TG* 74). She then returns to this image when she sums up the conditions that would result if women were able to create disinterested culture, this time returning to the word "ring":

Not to subscribe to papers that encourage intellectual slavery; not to attend lectures that prostitute culture; for we are agreed that to write at the command of another what you do not want to write is to be enslaved, and to mix culture with personal charm or advertisement is to prostitute culture. By these active and passive measures you would do all in your power to break the ring, the vicious circle, the dance round and round the mulberry tree, the poison tree of intellectual harlotry. The ring once broken, the captives would be freed. (*TG* 99)

The echo in these circular images of the ring left by the "Jew in the bath" in *The Years* helps to corroborate Woolf's claim that the novel and the polemic are really "one book."²²

In fact, the similarities in the way she treats the theme of money interest in the two texts are greater than they first appear. While *The Years'* "Jew in the bath" leaves a ring that represents enslavement by financial need, *Three Guineas* initially seems to have discarded the inappropriate metaphor of Jewishness, showing exasperated commiseration with male Jews and democrats instead. But in the same paragraph as the renewed description of the "ring" of "intellectual harlotry," Woolf compares the slaves "who are now kept hard at work piling words into books, piling words into articles" to "the old slaves [who] piled stones into pyramids" (*TG* 99). This reference to Hebrew slaves is the faint imprint in *Three Guineas* of Abrahamson's Jewishness in its sister-text. While the comparison to Hebrew slaves sounds sympathetic, we cannot forget that enslaved people in Woolf's argument threaten liberty and culture as they and their "diseased progeny . . . infect and corrupt and sow the seeds of disease in others" (*TG* 93). Jewishness is again, more covertly, linked to intellectual harlotry and associated with the conditions that menace free culture.

And so the terms in which Woolf casts her antidote to such enslavement begin to resonate more powerfully. Woolf offers in *Three Guineas* a recipe for what we might call cultural regeneration: that women should "refuse to be separated from the four great teachers of the daughters of educated men – poverty, chastity, derision, and freedom from unreal loyalties" – while combining these "teachers" with conditions that will turn them from affliction to freedom: "some wealth [so as to remain free from manipulation by financial power], some knowledge, and some service to real loyalties" (*TG* 79). Of the four "teachers," chastity is of course most directly related to what she has been calling intellectual harlotry.

By chastity is meant that when you have made enough to live on by your profession you must refuse to sell your brain for the sake of money. That is you must cease to practise your profession, or practice it for the sake of research and experiment; or, if you are an artist, for the sake of the art; or give the knowledge acquired professionally to those who need it for nothing. But directly the mulberry tree begins to make you circle, break off. Pelt the tree with laughter. (*TG* 80)

The proffered antidote was inspiring to many of Woolf's contemporaries, for understandable reasons. It is invigorating to imagine being released from chains of professional, financial, and advertising motives and set free to pursue disinterested art, science, or journalism. And the rhetoric has the advantage of religious solemnity, enlisting discourses of Christian asceticism and evoking the "evangelical counsels," vows taken by nuns and monks to embrace "poverty, chastity, and obedience."

Given that a corrupting money interest is linked with "the Jew in the bath" in *The Years* and Hebrew slaves in *Three Guineas*, the fact that the withdrawal from such pernicious influences is given in terms of a "feminist version of monk's vows" gathers ideological import.[23] That which is inadequate and harmful, associated with Jewishness, can be replaced by that which is enlivening and free, associated with a Christianized retreat into "poverty, chastity, derision, and freedom from unreal loyalties." We can see this progression from entrapment within the rings of financial enslavement to the freedom of detachment as a form of supersessionist discourse. Such a progression is structurally analogous to Paul's claim in Romans that Christians are freed from the deadening, "obsolete" Judaic law to live in the "newness of spirit": "For when we were in the flesh, our sinful passions, awakened by the law, worked in our members to bear fruit for death. But now we are released from the law, dead to what held us captive, so that we may serve in the newness of the spirit and not under the obsolete letter" (Romans 7:5–6).

Woolf disavows "religious pride" in *Three Guineas*, citing it as one of the "unreal loyalties" of which women must "rid" themselves (*TG* 80). So it is deeply ironic that in order to make her argument for freedom and detachment, she relies on an overarching movement from a Jewishness that represents mental slavery and money interest to a Christianized rhetoric of disinterested intellectual liberty. The fact that Woolf was not a religious Christian, that she disdained "religious pride," only underscores the wide circulation of supersessionist discourses in her modern, secular society.

Dorothy Richardson was more interested in Christianity than was Woolf. She seems to have found that a belief in Christian redemption could harmonize with a belief in the redemptive power of art, and, indeed, of feminist art. In the final two books of *Pilgrimage*, she brings Miriam Henderson's spiritual journey to the fore, making clear (as it was not necessarily clear throughout) that the title refers not only metaphorically to Miriam's journey into writing, but also to a pilgrimage in the denotative sense of a movement into Christian commitment.[24] In *Dimple Hill* (1938), the penultimate novel-chapter, Miriam goes to a Quaker farm for a long visit, becomes entranced and influenced by Quakerism, and moves toward a deeper affiliation with Christianity. In the final novel-chapter, *March*

Moonlight (published posthumously in 1967), Richardson "saves" Miriam from Quakerism's "insufficiencies" by moving her into a Christian life that cannot be circumscribed within a single denomination (*W* 347). Miriam's most important interlocutor and companion in this final novel-chapter is Jean, whom she has met during a visit to a Swiss inn. In Jean's "immortal love" (*P* IV, 584) Miriam believes she has found her "passport to eternity" (*P* IV, 580).

Jean Radford points out that "[u]nlike the other characters there is apparently no known prototype for [Jean] in Richardson's own life; she seems to be an imaginary composite (possibly named for 'John' of the Gospels)."[25] As Miriam looks back on her time in Vaud, Switzerland, she thinks, "Jean. Jean. Jean. My clue to the nature of reality. To know that you exist, is enough" (*P* IV, 612). With comments like these, Richardson does seem to suggest that Jean provides a conduit for God's love, or at least serves as a means to Miriam's long-awaited spiritual satisfaction. Radford highlights the spiritual component of Jean's role:

In psychoanalytic terms [Jean's love] might be called a fantasy of unconditional love[;] in religious terms "Jean" reads as the embodiment of human love which most nearly approaches God's love for human beings, "perfect love."
By struggling to see herself as Jean "the permanent forgiver" ([*P*] IV, 607) sees her and loves her, Miriam begins what for her are the most difficult tasks: loving herself and loving others as herself, with full forgiveness: "From hell, heaven is inaccessible until one has forgiven oneself" ([*P*] IV, 607) . . . In other words, Miriam comes to realise that the only God she will find in church, is the one she brought in with her.[26]

March Moonlight, then, is a deeply Christian novel in which Miriam's primary tasks are no longer emotional, sexual, or professional, but spiritual. In this novel-chapter Miriam remembers communing with Jean as Jean read her Oxford Bible. Watching her, Miriam decided that she would rather live alongside the most "hypocritically sanctimonious pietists" (she has temporarily moved into a Young Women's Bible Association House by the narrative present) than the most "enchanted and enchanting humanists" (*P* IV, 565). Christianity has become an essential element in Miriam's life, and one that will, as far as we can tell by the *Künstlerroman*'s end, give shape to rather than be displaced by her emerging identity as a writer.

Miriam's path to this Christian fulfillment, like any pilgrimage worth the name, has been long and indirect, punctuated with false starts. The forward movement inherent in the notion of the pilgrimage – and indeed, in the genre of the *Künstlerroman* itself – encourages a teleological reading of each event along the way: everything Miriam has experienced has, it seems in hindsight, propelled her forward toward this place of religious satisfaction and artistic inauguration. So to say that Jewishness or Judaism is *the* element Miriam has transcended in arriving at this place of endings and beginnings would be overstating the case, not taking into account the progressive structure of the genre. Yet in the narrative of *Pilgrimage*, while there are many obstacles that Miriam must surpass, Judaism is linked to the most pernicious. It represents the obstacles past which Miriam must most crucially progress.[27]

Jewishness in *Pilgrimage*, as I will demonstrate in chapter 4, is linked to an emphasis on racial continuity, biology, and procreation, making it a potential trap for the individualist, feminist protagonist to evade. This racialized portrayal of Jewishness rests in gentle tension with a related but distinct view of *religious* Judaism which I consider here. The relation between the racial and religious representations is established when Miriam's response to her suitor Michael Shatov's Jewishness, seen as a racial flaw, incites her to seek a more perfect love than he can provide.[28]

When Miriam is considering whether to marry Michael, she tells herself that her friends might not realize he is a Jew, but could take him for a cosmopolitan Frenchman: "The mysterious fact of Jewishness could remain hidden in the background . . . the hidden flaw . . . as there was always a hidden flaw in all her possessions" (*P* III, 193; original ellipses). Radford describes this realization that all love objects are flawed as a transition in Miriam's pilgrimage; from seeking fulfillment in humanity, she turns to seeking it in God:

Paradoxically, this deadlock leads to a new realisation: that the "flaw" is not just in Shatov but in any object she may take as her desire ("all my possessions"), since any love-object, male or female, will be lacking or "flawed." Only God, the image of perfect love, is not. The point prepares the ground for the next stage of Miriam's spiritual and emotional journey: not only are all human love objects "flawed", desire is necessarily unattainable.[29]

By focusing on the idea that all love objects are flawed, Radford downplays the fact that it is the particular flaw *of* Jewishness (and not a specific flaw *in* an individual Jew) that sets Miriam off on her quest for God. In fact, when Miriam is recovering from a nervous breakdown, Michael writes to her about a Quaker family willing to rent her a room. She imagines the scene: "Far away within the cool twilit deeps of her innermost consciousness, she went up a pathway towards a farmhouse within whose doorway stood a little group of grey-clad Quaker women, smiling a gentle welcome. Michael's gift" (*P* IV, 430). With the image of the pathway, Miriam suggests a motion away from Michael and toward Quakerism. Her journey to the farm at Dimple Hill is the "gift" of the Jewish Michael. With this Quaker family Miriam finds not perfect Christianity, but something closer than she has ever before known. That Michael's "flaw" prompts Miriam's religious quest and that he literally sends her off to pursue it are two of the most general symbols of a plotline in which Miriam advances past all that Jewishness and Judaism come to mean.

But Miriam overcomes the meanings that have accrued to Judaism more specifically as well. One of the elements associated with both religious Judaism and racialized Jewishness is an emphasis on generalities, unequivocal statements, "the letter" (as Paul has it) as opposed to the "spirit." At several points in the text, Miriam is frustrated because Michael relies too heavily on unequivocal statements, general principles, "quoted opinions," and "the cage of his fixed ideas" (*P* III, 191–192, 295, 474). Miriam also remembers him trying to convince her of the priority of racial continuity. "'The whole, Miriam, is greater than the parts.' That had sounded unanswerable. But now I see the catch in the metaphor . . . Are all the blind alleys and insufficiencies of masculine thought created by their way of thinking in propositions, using inapplicable metaphors?" (*P* IV, 427). Miriam weaves this critique of Michael's metaphoric thinking into her search for Christian redemption. In *March Moonlight* she imagines telling Jean

about thought. About the way its nature depends upon the source of one's metaphors. We all live under a Metaphorocrasy. Tell her I'm giving up words. She will understand. Will agree that thought is a cessation, cutting one off from the central essence, bearing an element of calculation. "Ye must become as little children." (*P* IV, 607)

Describing the sort of metaphoric thought associated with Michael as "calculation" not only prefigures recent feminist critiques of metaphoric language, but also draws upon discourses that link Jews to materiality. Miriam connects her desire to overcome such limited thinking to the line from Matthew, distinguishing a live, childlike, Christian intuition from the dead (cut off "from the central essence"), calculating, literal thought associated with Judaism and the Jewish Michael.

When Miriam wishes to give up words, of course, she is not abandoning meaning. Instead, this distinction is part of *Pilgrimage*'s feminist turn away from masculine "statements" and metaphors (embodied in "the current masculine realism"), and toward that part of language that can embody experience, that cannot be literalized in letters and sounds. Daniel Boyarin discusses Paul's hermeneutics in these terms:

> Just as the human being is divided into a fleshy and spiritual component, so also is language itself. It is composed of outer, material signs and inner, spiritual significations. When this is applied to the religious system that Paul inherited, the physical, fleshy signs of the Torah, of historical Judaism, are re-interpreted as symbols of that which Paul takes to be universal requirements and possibilities for humanity.[30]

By hoping to give up words, Miriam gestures toward this sense that language has "inner, spiritual significations." Her confidence that the Christ-like Jean will understand this desire stems from her feeling that true Christianity focuses not on words but on meaning, on the spirit behind the words. Judaism, Pauline discourse and *Pilgrimage* assert, entails too deep an involvement with the letter at the expense of the spirit. For Miriam to progress, then, toward a feminist modernism that eschews surfaces of language, thought, and plot, she must avoid mental and spiritual dangers marked, both within and outside the text, as "Jewish."

In addition to its alleged focus on the letter, Judaism in *Pilgrimage* is seen as especially patriarchal. It is viewed as masculinist not only because of Michael's typically masculine attributes – his emphasis on generality, continuity, and literal meaning – but also because Miriam associates the Jewish God with an obsolete patriarchy, the Christian God with feminist advances. In this linkage Miriam joins many others, from nineteenth-century missionaries to feminist modernist writers (I describe this phenomenon in chapter 4). In *Revolving Lights* (1923) she characterizes the Jewish God as masculinist and refers to the "surface misery" expressed by a man who has never "got beyond the angry, jealous, selfish, male God of the patriarchate" (*P* III, 328). In *Deadlock* (1921) she tells Michael that "Christ was the first man to see women as individuals" (*P* III, 221). Richardson seems to share this view, linking a spurious religious critique to Orientalist discourse in a letter to John Cowper Powys. Just after the Second World War, she writes that Milton's God is drawn too much from the Hebrew Bible: "And is not Milton's God inferior to Satan because he is the male Jewish, and Protestant, fire-breathing, vengeful oriental despot?" (*W* 531). The same attitude toward the God of the Torah may animate Woolf's description in *A Room of One's Own* of scribbling over the angry face of the professor/patriarch she has drawn: "[I] began drawing cart-wheels and circles over the angry professor's face till he looked like a burning bush" (*Room* 32).

Miriam also links Jewishness to masculinity when, in a conversation with Hypo Wilson, she denies her antisemitism: "And I'm not anti-Semite. I think Jews are better Christians than we are. We have things to learn from them. But not by marrying them, until they've learnt things from us. Women, particularly, can't marry Jews. Men can marry Jewesses if they like" (*P* III, 260). English women ought not to marry Jewish men, she suggests, because they would be caught in their more severely patriarchal system. Jews may have a sense of morality that Miriam condescendingly labels "Christian," but they have not overcome the patriarchal selfishness of their God.

Christianity, for Miriam, is an improvement upon Jewish ideas, and her own pilgrimage must replicate this motion forward. She does consider, however, whether Jesus himself personified the selflessness he preached. "But all the time he was alone with a certainty . . . Now if he had sacrificed paradise. But he couldn't. Then where was selflessness?" But she believes that even with this imperfection – that Jesus knew all along he would be saved – Christianity is preferable to the world of either Greek or Jewish gods. "Yet if Christ had never been, the sky would look different. A Grecian or a Jewish sky. Awful." In either non-Christian sky, there would be "[n]othing held on to but the endless pouring down of time" (*P* III, 358). Miriam objects here to what she sees as an absence of redemption or eternity in Jewish religion. Viewing time as an endless procession of moments leading toward no redemptive telos, both the Jew Shatov and the socialist Wilson lack a belief in eternity: "In Hypo there was no sense of eternity; nor in Michael, except for the race, an endless succession of people made in God's image, all dead or dying" (*P* IV, 155). With her Christian friend Jean, on the other hand, Miriam finds that silences are "fragments of a shared eternity" (*P* IV, 567).

Miriam's description of Jewish continuity as "an endless succession" of "dead or dying" people associates Jewishness with an empty, past time rather than a present infused with eternity. In this linkage *Pilgrimage* combines the supersessionist notion that Christianity has made Judaism obsolete with racial discourses that linked Jews with antiquity. *Pilgrimage* does not present Judaism as a living religion; instead, Miriam repeats the words "dead and dying," insisting on the *pastness* of Judaism and Jewish people – they are "dead and dying particles with no depth of life in them, mere husks" (*P* IV, 427). When Michael talks about Polish Jews, Miriam wonders that they should still exist: "it was strange to think of Polish Jews going on in modern everyday life" (*P* III, 75). The only time the narrative presents Michael absorbed with his religion, it represents Judaism through the same lens of the ancient past.

When Michael visits Dimple Hill, Miriam, surrounded by Quakers, is briefly able to see that Michael's reading of a psalm is alive, rather than a "husk": "Not the pensive, devout recital of an ancient text embodying permanent truths, but the passionate intoning of a poem, so that it seemed an improvisation, carrying the tide of the reader's current emotion" (*P* IV, 520–521). Michael is able to bring forth the psalm's aesthetic beauty, transforming it from an ancient text into a living poem. But detached from the poetry of the psalm, Michael's Judaism reasserts itself as ancient. When Miriam hears about Michael dancing outside the next morning, she immediately imagines him in the biblical past, "rejoicing before the Lord, with the tablets of the Law invisibly held within his swaying arms" (*P* IV, 521).

In Quakerism, on the other hand, Miriam finds what seems to her a true medium for transmitting the Hebrew Bible. When the Roscorlas (the Quaker family who live at Dimple Hill), read the "Old Testament," they let its true spirit come through: "The deep, vibrant monotone, simple, childlike, free from unfelt, tiresomely elucidatory expressiveness, leaving the words to speak for themselves, was the very sound of the Old Testament, the wistful sound of Hebrew piety, trustfully patient within a shadow pierced only here and there by a ray of light ahead" (*P* IV, 474). By describing this family as "childlike," Miriam suggests that they have followed Matthew's advice to become "as little children," which (as we saw) Miriam associates with delving beyond surface meanings and reaching to the essence of experience. But even more striking, the sound of "Hebrew piety" is seen in overtly supersessionist terms: it operates "within a shadow"; it is waiting for the "ray of light" that occasionally "pierces" the Hebrew text. The word "pierce" reminds the reader of Jesus's sufferings, which are in fact the "ray" to which the Hebrew text supposedly looks forward. The piety of the Hebrew Bible is "trustfully patient," waiting only to be fulfilled by Christianity.

Christianity supersedes Judaism in *Pilgrimage* by replacing its focus on surfaces (the letter of the law) with insight into deeper meanings; its patriarchal strictures with an awareness of women's full humanity; its empty, successive temporality with a progression toward a redemptive eternity; and its ancient, "wistful" piety with a childlike, light-filled present and future. Much of this project of surpassing inadequate "Jewish" ideas and emotions comes together in the final scene of *Pilgrimage*, a scene that at first seems confusing and anomalous.

The last page of *March Moonlight* is filled with Miriam's thoughts about Michael and his new wife Amabel, another of Miriam's former romantic partners, who has married Michael with Miriam's encouragement. Miriam has gone to visit them and their baby – a boy who has, Amabel writes, brought "all of bliss to Mike and me" (*P* IV, 636). At the end of the novel, Miriam thinks of the fulfillment she felt when she found the baby sleeping and picked him up to hold against her body. She felt "the complete stilling of every one of my competing urgencies. Freedom. Often I had held babes in my arms: Harriet's, Sally's, and many others. But never with that sense of perfect serenity" (*P* IV, 658).

This scene has presented a problem to critics. It seems implausible that Miriam would suddenly endorse motherhood, after struggling so long to keep herself free from its burdens. Some critics do opt for that reading,[31] while Radford suggests a more sophisticated version: she argues that Miriam comes to recognize the "claims of the world and the other."[32] Gloria Fromm, on the other hand, dismisses the scene as Richardson's hurried attempt to finish the novel as her health declined. Fromm argues that *March Moonlight* effectively ends after Miriam spends a previous weekend with Amabel and Michael, finding them miserable. "After this, Dorothy has spun out a fairy tale, even solving the Shatovs' marital problems with the birth of a son."[33] Fromm bases her judgment in part on the fact that the novel-chapter was never revised to Richardson's satisfaction. But even if the end of *March Moonlight* is more developed than Fromm believes, it does seem that Miriam feels freed in part because the baby relieves her of the responsibility, weighing on her since she met him, to secure Michael's happiness. Her sense of freedom also comes in part from her continued connection to Amabel: "Still we remain to each other what we were when we first met" (*P* IV, 658). But Jean has become more important to Miriam than Amabel. This is demonstrated throughout *March Moonlight*, but in particular when Miriam wonders how Amabel would react if she knew that her place in Miriam's heart has been usurped by Jean: "If now she knew that Jean, unquestioning, trustful of all I may do, stood central in my being, she would rejoice with me? Rejoice that the day of her full power, recalled by the present retrospective radiance, is over?" (*P* IV, 604). So Miriam's intimacy with Amabel cannot explain Miriam's feeling that it is only Amabel's baby who could provide this serenity: in the novel's final lines, she questions whether she would feel the "same sense of fulfillment" "if Jean's marriage with Joe Davenport brought her a child" (*P* IV, 658).

Miriam's response to the baby seems less incongruous when we understand the scene as part of a Christian allegory. Her feeling of serenity has its allegorical source in the name change Richardson performs on the baby. Richardson's friends Benjamin Grad and Veronica Leslie-Jones, the models for Michael and Amabel, had a baby they named David.³⁴ In the novel Michael and Amabel name their baby Paul. Richardson changes a name essential to and glorified by the Hebrew Bible to one that marks that Bible's displacement. Through this Paul, Amabel reports finding bliss and Miriam freedom. In a book where Miriam finds "immortal love" in Jean the "permanent forgiver," envisions "a future that held no assurance of a fresh meeting [with Jean] and yet promised reunion," and embraces "pietists" rather than humanists, this change of names can hardly be coincidental.

It is Paul, after all, who carved the letter/spirit dichotomy so deeply into Christian thought. The opposition runs through his writings (for example, in Romans 2:29 and 7:6), as he admonishes the Hebrews to give up their alleged focus on "the letter" and embrace the spirit. In II Corinthians he asserts that "the letter killeth, but the spirit giveth life" (3:6). It is this dichotomy that undergirds both Miriam's new belief in the deeper meanings behind masculine "statements," and indeed Richardson's antilinear "feminine equivalent of the current masculine realism" (*P* I, 9). Moreover, this dualism about language, as Daniel Boyarin shows in *A Radical Jew*, is parallel to the more basic dualistic belief in a body distinct from its soul. Using this separation, Paul was able to claim that the soul of a Christian was without gender and free from other social categories. In Galatians 3:28 Paul writes that there is "neither Jew nor Greek, there is neither bond nor free, there is neither male nor female: for ye are all one in Christ Jesus." This promise seems to motivate Miriam's claim that Jews need to learn from Christians before English women ought to marry them. In Christianity, she believes, one can overcome not only race and social status, but the stark sex-gender system against which she has fought throughout the thirteen novel-chapters of *Pilgrimage*.

Holding Michael and Amabel's baby, then, paradoxically (and we have to assume temporarily) frees Miriam from the burdens of the flesh, because on an allegorical level, Paul Shatov promises transcendence of the letter, of gender, and of the body. From Jewish roots, Miriam finds, springs the source of Judaism's own displacement. This dynamic parallels Paul's strategies for rendering the Jews' links to the Bible bodily rather than spiritual. He claims that while Jews are the children of Abraham "according to the flesh," Christians are the children of Abraham "according to the promise" (Galatians 3:29).³⁵ In an analogous move *Pilgrimage* turns the fleshly baby of its Jewish character into a sign of that which surpasses Judaism as Miriam and Richardson have imagined it.

While Jewishness and Judaism are not the only obstacles overcome along Miriam's pilgrimage, they represent some of the most important: literal masculine language, gender rigidity and patriarchy, an empty temporality lacking redemption. In moving Miriam past these pitfalls, Richardson adapts the discourse of supersession. She uses the powerful cultural belief that Christianity is an advance over an obsolete Judaism as a framework within which she can assert the superiority of her own feminist modernism – defined as a belief in particularity rather than generality, in deeper meaning rather than surface description, in emphasis on the individual mind, in gender fluidity – over the obsolete materialism of masculine fiction. Judaism is thus a crucial foil for Richardson's work, and anti-Judaism a fundamental element in her creation of feminist modernism.

Although Richardson does not use the terms slavery or prostitution, her emphasis on the superiority of the spirit over the letter and her assumption that Judaism represents the letter draw upon the same discourses of freedom from entrapment that Woolf uses to construct her antidote to intellectual enslavement. Both these experimental modernists use supersessionist rhetoric to depict intellectual and spiritual freedom generally, and their own art in particular, as surpassing the art, ideas, and attitudes marked by the texts as Jewish. Both cast their call for feminist modernist detachment in triumphalist Christian rhetoric.

Such rhetoric, of course, is very different from overt hostility toward Jews, and could and did coexist with Woolf's and Richardson's genuine concern for Jews under Nazism. But it does deepen the problem I raise in chapter 1: how ought we to view feminist modernist projects we admire when they make use of anti-Jewish or antisemitic rhetoric? We cannot, of course, decide that because they are stained with supersessionist attitudes, we will dismiss out of hand Woolf's call for mental freedom or Richardson's liberating feminist aesthetic. What we can and must do, however, is refrain from celebrating these projects in sweeping terms, thereby implicitly endorsing the aspects of their projects built upon supersessionism and antisemitism. We must see clearly the flaws at the center of some of the most inspiring feminist literary projects. In the next chapter I consider another facet of modernist authors' representations of Jews: their use of Jews as signs of modernity itself, with all *its* pitfalls.

3

Adding bathrooms, fomenting revolutions: modernity and Jewishness in Woolf and Warner

In his analysis of antisemitism and modernity, Zygmunt Bauman writes that Jews, more than other groups, were "vulnerable to the impact of new tensions and contradictions which the social upheavals of the modernizing revolution could not fail to generate. For most members of society, the advent of modernity meant the destruction of order and security; and . . . Jews were perceived as standing close to the center of the destructive process."[1] Bauman is referring to modernity more broadly, but his points apply well to interwar British and American culture. In the first half of the twentieth century, Jews were often viewed as moderns *par excellence*. Like modernity itself, they were seen as cosmopolitan, rootless, and urban.[2] They were perceived as instrumental to whatever social-financial system seemed especially modern, whether mass market capitalism or revolutionary socialism. In his study of Freud, Germanness, and Jewishness, Peter Gay proposes that antisemitism was motivated by a fear of modernity:

Whatever else it was, German anti-Semitism was a way of confronting – or, rather, not confronting – the pressures of contemporary life [. . .]: specialization, mechanization, the crowding in of impulses and the speeding up of existence, the burgeoning threats posed by Godless morality, Socialist revolution, and cultural nihilism; anti-Semitism was, in short, an irrational protest against the modern world."[3]

Although antisemitism is motivated by multiple cultural forces and contains various thematic strands (and therefore the phrase "in short" is misleading), unease with regard to modernity did clearly constitute a major motif of nineteenth- and twentieth-century antisemitic thought.

Associations between Jews and modernity, however, did not mean that antisemitism was totally distinct from prior anti-Judaism. As I argue in the previous chapter, racial antisemitism shared much with Christian anti-Judaism, adapting earlier ideas and discourses into forms more suited to modernity. Todd Endelman describes a consistency at the heart of anti-Jewish animus:

> Whether or not men and women still attended church or read the Gospels, they continued to see the Jews in a negative light. The rise of nationalism, with its emphasis on the organic unity of the national community, encouraged this negative perception by reiterating the alienness of the Jews . . . In the medieval world, the Jew was the ally of the Devil and the sworn enemy of Christendom, poisoning its wells and murdering its children. In recent times, the Jew was the bearer of those forces transforming and threatening traditional society – capitalism, liberalism, secularism, urbanization, materialism. In either case, the Jew appeared as malevolent, rapacious, and aggressive.[4]

That many early twentieth-century Britons and Americans accepted the link between Jews and the "forces transforming and threatening traditional society" is confirmed by the popularity of the *Protocols of the Elders of Zion*. Published in Polish and German in 1919 and in English (in Boston and London) in 1920, it claimed that Jews aimed at world domination specifically through modern versions of democratic ideals. As *The Times* described it on May 8, 1920, the document claimed that Jews sought the destruction of "existent political states" by a process of "liberalism and radicalism, then by socialism and Communism, and finally by anarchy."[5]

This association between Jews and modernity was not the property only of antimodern, antisemitic segments of society, however. James Joyce is the best example of a sympathetic author for whom the association of Jews with modernity was an important theme. As Marilyn Reizbaum and others have shown, Joyce drew playfully upon ideas from Guglielmo Ferrero, Friedrich Nietzsche, and Otto Weininger when he made his quintessential modern, urban, secular, alienated human being a Jew.[6] Sylvia Townsend Warner follows Joyce along this track, using her Jewish character in the service of her equally sympathetic, clear-sighted portrait of modernity's possibilities. Inasmuch as modernist literature interrogates and comments upon modernity, Jews were defining figures within modernist texts.

Walter Benn Michaels's discussion of F. Scott Fitzgerald and Ernest Hemingway illustrates some of the ways authors could use Jews to explore their ambivalent responses to modernity. As he points out, in both *The Great Gatsby* (1925) and *The Sun Also Rises* (1926) the war has changed everything about the way people interact. Along with other forces of modernization, it wrought a massive social rupture that blurred the boundaries among social groups, allowing Jews to move into circles from which they had been excluded. It was the war that allowed Jimmy Gatz to get "within a mile" of Daisy: "he was wearing the 'invisible cloak of his uniform.'" And it was the war that "encouraged . . . inattentiveness" so that people like Robert Cohn could not distinguish between people who "really were nice and people who just looked or acted nice," where "nice" is Jake Barnes's well-bred synonym for being well-bred.[7] Authenticity is at issue in both novels, and Jay Gatsby's pose is incomplete unless he can claim an elite ancestry.[8] In this way he stands for a modernity cut off from any genuine past. In *The Sun Also Rises*, authenticity is associated with Spanish traditions, bullfights, Basques, and the past. Like Gatsby, Cohn is inauthentic, an imitation of "nice" people who turns green at the bullfight, writes his telegram in Spanish though he does not know the language,[9] and declines to go on the trip during which Jake and Bill Gorton talk and drink with the Basque men. While Cohn does not seem to *represent* modernity more than the war-injured Jake, his presence, and his similarity to Jake, are results of a modernity that confuses the real with the imitation and breaks down social boundaries that should have excluded him from Jake's circles.

Modernity is more dangerous in Mary Butts's novel *The Death of Felicity Taverner* (1932), where Butts puts her antisemitism in the service of her antimodern modernism. Jewishness for Butts represents an actively destructive force, robbing rural England of innocence and tradition. In the novel, the cousins of the dead Felicity seek to save her rural estate from her Jewish widower, Nick Kralin. Kralin is an art collector who views both art and women merely as means. Kralin is a "[s]uperficial scientific pornographer" for whom the only real pleasure is to thwart others' freedom, "to see its not-fulfilment, to bring it to his Nothing."[10] His goal is to base himself in his late wife's house and then buy up several estates in the surrounding countryside "which by judicious purchase could be made to link-up." He would then build a golf course, "a hotel and a row of bungalows along the low cliff, light the sea lane and drain it." When Picus Taverner listens to Kralin's plan, he hears "a lamentation from outside that never stopped. A mourning somewhere in creation that the freshest earth there is should lose its maidenhood, become handled and subservient to man."[11] Taverner casts Kralin here as a rapist who would violate the English countryside. And his destructiveness is viewed as essentially modern; he seems a "new variety of man," linked to both cities and machines: "About [Kralin] and his evil they sensed something urban and mechanical, as of a large intricate machine in full use."[12] Butts's novel is an extreme instance in modern British fiction. Its antisemitism is overt and powerful. But it is instructive in that it makes plain a sort of template for antimodern antisemitism within this body of literature. It uses a Jew to figure the destruction of rural life – described through the metaphor of sexual defilement – and to represent urban soullessness, mechanization, commercialization, and negation. (D. H. Lawrence's Loerke is a version of this type.) As we will see, these facets of Butts's representation of Jewishness cast an unpleasant light upon Virginia Woolf's milder use of a Jew in *Between the Acts*, published posthumously in 1941.

Although they viewed modernity somewhat differently, Woolf and Warner were among those writers who used Jewish characters to comment on what they saw as its promises and dangers. For both writers, modernity meant, in large part, the threat of fascism. This threat was especially personal for Woolf, married to a prominent Jewish political thinker. Nevertheless, Woolf seems to have viewed modernity for the most part in broad philosophical and social terms, and in *Between the Acts* in oppositional ones: as a political and economic force that gathered people into mass consumers, mobs, parties, and militant nations and yet also fragmented community and continuity. In her last novel she explores the value and dangers of these aspects of modernity. And in her critique of modernity's rupture, she enlists her otherwise minor Jewish character.

For Warner, modernity held the potential for Communist revolution. In *Summer Will Show* (1936), she uses both a specifically Jewish past – a pogrom – and Jewish aspects of the 1848 revolutions in France to demonstrate her commitment to revolution while critiquing its likely excesses. Her linkage of Jews with revolution was, unlike the writers and journalists Sharman Kadish documents,[13] a positive one: as a Communist, she valued the contribution some Jews were making to socialism and Communism.

While the protagonist of *Summer Will Show* never quite abandons her antisemitic responses to the woman who becomes her lover, the novel itself, as I argue in chapter 1, works against antisemitism, using Jewishness to disrupt dominant stereotypes. In this chapter I demonstrate additional ways in which the novel uses Jewishness for what could (perhaps ironically) be called liberal humanist ends: to underscore the value of art, even within revolutionary societies. Woolf's *Between the Acts*, on the other hand, moves congruently with those of its characters who long for a simpler past and view the Jewish Ralph Manresa as a sign of a negative modernity. As will become clear, I do not claim that the novel is primarily nostalgic; it incisively critiques both the present and the past. But there remains in the novel a grief over lost continuity, and it is in that strand that the Jewish character is most useful to the novel.

In *Between the Acts*, one of the fundamental features of modernity is the way it separates and isolates people, fragments community and ruptures continuity. This overriding sense of fragmentation is echoed in the book's multivoiced structure and choppy narrative. *Between the Acts* portrays such discontinuity as liberating – as working against the herd instinct – yet also evinces nostalgia for older modes of maintaining community. Not surprisingly, the novel meditates on the results of fragmentation in part through references to a Jewish character. Ralph Manresa, the offstage Jewish husband of the vibrant Mrs. Manresa (whose first name we never learn), represents a parvenu mentality that becomes a significant site of the text's nostalgia, its critique of modernity.

That the dichotomy of continuity and discontinuity is central to the novel is made plain throughout. On one hand, Lucy Swithin, an elderly inhabitant of Pointz Hall, is reading about the prehistory of England, when the continent was a single whole. The view from the house in 1939, when the novel is set, is the same as it was in 1830. The same families show up for the pageant as would have been represented a hundred years before. Miss La Trobe's play presents English history using unmistakable present-day villagers (the aptly named Eliza Clark "look[s] the age in person" when she plays Queen Elizabeth (*BTA* 83)), emphasizing the relationship of the present to the past. Yet references to technology, science, and the impending war abound, interrupting the sense of continuity provided by the unchanging view and old families. People forget the lines to nineteenth-century poetry; they wonder what to do about the refugees; they ask whether machines are "the devil" (*BTA* 201); they discuss "the very latest notion [that] nothing's solid" (*BTA* 199). When the Reverend Streatfield steps up to summarize and interpret the play, "a zoom sever[s]" his talk: "twelve aeroplanes in perfect formation like a flight of wild duck came overhead" (*BTA* 193). The dichotomy is taken up by the gramophone that plays the pageant's musical score. Repeating "*Dispersed are we*" throughout the novel, the gramophone ends by adding the possibility of unity: "The gramophone gurgled *Unity – Dispersity*. It gurgled *Un . . . dis . . .* And ceased" (*BTA* 201). As Susan Dick and Mary Millar put it, the design of the novel "is shaped by the rhythmical interplay between unification and separation."[14]

How to read the novel's valuation of these dichotomies, however, is less clear. The gramophone lays out the problem: "*Dispersed are we*, the gramophone triumphed, yet lamented, *Dispersed are we* . . ." (*BTA* 198). On one hand, dispersal is a triumph, freeing individuals from being tyrannized by tradition, stifled by the rural English community to which the Oliver family, having lived in the area only 120 years, is a recent addition. The people here have "taken indelibly the print of some three hundred years of customary behavior," leaving little room for independent or imaginative thought (*BTA* 27). The repetitiveness of the view is itself "senseless, hideous, stupefying" (*BTA* 67). At one point during a break in the play, the audience thinks together: "We aren't free, each one of them felt separately, to feel or think separately, nor yet to fall asleep" (*BTA* 65).

On the other hand, the dispersal ought to be lamented, since without community individuals are isolated, communication is broken. The audience continues its collective meditation: "We're too close; but not close enough" (*BTA* 65). Their collective musing itself demonstrates a reason to lament "dispersity" – here is a genuine community, feeling similarly about its relation to the play, about its members' links to each other, collectively fearing the growing violence across the Channel. That they should be dispersed, that the play should not touch and move them, that communication should founder, is a failure, as La Trobe thinks at the end of the pageant. Indeed, La Trobe and the other homosexual in the novel, William Dodge, reveal the pain of isolation. Both are outcast and yearn for community. William longs to connect with Lucy more deeply, to tell her about his sexuality and his victimization at school. La Trobe, since she quarreled with the "actress who had shared her bed and her purse," feels the "horror and terror of being alone" (*BTA* 211).

Nevertheless, disruption seems to serve as an enlivening force overall, particularly in the last scene of the pageant, entitled "Ourselves." As the music changes to "Foxtrot, was it? Jazz?," the audience is offended by the jarring sounds: "What a cackle, a cacophony! Nothing ended. So abrupt. And corrupt. Such an outrage; such an insult; her game? To disrupt? Jog and trot? Jerk and smirk? . . . The young, who can't make but only break; shiver into splinters the old vision; smash to atoms what was whole" (*BTA* 183). This passage recalls Woolf's description in *A Room of One's Own* (1929) of Mary Carmichael's *Life's Adventure*, in which "[s]omething tore, something scratched" (*Room* 80). Readers of *Room* will find it hard to sympathize with an audience offended by the jerkiness of art that "[breaks] the sequence" (*Room* 81). And in fact a megaphonic voice in *Between the Acts* admonishes the audience to "break the rhythm and forget the rhyme" (*BTA* 187). Without individual thought, without people able to break the rhythm of the patriotic ballad, history will continue to repeat itself ("1830 was true in 1939"). And history now means the Great War, whose second act is being rehearsed across the Channel. The stakes are high. As Woolf makes clear in *Three Guineas* (1938), too much uniformity, too much group-think, too much adherence to a militaristic collective, and Britain, in fighting Nazism, will capitulate to Nazism's principles and modes of operating, will become the enemy.

This is why Michelle Pridmore-Brown's 1998 *PMLA* article on *Between the Acts* is so compelling. Pridmore-Brown argues that Woolf performs antifascism by "exploiting the noise or static inherent in communications technology" which short-circuits the "instantaneous connection among rhythm, emotion, and collective action" that empowered dictators like Adolf Hitler.[15] It is crucial for this reading that the audience not become a unified whole, responding with one mind and heart to patriotic songs, but instead be fragmented and made aware of its fragmentation. In the final scene, "Ourselves," the cast comes forward with mirrors and scraps of reflective surfaces, to show the audience themselves. The voice through the megaphone sums up "ourselves" as "orts, scraps and fragments" (*BTA* 188). Pridmore-Brown describes La Trobe's play, with its inaudible passages and "chuffing" gramophone:

By increasing the noise in the communication channel, La Trobe deliberately draws attention to the channel itself, thus attenuating the link between sound waves and emotion . . . After each grand moment of unity (in which the audience is united in the patriotic "we"), she abruptly "dissolves" or "spills" the emotion by either warping the sound waves (changing the key, for instance) or severing them.[16]

This wavelike consolidation and dissolution echoes the gramophone's refrain, "*Unity – Dispersity.*"

In this reading the novel's antifascism is encapsulated in the breakdown of communication and thereby of collective thought and action. So we read these breakdowns as unambiguously positive. Community entraps, tradition enslaves; only their interruption makes space for individual thought and disrupts the power of the dictator's charisma. This seems to me accurately to describe a major component of *Between the Acts*. But it neglects the nostalgic strain I also see in the novel. When Woolf first conceived it, she described its setting in the English countryside and its emphasis on community in more positive terms. She wrote that (what was then) Poyntzet Hall would be a "centre":

all lit. discussed in connection with real little incongruous living humour; & anything that comes into my head; but "I" rejected: "We" substituted: to whom at the end there shall be an invocation? "We" . . . composed of many different things . . . we all life, all art, all waifs & strays – a rambling capricious but somehow unified whole – the present state of my mind? And English country; & a scenic old house – & a terrace where nursemaids walk? & people passing – & a perpetual variety & change from intensity to prose. & facts. (*Diary* V 135)

In this description the "We" can accommodate difference, can be "composed of many different things," can be "rambling capricious." The countryside is not pictured as stultifying, as it will later become. There is no herdlike and threatening uniformity in this world, but "perpetual variety."

It may be that Woolf changed the focus and tone of her "centre," Pointz Hall, in response to the war. After all, that diary entry was written in 1938, but she was still working on the novel throughout 1939 and 1940. This scenario would bolster Pridmore-Brown's assertion that the text's interruptions of a dangerous uniformity comprise an antifascist argument.[17] But even if that is true, the former focus, the strand of the novel in which the rural Pointz Hall is various and alive, in which community is substituted for individuality, in which "We" does not stamp out but encompasses difference, remains a potent if subtle force in the text. As Jed Esty points out, critics of this novel have generally "underemphasized the appeal of a ritualized nativism that reintegrates artist and audience into a common culture."[18] There are, he notes, "moments of communal longing and national sentiment that run against" the grain in which *Between the Acts* deflates nationalism.[19]

In keeping with the text's interest in rupture, La Trobe longs for a play without an audience; yet Woolf's comment in her diary that she lacks an audience sounds far more sorrowful. On June 27, 1940, when she was working on *Between the Acts* (then entitled *Pointz Hall*), she lamented that "no echo comes back. I have no surroundings. I have so little sense of a public . . . Those familiar circumvolutions – those standards – which have for so many years given back an echo & so thickened my identity are all wide and wild as the desert now" (*Diary* V, 299). Two lines later, she writes that she cannot "conceive that there will be a 27th June 1941." Other diary entries and letters from 1940–1941 repeat this worry that she lacks an audience and an echo.[20] This despair is not absent from the novel, and neither is its obverse, the sense that wholeness, communication, and unity might be desirable, might heal.

This seems particularly true of the community formed among the servants, and between the cook and Lucy. When the nursemaids "trundle the perambulator up and down the terrace" after breakfast, for example, the novel celebrates their effortless communication that employs not "pellets of information" but "rolling words, like sweets on their tongues" (*BTA* 10). When Mrs. Sands and Lucy Swithin cook together, "it was soothing, it was consolidating, this handwork together" (*BTA* 34). Scenes of nature, too, evince a longing for simplicity and meaning, as when the trees form an "open-air cathedral" where swallows make patterns (*BTA* 65), and for unity between humans and other species, as when the cows play their part in the pageant. "It was the primeval voice sounding loud in the ear of the present moment . . . The cows annihilated the gap; bridged the distance; filled the emptiness and continued the emotion" (*BTA* 140–141). When Lucy and William are touring the house, the nursery seems to validate the nostalgic painting of a Newfoundland dog he sees there: "the room smelt warm and sweet; of clothes drying; of milk; of biscuits and warm water. 'Good Friends' the picture was called" (*BTA* 71). As they walk through the house, Lucy and William experience moments of communion that seem all the more valuable for their rarity. And Lucy's conviction that "We live in others, Mr . . . we live in things" (*BTA* 70) suggests a sort of mystical unity reminiscent of Clarissa Dalloway's belief in a "mist" that connects people and makes them survive in each other.[21]

In her diary Woolf describes the contradictory effects of the coming war: both severance and community. Here the sense of community is positive, a respite from meaningless anxiety. "[W]hats odd . . . is the severance that war seems to bring: everything becomes meaningless: cant plan: then there comes too the community feeling: all England thinking the same thing – this horror of war – at the same moment. Never felt it so strong before. Then the lull and one lapses again into private separation" (*Diary* V 215). The dynamic Woolf describes in this diary entry is the very rhythm of the novel ("Unity – Dispersity"), where unity is represented by the community of old families around Pointz Hall. But such meaningful unity is threatened by a rupturing modernity associated with Ralph Manresa.

In early drafts of the novel, Ralph was present at Pointz Hall on the day of the novel's action. In the published novel, however, he is absent, excluded from the community that has come together to hear the pageant. He is first described when the narrator details the rumors about Mrs. Manresa's history:

Also it was said her diamonds and rubies had been dug out of the earth with his own hands by a "husband" who was not Ralph Manresa. Ralph, a Jew, got up to look the very spit and image of the landed gentry, supplied from directing City companies – that was certain – tons of money; and they had no child. But surely with George the Sixth on the throne it was old fashioned, dowdy, savoured of moth-eaten furs, bugles, cameos and black-edged notepaper, to go ferreting into people's pasts? (*BTA* 40)[22]

The fact that Ralph is "got up to look" like the gentry depicts him as a parvenu, one of the most common and powerful stereotypes applied to middle-class British and American Jews since the middle of the nineteenth century. Parvenu Jews can be found in Anthony Trollope, Willa Cather, Edith Wharton, Djuna Barnes, Elizabeth Bowen, and others and form a subcategory of the stereotypical materialistic Jew. Ralph's "tons of money" adds to this picture of a Jew who uses newly accumulated wealth to approximate the standing of old English families.[23] The fact that his businesses are in the "City" stresses the urban origins of his pretended "county" status. (Giles Oliver's associations with money and London add to his negative portrait, too.) The Manresas' childlessness reinforces the sense that Ralph is cut off from continuity, especially the kind of continuity evidenced in this rural community where people might assert that they are present "in place of" their grandparents (*BTA* 75).

Two earlier drafts of this passage appear in the typescripts. In the first Ralph's Jewishness is not mentioned, but we get a hint of racial non-belonging in the way the passage ends:

And it was also said that her diamonds and emeralds had been dug out of the earth with his own hands by a "husband" who was not Ralph Manresa. But with George the ~~Fifth~~ Sixth on the Throne, it was old-fashioned, dowdy; it savoured of moth eaten furs, cameos and black-edged notepaper ~~was a spot~~ only fit for old maids in cathedral closes – this interrogation of ancestry.[24]

This "ancestry" ostensibly refers to Mrs. Manresa, since the passage is about her background, beginning with the rumor that she was born in Tasmania. But Mrs. Manresa's *ancestry* in the sense of ethnic or national identity is not in doubt. Her grandparents were definitely English, but the rumor is that her grandfather may have been transported for his involvement in a scandal. The word "ancestry" is therefore an odd choice, making little sense except insofar as it raises the specter of her husband's ancestry. Woolf changed the phrase first to "ferreting into facts"[25] and then, in the published novel, "ferreting into people's pasts," which more clearly refers to Mrs. Manresa and her family's history.

From these early drafts, it was clear that Ralph Manresa would not fit in with the rest of the community. In scene twenty-one of the early typescript – the scene where Mrs. Manresa is leading Giles "down the Barn, in and out" (*BTA* 107) – Mrs. Manresa considers her views of those present and their views of her:

Everyone was a thorough good sort; had money in the savings bank; didn't she know it? She was their pal; though as she knew, they regarded thin Ralph Manresa, her husband, in perfect riding breeches talking to the Parson, with suspicion. It was partly his clothes. But the wild child they felt one of themselves; coming down from town, with a boxfull of goodies; and a boy or two to keep her company.[26]

In this earlier version of the description of Ralph "got up to look the very spit and image of the landed gentry," Woolf does not enumerate the reasons those gentry regard Ralph "with suspicion." It is only "partly his clothes." His ethnic difference, if Woolf already had it in mind (as his foreign name indicates), is most likely a factor as well. His "perfect riding breeches" show his insecurity about his class status: Ralph must adhere strictly to convention lest he be excluded from upper-class society. Mrs. Manresa, on the other hand, displays her difference from the others, those who judge her husband, by accepting "money in the savings bank" as evidence that people are "thorough good sort[s]," as well as by marrying Ralph. While it does not explicitly state that he is "new money" or that the local gentry mistrust him for that reason, this passage certainly sets the stage for the more fully developed description of Ralph as a parvenu, which by the later typescript is almost in its published form.[27]

In addition to his clothes, Ralph's car exhibits his pretensions to aristocratic status. The car is described from Giles's point of view: "He had seen the great silver-plated car at the door with the initials R. M. twisted so as to look at a distance like a coronet" (*BTA* 46). Not only is the car showy with its silver plating, but Ralph has had his initials styled to resemble the crown worn by English dukes and other nobles. The word "twisted" emphasizes the distortion inherent in this attempt to appear what he is not.[28] Ralph's use of his wealth recalls Cather's Louie Marsellus from *The Professor's House* (1925), who drives a Pierce-Arrow with a chauffeur, chooses all his wife Rosamond's elegant clothing, and publicly presents her with "out of scale" rubies.[29] Like Marsellus, Simon Rosedale in Wharton's *The House of Mirth* (1905), and Felix Volkbein in Barnes's *Nightwood* (1936), Ralph Manresa's ostentation serves only to reveal what it is trying to conceal: in his case, exclusion from established, aristocratic Englishness.

Beyond simply being a parvenu himself, Ralph acts upon the English landscape by modernizing his house. As the audience gathers, the guidebook writer "Mr. Figgis might have observed" the old families: "Some had been there for centuries, never selling an acre. On the other hand there were the new-comers, the Manresas, bringing the old houses up to date, adding bathrooms" (*BTA* 74). This reference to updating old houses at first seems neutral, and Dick and Millar point out that Woolf hoped in 1925 to earn enough money to add a "bath & hot water range" to her Rodmell house (*Diary* III, 9).[30] But the process sounds more threatening when, at the end of the passage, the company discusses the "hideous new house at Pyes Corner! What an eyesore! And those bungalows!" (*BTA* 75). Woolf uses the same phrase, "hideous new house," in her diary in a complaint about "Hancock's horror," a house built near Rodmell (*Diary* IV, 17).[31] While the Manresas seem not to have built a new eyesore of a house, only updated an old one, the paragraph associates modernization with blights on the English countryside. The lack of a phrase like "for instance" after "the Manresas" contributes to the sense that this couple is representative of modernization, not only an instance of it. "[B]ringing the old houses up to date, adding bathrooms," in its plural form, suggests a general, ongoing project more than a discrete set of renovations to a single house.

It is not only nameless villagers who associate modernization with destruction. La Trobe includes modern bungalows in her critique of contemporary culture at the end of the pageant, when the megaphonic voice asks the audience to consider its similarities to warmakers. "*Consider the gun slayers, bomb droppers here or there. They do openly what we do slyly. Take for example* (here the megaphone adopted a colloquial, conversational tone) *Mr. M's bungalow. A view spoilt forever. That's murder . . .*" (*BTA* 187). This Mr. M may not be Ralph Manresa, but it certainly alludes to him, reminding readers of the earlier passage. And it may seem extreme to equate a ruined view with murder, but the passage bears metaphoric weight. It is beauty that is being destroyed, and modern efficiency and commercialization that are destroying it. Viewed that way, the accusation seems justly serious. Indeed, it would have to be in a novel where England is "scarred" (*BTA* 4) and where the rape of the girl by the soldiers, while devastating in itself, is also part of an allegory in which England is raped by soldiers, by war – in which both parties to war are crushed under the boot of the military as the snake is crushed by Giles.[32] In this sense *Between the Acts* uses, in a milder way, the same link between Jews and the destruction of rural England that serves as a major theme of Butts's antisemitic novel *The Death of Felicity Taverner*.[33]

Moreover, the association of bathrooms with a Jewish man is eerily reminiscent of the "Jew in the bath" scene in *The Years* (1937), in which, as I have shown, the refrain "all because of a Jew in my bath" signals the introduction of money interest into spheres that ought to be disinterested. The question of disinterestedness comes up in *Between the Acts* as well, and again the Jewish character is tangled up in it. When Bart Oliver, Giles's father, "snort[s]" that all the village festivals " 'end with a demand for money,' " Mrs. Manresa "deprecate[s] his severity." He continues, " 'Nothing's done for nothing in England.' " But Mrs. Manresa protests:

"It might be true, perhaps, of the Victorians; but surely not of ourselves?"
"Did she really believe that we were disinterested?" Mr. Oliver demanded.
"Oh you don't know my husband!" the wild child exclaimed, striking an attitude. (*BTA* 177)

But Mrs. Manresa is romanticizing her husband. Bart's response recognizes the defensive, knee-jerk quality of her praise: "Admirable woman! You could trust her to crow when the hour struck like an alarm clock; to stop like an old bus horse when the bell rang" (*BTA* 177). Moreover, Mrs. Manresa "strik[es] an attitude" as she praises her husband, suggesting that the whole statement is a pose. Finally, while Bart says nothing, "Mrs. Manresa had out her mirror and attended to her face" (*BTA* 178). It is her own image that concerns Mrs. Manresa; she claims that her husband is disinterested because it reflects well on her.

The early typescript confirms that Woolf did not conceive Ralph as disinterested. In that version, although he is at the pageant, he is mentioned rarely. He is named, however, at the end of the pageant. While the megaphonic voice asks the audience to consider itself, the mirrors expose those present:

"Let's break the rhythm and forget the rhyme. And calmly consider ourselves. Ourselves. Bony or fat." (The looking-glasses kept rough pace with the words, ~~illustrating~~ illuminating them.) "Liars and thieves." (Ralph Manresa. Manresa was here exposed to view.) "The poor are as bad as the rich. Don't hide among rags; or let our cloth protect us." (The Rev. Streatfield faced the cheval glass from the rectory.)[34]

The text uses Ralph, then, to represent the general state of affairs Bart is deploring, that English culture is invariably interested, made up of "liars and thieves": that everything ends with a "demand for money." This link between Jews and the commercialization of modern society is quite of a piece with the drafts of the scene in *The Years* where Elvira uses the phrase "the Jew's in his bath" to indicate the corruption of those who write for pay. In fact, the money to be collected at the end of the pageant is to go toward "installing electric light in the Church" (*BTA* 177). This detail extends Woolf's critique of modernization: it is associated not only with Jewishness but with money interest more directly.

The only aspect of Ralph's characterization that counters dominant stereotypes is that he served in the army. We learn of his military service when Mrs. Manresa informs the Olivers and their friends that she knew "that Ralph, when he was at the war, couldn't have been killed without her seeing him – 'wherever I was, whatever I was doing,' she added, waving her hands so that the diamonds flashed in the sun" (*BTA* 44). Again, Mrs. Manresa's boast primarily bolsters her own image, as the flashing diamonds imply. But her husband appears to have served in the Great War. For many writers, this characterization would indicate an effort to defend Jews from ubiquitous charges of disloyalty and femininity. But for Woolf, of course, militarism is harmful, the most destructive form of masculine aggression. Through his link to war, as well as his urban, commercial occupation, Ralph here is associated with Giles. Although one is excluded from and the other solidly ensconced within English culture, both men represent aspects of modern, soulless, and violent masculinity.

Not only is Ralph a parvenu, linked with money interest, and associated with destructive modernization, but he is also emasculated by his wife's gallivanting around the countryside with other men. In the published novel she has been driving "through June lanes, along with Bill it was understood" since the previous night (*BTA* 42). Since William is homosexual, there is no suggestion of an affair. But her journey with him could be seen as ousting Ralph even further from the community that gathers at Pointz Hall – even the homosexual outcast finds some sympathy (from Lucy and Isa Oliver) where there is no place for Ralph. As for Mrs. Manresa's sexual liaisons, she ogles Bart and the servant Candish (*BTA* 40, 41) and commits infidelity quite casually with Giles; in the passage from the drafts I quote above, she is said to "come down from town" always with "a boy or two to keep her company." This behavior of hers, as much as his too-perfect clothes, makes Ralph ridiculous.

On the other hand, he is paradoxically associated (though differently from Giles and Bart) with patriarchy: since we never learn her first name, his identity defines his wife completely. And she is so male-identified that her actions confirm as well as undermine his authority over her. Mrs. Manresa's willingness to play up to men, to define herself by her sexual appeal, recalls

Dorothy Richardson's *Pilgrimage* (1915–1967), in which the protagonist believes that Jewish men have greater power to define "their" women than Christian men. Miriam Henderson tells her Jewish suitor Michael Shatov, "'I can't bear Jewesses, not because they are not really like other women, but because they reflect the limitations of the Jewish male. They talk and think the Jewish man's idea of them'" (*P* III, 221). We can see Ralph's retention of patriarchal power as well as his wife's subversion of it as part of Woolf's portrait of a modernity in which old forms are crumbling without anything positive to replace them. Much as the village play, and even "ourselves," are reduced to "orts, scraps and fragments," so modern married women have new freedom to travel and explore but for the most part still depend for their entertainment and their identities on their relations to men.

The novel suggests another way in which modernity creates a problem that is nevertheless "the same" as it has always been when it refers to "the refugees." During a break in the pageant, the audience briefly discusses the refugees. As with most of the conversations, we get only "scraps and fragments" of what was said. "'And what about the Jews? The refugees . . . the Jews . . . People like ourselves, beginning life again . . . But it's always been the same . . . My old mother, who's over eighty, can remember . . .'" (*BTA* 121). The characters here acknowledge that the refugees are people like them – the most important positive statement in a text and community that ousts the Jewish Ralph from its midst. On the other hand, the assertion that "'it's always been the same'" removes the urgency from the situation, freeing the speakers from the burden of potential action. Sympathy for the plight of these refugees is, it seems, easier for the community than accepting Ralph; they can pity the Jews at a distance without wishing to integrate them into their own lives. Indeed, as I mention in the introduction, Andrew Sharf finds a parallel set of reactions in his analysis of the British press's responses to news from Germany. While from 1933 to 1945 the press was "virtually unanimous in its denunciation of what was happening to Jews under Nazi rule," it also expressed a great deal of reluctance to accept German Jewish refugees, for fear they would destroy the British economy and lower standards of living.[35] Even after the November pogrom of 1938 (*Kristallnacht*), the press, like the characters in *Between the Acts*, "did not appreciate that aspect of the refugee problem which had become fundamental even earlier – its urgency."[36]

Judith Greenberg reads the refugee passage as signaling a crucial question: whether people are able to listen to the traumas of others (assuming those others can speak them). "Between the lines and in the fragments of overheard phrases emerge such questions as 'What about the Jews?' How much are people willing to be unsettled by the voices of others? Is this community willing to challenge a sense of harmony, complacency, and solipsism and listen instead to the cacophony of deeply unsettling messages?"[37] Woolf herself certainly listened to these messages, but she also felt a "strain" in response to their demands. Natania Rosenfeld describes Woolf's account of her meeting with Sigmund Freud in January 1939 in terms that resonate with this passage of *Between the Acts*. Woolf recorded "[a] certain strain: all refugees are like gulls with their beaks out for possible crumbs . . . The strain on us too of being benefactors" (*Diary* IV, 202). Rosenfeld writes that Woolf

> clearly felt her sympathies being enlisted in a way she was inclined to resist. She uses the word "strain" twice to describe the aura of the visit, as if to indicate a conflict of wills . . . In *Three Guineas*, she easily identifies herself as an outsider, excluded from the society men have constructed; yet she uneasily confronts her other identity, that of potential benefactress, withholding her guineas while the beaks clamor.[38]

Rosenfeld points out here the difficulty with which Woolf occupied positions of power. It would be easier to cling to her "outsider" status, her stance that "uneducated and voteless, I am not responsible for the state of society," but Woolf knows that in comparison with some others, especially stateless refugees, she *does* bear nationality and its attendant responsibility.[39]

That sense of responsibility surfaces in the draft version of the refugee passage, where caring about the Jews is viewed as a dull obligation and then, as in the published version, distanced with the complacent line "It's always been the same." In the early typescript the passage begins with someone preferring a play to a book because it helps her to forget – or perhaps to remember. This vacillation itself demonstrates an uneasiness, an ambivalent response to the question of engagement or disengagement with social reality.

> I'm very fond of the play, myself. It takes one out of oneself – more than a book. And that's what one wants. Something to make one forget. Or perhaps I should say, remember. I feel, though I wouldn't say it in public, half the time we worry about what doesn't matter. People saying the end of the world's come. And it hasn't. It's by way of an excuse mostly. <Isn't it an excuse for not doing well what one ought to?> An excuse for not doing what's dull, you mean. But what about the Jews? And the refugees? People like ourselves beginning life over again – people who've been used to every comfort. It's always been the same . . . Well, perhaps.[40]

Here the characters acknowledge that doomsday pronouncements are sometimes used to excuse inaction. But that excuse seems flimsy when they think of the Jews and the refugees (not equated here, as they are in the published passage); clearly something needs to be done for them. But what? Instead of answering that question, the speakers let the question drift away using the opposite tactic from the "end of the world" excuse: "It's always been the same." This speaker's dismissal and the interlocutor's easy acquiescence ("Well, perhaps") allow the return of the very complacency they have been discussing.

The effects of the published version of this passage are minimal, both because of the line "It's always been the same" and because the conversation turns so quickly to another topic. This fragmented quality of all the conversations helps the text to portray how communal life is reduced to ineffective "scraps." And in this reduction readers can see an aspect of the loss that modernity brings: there is not enough unity for genuine engagement and debate, and there is too much unity for genuine engagement and debate. The fragmentation of tradition, continuity, and community that most powerfully defines modernity in *Between the Acts* is Janus-faced. It is productive in the ways Pridmore-Brown describes, in the ways the novel itself describes when it tacitly compares its own "jarring" rhythm to La Trobe's pageant. Yet it is alarming to be cut off from one's moorings, to have one's shelter dissolve as it does for Giles and Isa at the end of the novel. To repeat the Victorian past would be stultifying, but there is a loss, too, in *not* hearing the poets sing to each other over lunch as the narrator of *A Room of One's Own* imagines (*Room* 12–15), or (to stay with *Between the Acts*) to abandon faith in what the view and the tune are "saying": "how after toil men rest from their labours; how coolness comes; reason prevails; and having unharnessed the team from the plough, neighbors dig in cottage gardens and lean over cottage gates" (*BTA* 134).

As Patricia Laurence points out, "[t]he structure of oppositions and the rhythm of alternation . . . are often ignored in Woolf's work: one critic emphasizing the unity, another, the fragmentation; one highlighting the optimism, another the pessimism."[41] Laurence proposes a fugue as a metaphor for the alternating structure. This complicated musical form seems an appropriate figure for a novel that so thoroughly explores fragmentation and unity, tradition and modernity, and lays bare both invigorating and threatening aspects of each. What I want most to point out here is not simply that Woolf includes an antisemitic portrait of a Jewish man in *Between the Acts*, but that the portrait serves to focus important aspects of Woolf's critique of modernity. The damaging and dangerous side of modern fragmentation and discontinuity, England's enslavement to financial and military interests – these threats come together in Ralph Manresa, the Jew who adds bathrooms, ruins views, and disrupts class and national community.

The link between Jews and modernity takes a very different form in Warner's *Summer Will Show*. In this novel Jewishness is linked to ethical action, and ethical action to revolution – not to revolution as it has historically been carried out, but to a revolutionary society that would maintain some aspects of liberal democracy: most crucially its room for and appreciation of art and artists. The Jewish artists in this novel are victims of revolutionary excess, and Warner uses that victimization to evoke sympathy for artists and Jews and to remind her leftist comrades that revolution ought to be a means to a free society, not an end in itself.

In linking Jews to revolution, Warner was drawing upon one of the most prominent threads of antisemitic thought in the modern period: that Jews were socialists and Communists bent on destroying traditional culture. In his *Roots of Hate* (2003), William Brustein analyzes what he argues are the four components of antisemitism: religious, racial, economic, and political hatred. He attributes the rise of political antisemitism in part to the threat posed by international socialism:

Political anti-Semitism, defined as hostility toward Jews based on the belief that Jews seek to obtain national and/or world power, experienced a momentous upsurge after 1879 in Europe. We can largely attribute the dramatic rise in political anti-Semitism between 1879 and 1939 to the emergence and rapid development of an international socialist movement and, concomitantly, to the popularization of the notorious "Protocols of the Elders of Zion" in the aftermath of the Bolshevik Revolution.[42]

As a Communist herself, Warner of course reverses the value of the link between Jews and revolution. For her, the link reflected well on both Jews and socialism. This is one strategy, not without its pitfalls, for working against the antisemitic accusation that Jews were trying to undermine the social order through revolutionary socialism. And although it reaffirms the link between Jews and socialism far more often made derisively, it was Warner's only option if she were to remain true to her political beliefs *and* write against antisemitism.

Warner wrote *Summer Will Show* during the years 1932–1936, a period when she was seriously considering her leftist political affiliations and drawing toward the Communist Party, which she joined in 1935. The novel is in part the product of this political soul-searching: set during the 1848 revolutions in Paris, it portrays various types of revolutionaries and Communists, and it ends with an excerpt from Karl Marx and Friedrich Engels' *Communist Manifesto* (1848). By setting the novel almost ninety years before her own time, Warner creates a space for herself to think through political issues at a safe and instructive distance. Her aim seems less to analyze the specific historical causes or consequences of the revolutions than to imagine them through the lens of the present, creating a sort of fable, a warning about the dangers that any revolution courts. As Arnold Rattenbury notes, "the book's real greatness lies, I think – perhaps with historical novels it always does – in its encapsulation not so much of the 1848 Revolution as of the 1930s of its writing."[43] This assertion raises the question, why 1848? In what ways did that particular event serve as a meaningful past, a past that could encapsulate the present, for a left-leaning and then newly Communist writer in the early to mid-1930s?

One of the salient features of the 1848 revolution for Warner was surely its failure. The Paris revolution of 1848 began in February, the month Warner's protagonist Sophia Willoughby arrives in the city; it failed, with many arrests and much bloodshed, in June, the month in which the narrative ends.[44] Of the many February reforms, only universal male suffrage survived the counterrevolutionary ferment. Circumscribing her narrative within a historical revolution that initially burst with hope and then failed brutally allows Warner to speculate, in the midst of her love story, about the risks facing a possible revolution in the 1930s. It offers her a way to display hope for progressive change without seeming utopian. The failed revolution provides a realistic, not romantic, political narrative, and *Summer Will Show* follows suit. At the end of her novel, Warner abruptly replaces the romance plot with one of political transformation. Moreover, the text maintains a satiric distance from the revolution, presenting ruthless Communists as well as idealistic socialists and unaffiliated supporters. The satiric tone manifests Warner's concern to portray herself as hard-headed, knowing the costs of revolution.

The 1848 revolution also resonated for Warner because of the position of the middle-class vis-à-vis the revolutionary proletariat. In the February revolution, sometimes referred to as the "bourgeois revolution," many people from the middle classes supported the workers (if not by fighting, at least by donating food, weapons, and supplies to the people at the barricades) and the bourgeois National Guard "at a critical moment on 23 February" refused to defend the king, who was forced to abdicate.[45] But by the "June days," according to Geoffrey Ellis, "the ranks of the counterrevolutionaries were swelled by large numbers of Parisian bourgeois, now willing to be counted on the streets, as they had not been in February."[46] The difference between the February revolution and the "June days" was sufficient for Marx to view the latter as a civil war which "marked the victory (if only provisional) of 'bourgeois terrorism.'"[47] Such a conflicted history of middle-class allegiance echoes through Warner's novel, giving subtle voice to her mixture of pride and guilt as a middle-class Communist artist. As her biographer Claire Harman points out, Warner's letters of the period show a parallel self-consciousness about her class status:

After a May Day rally in London [in 1935], Sylvia wrote to Julius Lipton, a young poet: "I appreciate how lucky we are, coming newly into the Party, and from such a dubious quarter, middle-class homes and genteel upholstery, to have met you so early and to have had your greeting and welcome" – the tone of which is almost apologetic. Later she was to write that in the early thirties, the Communist Party of Great Britain "was accepting new adherents from what it thought of as the Bourgeoisie and called the Intellectuals" . . . In *Summer Will Show* . . . Sophia Willoughby has a similar experience of finding her class and background difficult for the revolutionaries to overlook.[48]

Not only Warner, of course, but W. H. Auden and his circle also wrestled with what their class background meant in relation to their various degrees of Communist affiliation.[49] It was this self-conscious distance from the workers they wished to support that Woolf pointed to when she labeled them the "leaning tower" generation ("The Leaning Tower" [1940]). Portraying the events of 1848 in both their February and June aspects, Warner captures the conflicted, sometimes guilty support for Communism of leftist bourgeois English writers of the 1930s.

A more particular aspect of the 1848 revolutions that echoed in 1930s Europe was their link to Jewish emancipation. Although French Jews had been formally emancipated in 1791, the revolutions of 1848 lifted the disabilities imposed on the Jews of the Italian and German states and across the Austro-Hungarian empire (temporarily, as it turned out). When Warner was writing her novel, European fascism was already targeting Jews. Again like Auden, she was distressed by this aspect of contemporary history. She marched in protests against the British Union of Fascists,[50] and in 1937 she published a "fable" in the *Left Review* that criticized the government's negligible efforts, in the Public Order Act of 1936, to protect East End Jews from Oswald Mosley's thugs. By including several Jews in Minna Lemuel's revolutionary circle, *Summer Will Show* hints at what Howard Sachar notes of the period – that in the liberal meetings and clubs of 1848–1849, Jews were suddenly "everywhere welcome, everywhere active."⁵¹

That this aspect of 1848 was crucial to Warner's aims is reflected in the significant presence in the novel of what we might call its Jewish content. Sophia Willoughby's rival and then lover, the storyteller Minna Lemuel, is Jewish, a fact that (as I discuss in chapter 1), Sophia consistently misreads and seems never to forget. Minna has an important Jewish friend, a composer named David Guitermann. And arguably the most vivid part of the novel is Minna's narration of the pogrom that killed her parents when she was a child. Since Warner was clearly dismayed by the antisemitism she saw rising around her in 1930s Europe (including in Britain), it seems plain that her use of these Jewish characters and subjects is related to her critique of the political and social climate and her commitment to changing it. But what remains ambiguous is just *how*, aside from expressing her disapproval of antisemitism, the Jewish content relates to her political commentary.

The first sign that Jewishness contributes meaningfully to the novel is the narrative importance given to Minna's story of the pogrom. Part I ends with Sophia preparing to listen to Minna's story. Part II begins with that story *in medias res*: "'But the first thing I can remember is the lighting of a candle'" (*SWS* 119). Minna starts her tale by casting Jewish religion in a mysterious setting. She recalls awakening to her father lighting a sabbath candle secretly in the darkness, and softly chanting "in a language which [Minna has] never heard before." He is wearing tifillin (phylacteries) and a tallit (prayer shawl), which she describes from the child's perspective: "'On his forehead is a little box, and over his head is the praying towel.'" Although this is her first encounter with her family's Jewishness, she can "'understand it well enough to know that it is something secret and precious, a jewel that can only be taken out at night'" (*SWS* 119). Having established the religious setting, Minna moves on to describe the natural environment, telling a romantic and engaging story of coming to understand "Liberty" through the debacle of a frozen river (*SWS* 123). The next spring, seeking that feeling again, the young Minna returns to the river with her father, but this time there are bloody men and horses "'half frozen into the ice'" (*SWS* 125). With this image Minna injects into the tale of the "precious jewel" of Judaism and the freedom of the spring river a sense of foreboding that sets the stage for her description of the pogrom itself.

This narrative takes up more than fifteen pages of the novel. It is given poignancy by the skill with which Minna weaves into the narrative her younger self's innocence about what was happening. When she learned from her mother's "'wild despairing cry'" (*SWS* 130) that the "'Christians were coming,'" she volunteered to warn her neighbors.

"Through the heavy dusk I ran from house to house. Many houses were closed and shuttered, I had to bang and shout to be admitted. I stopped only to say, 'The Christians are coming.' It was all I knew. In every house it was the same. A cry, a lamentation! And then the same desperate haste, and smooth making ready to fly, as though, waking and sleeping, winter and summer, a life-long, a nation-long, this had been expected and rehearsed." (*SWS* 131)

Moving from the child's point of view to her own commentary ("'a life-long, a nation-long'"), Minna captures her audience's attention so well that Sophia forgets at every pause to look for her husband Frederick, whom she came to Minna's flat to find. Toward the end of the narrative, Minna describes finding her mother's wig "'like a fallen bird's nest, cold and stiff with frost, and rocking lightly in the wind'" (*SWS* 134). Her parents have both been killed. She is taken in by a priest for the alleged purpose of saving her soul. "'I shall not forget what I suffered in the priest's house,'" she says, and is about to continue when "[i]nto that silence broke a preliminary cough, and a dull snuffling voice said, 'Excuse me, ladies and gentlemen. But the people in the street are demanding the carriages for their barricade'" (*SWS* 135). The revolution is beginning.

The length, power, and positioning of this narrative indicate its importance to the novel. Harman describes its intensity:

When, at the beginning of Part II, we are plunged into Minna's narrative of escape from the pogrom in Lithuania, Sylvia Townsend Warner achieves an important coup; having told us that Minna is a spell-binder, she makes her one. The narrative, with its complete change of pace and tone, pushes the reader into that Parisian drawing-room with Sophia. One is, for its duration, more of a listener than a reader. (*SWS* vii)

The tale's placement at the beginning of part II and its position as the setting for the revolution's prosaic beginnings imply that it is an introduction to what follows: to Sophia's emancipation from the world of "oughts" (discussed in chapter 1), to the love affair between Sophia and Minna, and to the revolution itself. In its role as introduction, the narrative of the pogrom suggests that oppression of Jews is a key component of the injustice a revolution would target. The narrative as lead-in to the revolution represents the hope for freedom from oppression of any sort. Not untypically, this interwar novel views Jews as almost archetypal victims, weaving their history into a larger consideration of revolutionary politics, using them as icons of bravery in persecution. In conjoining this narrative with the beginning of the revolution, Warner captures both the hopeful idealism of February 1848, and that of the nascent Communist Party in Britain in the early 1930s.

But this general assent to Communism in the novel and Warner's own induction into the party may lend false clarity to the novel's ending, in which Minna is apparently dead and Sophia begins reading the *Communist Manifesto*. It may seem as though Sophia had to be freed from Minna's romantic socialism, and even perhaps from the women's romantic (in the other sense) entanglement, in order to become a more orthodox and effective revolutionary. If this is an accurate reading of the novel, admirers of Warner have new political problems. First, such a plot might contain hints of lesbian panic (suggesting that the women's relationship is degrading or threatening). Second, it might suggest an antisemitic strain in the novel, one that finds it easy and appropriate to kill off a Jewish character once she has fulfilled her function of mirroring the English protagonist's loss and alienation so that the protagonist can move forward. Third, if the plot depends on killing off Minna to free the orthodox Communist in Sophia, the novel sounds, in Robert Caserio's description, rather Stalinist.[52]

The fact that the lesbian lover of our aristocratic protagonist dies at the end of this novel has raised suspicions that the ending is motivated by internalized homophobia. Julie Abraham, for instance, reads Minna's death as a typical ending to a lesbian novel, as "the punishment that completes the representation of lesbianism."[53] Gay Wachman argues against this view in her comparison of *Summer Will Show* to Radclyffe Hall's *The Well of Loneliness* (1928), pointing out that the former contains little of the grotesque that haunts *The Well*.[54] She footnotes a reference to Abraham, and argues that such a reading "involves a drastic oversimplification of Warner's novel. Minna dies as a result of the class war and of Sophia's arrogant, racist refusal to take Caspar's infatuation seriously. Caspar kills Minna because Sophia loves her and neglects him and because he has absorbed the values of the patriarchal imperialism that brought him into the world."[55]

I ultimately agree with Wachman, both for the reasons she gives and because there is nothing in Warner's diaries, letters, or other fictions to indicate a horrified reaction to her own initiation into a lesbian "marriage" with Valentine Ackland, to whom she dedicates *Summer Will Show*.[56] (Of course, one might conceivably "write out" such anxieties in fiction in a successful attempt to keep them from infecting one's own emotional life.) Nevertheless, I find it difficult to dismiss Abraham's sense that something more than the plot elements Wachman mentions motivates Minna's death.

The most unsavory possibility for anyone interested in the literary and political roles assigned to Jews in modernist literature is that Minna serves the novel merely as a means: a means to reflect Sophia's displacement from England and the painful detachment from her role as mother (her children have died of smallpox), and to convert Sophia to Communism. When she has accomplished these functions, such an interpretation would hold, she is no longer necessary. In fact, the ending might imply, she should be gotten out of the way so that Sophia might deepen her commitment to an orthodox Communism to which the romantic Minna could never assent. The possibility that Minna is sacrificed to Sophia's conversion to Communism is mentioned by several critics, Wendy Mulford and Caserio among them, but without reference to its antisemitic implications.

Mulford suggests three possible reasons for Minna's death. Two of these are quite similar, the first a milder form of the second: Minna may die because Warner wanted to emphasize Sophia alone with her "dedication to her chosen politics" or "because Minna as romantic revolutionary had to be swept aside for the forces of new Communist realism represented by Sophia."[57] But these explanations do not satisfy Mulford: "If, in *Summer Will Show*, Sylvia attempted to stifle the artist in order to free the dedicated revolutionary, her unconscious was unable to consent to such a move. The death of Minna remains a botch, an unsatisfactory imposition on the artistic unity of the novel."[58] Mulford's other suggestion, not finally endorsed any more than the former two, is that "Minna as Jewish victim must exemplify the doom of her race."[59] This is the only explanation I have found that takes Minna's Jewishness into account. But it is not clear what this explanation would mean: would it point to Warner's sympathy with persecuted Jews or a requirement of realism or both? Mulford does not explain how this exemplified doom might contribute to the novel's political effects. Her use of the word "doom," in fact, unwittingly treats the Holocaust as a foregone conclusion, as if Warner could know by 1935 the extent to which European Jewry would be destroyed.[60] As I describe below, my interpretation of the novel's ending does encompass Minna's status as Jewish victim, but it reads her death not as a statement of doom but, on the contrary, as an evocation of compassion and a call-to-arms for antifascist work. At the same time, Minna's death contributes to a critique, in the midst of Warner's affirmation of socialist ideals, of single-minded, ruthless Communism that leaves no room for art.

Caserio's compelling but ultimately unconvincing reading of the end of the novel is premised on Minna's romanticism and her consequent unfitness for Communist insurrection.[61] That the artistic Minna would not be able to adhere to strict Communist doctrine is implied by the way the novel presents her artistry. As I describe in chapter 1, Warner uses Minna to represent disinterested art and love; unconcerned with money, political power, or social position, her only greed is to experience her tales' effects on their audiences. This delight in artistic effect is portrayed as that which prevents her from being a proper Communist. Minna is just the kind of passionate but erratic revolutionary described in the treatise being written by Ingelbrecht, a rather severe character based on Engels. "'What have you written about Minna?'" Sophia asks him. He reads from his treatise:

"'There are some revolutionaries . . . who seem incapable of feeling a durable anger against the conditions which they seek to overthrow. In these characters the imagination is too rich, the emotional force too turbulent. The anger which they undoubtedly feel is neutralised by the pleasure they experience in expressing it . . . [W]hen they have finished their speech, or poignarded their tyrant, they are in such a mood of satisfied excitement that they are almost ready to forgive the state of society which allows them such abuses on which to avenge themselves.'" (SWS 268–269)

Through this treatise the text establishes a conflict between artistic mastery and political efficacy and reflects on Warner's own artistry. Warner has framed a question that worried Auden and his circle in reverse: instead of expressing anxiety that politics might impinge on her art, drag it down into propaganda, she seems to worry that her artistic commitments would dilute her Communist ones. Whereas Auden later regretted in his "New Year Letter" that he had "adopted what I would disown / the preacher's loose immodest tone,"[62] Warner seems to have doubted, at the outset of her political career, whether her passion for the cause could endure apart from her passion for art.

Ingelbrecht's treatise becomes the focus for Caserio's tentative interpretation of the end of the novel, one that coincides with Mulford's two versions of the same claim:

And there is above all – where classic Marxism is concerned – the potential Stalinism of the segment of plotline identified with the revolutionary named Ingelbrecht, who is writing a treatise "on the proper management of revolutions." The portions of his treatise embedded in *Summer Will Show* deride a type of revolutionary who "seem[s] incapable of feeling a durable anger against the conditions which they seek to overthrow . . . " It appears that Minna Lemuel, the Jewish bohemian artist, is such a character. She is wounded (probably fatally) as the result of her extending a moment of forgiveness to a representative of the reactionary state. In arriving at Minna's probable death the narrative might seem especially to be endorsing Ingelbrecht's character analysis, and in this light Sophia's absorption in the *Communist Manifesto* equally seems to be a critique of Minna.[63]

He goes on to point out that Sophia's loss of Minna can be read as Sophia's "politically correct separation from Minna's allegedly amateurish revolutionism."[64]

Such interpretations assume that Sophia's love for Minna the "romantic charlatan" (*SWS* 178) is in conflict with her potential political commitments. But from Minna's admittedly romantic point of view, Sophia's interest in her is consistent with her commitment to revolution: "though you may think you have chosen me, Sophia, or chosen happiness, it is the Revolution you have chosen" (*SWS* 277). Besides, Ingelbrecht's treatise has labeled revolutionaries of Sophia's type *"undesirable recruits from the bourgeoisie . . . These miserable camp-followers clog action, talk incessantly, make the movement ridiculous, and, parasites themselves, harbour further parasites"* (*SWS* 270). This makes it seem unlikely that, at least from Ingelbrecht's (representatively orthodox) point of view, being separated from Minna's insufficiently dogmatic interest in the revolution would make Sophia a useful Communist or purge her bourgeois sympathies, acquaintance with the *Communist Manifesto* notwithstanding. Moreover, it is Minna whose Judaic ethics seem endorsed by the novel. As I quote in chapter 1, Minna tells her friends that as a child, "'I learned some Hebrew, and one of the things I learned was, that in our Hebrew language there was no word for charity. The word I must use, my father said, was Justice'" (*SWS* 361). It is Minna's generosity – her sense of "Justice" – that creates the joy between herself and Sophia. By describing this ethical view in terms of giving away money, Warner links Minna's ethics to the redistribution of wealth that the revolution would inaugurate. She thus reminds readers that the purpose of a revolution is to create a just society, not to create a uniform, orthodox approach in those who seek it.

In addition, when we consider the emotional force of the novel's final section, in which Sophia becomes delirious and paralyzed with grief, and then breaks out of her paralysis to search fruitlessly for Minna, hoping she may still be alive, we may find it very difficult to view Minna's character as a means only. It is not that the plot of transformation is not important.

One of the novel's most resonant lines is Sophia's when she refuses to accompany her great-aunt back to her expensive flat: "'I have changed my ideas. I do not think as I did'" (*SWS* 403). But Minna's compelling presence, and Sophia's longing for her when she is gone, are integral to that plot: Minna's ideals, romantic as they were, seem too much of a piece with Sophia's transformation to be superseded by it.

But the argument that Minna's death frees Sophia for stricter adherence to Communism hinges most on the question of the text's attitude toward doctrinal, purely economic Communism and toward such heartless, anything-for-the-cause maneuvers as the text might seem to enact in killing off Minna for the sake of Sophia's conversion. The text first indicates that it condemns the latter just after the February revolution has begun. Minna's friend Gaston arrives at her flat and describes his plan. In order to gain public support, he tells her, the revolutionaries will incite troops to fire on "'a procession of the citizens with their children – children are essential for the right feeling, and I have arranged for the children'" (*SWS* 149). Sophia finds such talk "repulsive and silly," and the text's repetition of the word "children" makes it impossible to approve the proceedings. Indeed, this scene seems to be included in part so that the text might endorse Minna's later comments that certain kinds of Communists are "'dangerous, deadly,'" that "'there must be death . . . in any such earnestness'" (*SWS* 323). Warner's own later description of her politics corroborates such skepticism: she said that she became a Communist because she was "agin the Government," a position she acknowledged was closer to anarchism than orthodox Communism.[65]

Condemning such cold-blooded plots does not necessarily mean that the text also condemns doctrinal Communism; after all, it is not Ingelbrecht, the representative of Engels, who concocts the scheme to have the families fired upon, but Minna's friend Gaston. But Warner also seems to criticize orthodox Communism on two counts: its exclusive focus on economic injustice both dismisses the distinct power of racism and views art as a luxury, fittingly sacrificed.

Warner's suggestion that race must not be subsumed under class antagonism is centered in Minna's murder by Sophia's young black colonial cousin Caspar. The novel portrays these two characters at odds in spite of Minna's deep sympathy for Caspar (she tries in vain to prevent Sophia from sending him away to school; she brings him food and presents). The potential bond between this illegitimate colonial boy sent to England by his white father, and the poverty-stricken Jewish bohemian Minna is foreclosed by Sophia's racist indifference to Caspar's emotions and by the antisemitism that Caspar absorbs in his European surroundings. First, as Wachman points out, Sophia fails to take Caspar seriously because of her own racial prejudices.[66] Although it is clear that he adores her and is jealous of Minna, Sophia dismisses him as childish. She insists that he cannot live with them, and asks her estranged husband to find him a school in France, since he has run away from the oppressive school she had sent him to in England. Instead, Frederick secretly enlists Caspar in the counterrevolutionary *Gardes Mobiles*. Sophia's mistreatment of Caspar, her underestimation of his passion and power, and her unwillingness even to find a school for him herself, prove fatal to Minna.

Second, Caspar seems hungrily to accept an antisemitism that provides him with another rationale for his dislike of Minna. If he did not learn antisemitism in the English school to which Sophia sent him, he is certainly taught it by the caretaker of Minna's building, Madame Coton, with whom he is staying. When he awakens from nightmares about the school, Madame Coton hugs him "in her scrawny arms, deepen[s] her grudge against the English and warn[s] him to beware of the Jewess" (*SWS* 298). Sophia knows this, but says nothing. Madame Coton's repeated warnings against "the Jewess" (*SWS* 311) seem to take effect: we learn that Caspar has rudely turned away Minna's friend, the composer David Guitermann. Caspar tells Sophia and Minna "that during their absence a wretched Jew – a Jew with a hump-back, moreover – had come to the door, enquiring for Minna, but had been routed by Caspar's assurance that there were no old clothes for sale today" (*SWS* 309).

After Caspar is enlisted in the *Gardes Mobiles*, his antisemitism finds far more serious expression. As a counterrevolutionary soldier, he comes bounding over the June barricades and, in spite of Minna's warm cry, "'Why, it's Caspar!,'" stabs her "with a howl of rage," crying, "'Drab! ... Jewess! This is the end of you!'" (*SWS* 382). Sophia then, with eerie calm, shoots and kills Caspar. Sophia's indifference to Caspar's antisemitism and the racial prejudice that causes her to devalue and underestimate him distance readers from her character, revealing her blindness to the role of racism in larger systems of oppression. As Robin Hackett argues, the end of the novel "is Warner's utterly coherent propagandistic warning. Because Sophia does not incorporate Caspar and racism into her class analysis soon enough to prevent tragedy, she suffers the loss of Minna, the source, she says, of everything that has ever made her happy."[67] In this strand of the novel, Warner seems to suggest that the class struggle cannot succeed by itself – that racial hatred must be attacked as well, and racial equality part of the Communist agenda.[68]

Warner extends her critique of narrowly economic Communism through her portrayal of Guitermann, the "hunchback" composer. The similarities between his death and Minna's indicate that the novel may be asking its readers to consider the costs of revolutionary Communism. As Caspar's final words to Minna make clear, Minna dies as a woman and a Jew. She also dies in the midst of her kindhearted refusal to see Caspar as the counterrevolutionary soldier he has become: for her, he is still the young man who loves Sophia, and for whom she feels responsible. The other artist figure in the novel, the tubercular Guitermann, also dies with his integrity intact. Minna learns that he moved out of his family's house after he refused to help with a metalwork project assigned to his father by the army. As Minna explains, "'[H]e would not work for the army, he said. He had had enough of their trumpets, he had his own music to attend to. There was a bitter quarrel, and David, wrapping himself in a bloodspitting as in a royal mantle, walked out of the place'" (SWS 358). Guitermann soon dies in a rented room, blood blotting out his unfinished score. Like Minna, he dies as a revolutionary, but also as an artist, both because he has refused to work against the revolution and because his health has declined, since "revolutions ha[ve] no need for symphonies" (SWS 200). Hearing of his death, Sophia comments, "'I begin to think we must all be damned . . . The way we can endure to hear of these things'" (SWS 360).

Earlier, when Sophia encountered him between the February and June revolutions, Guitermann was playing guitar on the street. He told her that he was "'one of the luxuries that have been lopped off [by the revolution]. And sometimes I tremble for the threat to the essentials . . . to the greatest of essentials, to art'" (SWS 200). The emotional weight of Minna's murder has its precursor in the harrowing tale of Guitermann's death, and, taken together, these aspects of the novel seem to demonstrate Warner's sympathy with Guitermann's fear for the future of art. His lament for the "essentials" is a serious version of Warner's sarcastic comment about the Great War in her diary in 1933: she describes an August day as "interminably gloomy . . . with nothing to show for it, except reading [Charles] Sorley's poems, who died in the war: which was to make the world safe for democracy, so very properly killed all the poets it could lay hands on."[69] Like Woolf, whose *Three Guineas* focuses on mental autonomy as the antidote to fascism, Warner implies that political solutions that do not protect imaginative freedom, that do not make the world safe for *artists*, are little better than the fascistic threats they are intended to oppose. The parallel between Minna's and Guitermann's deaths suggests that Warner's brand of revolutionary passion resembles not Ingelbrecht's but Minna's, romantic faults and all.

Although Warner inverted the terms of one of Auden's central questions, I would argue that she has arrived at a similar answer, approaching the question of the artist's role in revolution in a vein similar to the "Auden Generation." Their critical writings of the mid-1930s, in Samuel Hynes's words, amounted to "a series of defences constructed to protect literature and writers from the pressures of the time – pressures to be politically orthodox, to make art a class weapon, to abandon the traditional past, to simplify the complexities of art in the service of an urgent cause."[70] Far from endorsing Ingelbrecht's claim that Minna is the wrong kind of revolutionary, *Summer Will Show* suggests that a revolution that kills its artists is the wrong kind of revolution. To the degree that it performs a political summons, it demands a more just, perhaps more circumscribed, revolutionary process than that so brutally suppressed in 1848: one that would find use both for symphonies and for storytellers.

Moreover, read in 1936, the story of two Jewish artists' deaths, narrated after a vivid description of a pogrom, would conjure the threat of Nazi oppression, and it was to combat Nazism and the British government that appeased it that many left-leaning artists and intellectuals were becoming Communists. Since the British Communist Party was founded only after the First World War, its dogmas and their implications for literature were still being determined. As Hynes puts it, the 1930s "was not a time of political orthodoxy, but a time when orthodoxy was being worked out."[71] In an article about socialist fiction in the 1930s, H. Gustav Klaus points out that what bound socialist writers together in groups such as the Writers' International was primarily the aim of defending European culture from fascism, rather than a positive desire to promote a revolutionary proletarian literature.[72] This seems to be true of Warner. As she and Ackland considered their politics in the year before they joined the Communist Party, they weighed the need to combat fascism against their fear of collective action, which Ackland labeled the "ant-and-bee society." All Warner was sure of was what she *dis*liked: "priests in their gowns, anti-Semitism, the white man who is the black man's burden, warmongers."[73] Warner's novel ought to be read as arising from and partaking in this general defensive climate of the British left. *Summer Will Show* does not casually use Jewishness and then sweep it away for the sake of Sophia's conversion to orthodox Marxism; instead, it uses the sorrow of its ending to call up sympathy with artists and with Jews, to evoke just the sort of protectiveness that prompted Warner and many of her contemporaries to join the Communist Party.

Warner and Woolf, then, both use Jewish characters to express negative attitudes about certain features of modernity: Warner criticizes revolutionary excess and Woolf critiques modern fragmentation and discontinuity. But neither of these writers was antimodern. Warner viewed revolution as a crucial, potentially liberating aspect of modern culture; she was, however, concerned about its intensity, scope, and tendency to view itself as an end rather than a means. Woolf viewed modern discontinuity as liberating, too: it freed people from herdlike uniformity and allowed them to think individually; but she also recognized the loss involved when unity becomes a danger and when modernization (efficiency, commercialization) takes precedence over aesthetics. Both Warner and Woolf believed in art as a powerful social force, necessary not only to personal and intellectual liberty, but to political liberty as well.

One crucial difference between them is the way in which they relate Jewishness to these critiques. Warner uses her Jewish characters' *deaths* to represent the negative features of revolutionary zeal; that is, she assumes that readers will sympathize with those characters, mourn their deaths, and perhaps reaffirm their own liberal democratic commitment to an autonomous artistic or cultural sphere even within revolutionary societies. Woolf, on the other hand, uses her Jewish character to *represent* the negative features of modernity. In spite of her generally promodern and antifascist convictions, she thereby expressed her mild, "polite" antisemitism in a way that parallels the antimodern antisemitism common to fascism. Analyzing these portrayals of Jews in texts that take the modern as their subject sheds light on the writers' multiform responses to a phenomenon itself so various and complex.

Coinciding with the pervasive notion that Jews were quintessentially modern was a cultural association between Jews and the past, and between Jews and a racial continuity which brings that past into the present. In the next chapter I turn to this facet of modernism's representations of Jews, analyzing the ways Dorothy Richardson and Djuna Barnes enlist Jews in their feminist critiques of historical and biological continuity.

4

The race must go on: gender, Jewishness, and racial continuity in Barnes and Richardson

Christian theological discourses about Judaism have long associated Jews with the body while identifying Christians with the spirit. As the previous chapters make clear, this association is integral to stereotypes of Jewish materiality and financial acuity as well as to supersessionist models of Christian theology. In her seminal study *Faith and Fratricide* (1974), Rosemary Ruether describes the larger context and philosophical underpinnings of this anti-Judaic claim. Ruether explains that while Hellenistic Jewish philosophers such as Philo worked to spiritualize and universalize Judaic ritual practices, they did not therefore devalue the Torah that commanded those practices. Jewish Hellenistic Midrash, Ruether shows, "sought rather to invest the letter with a spiritual and ethical significance that would make it meaningful to those who had learned to think of truth in philosophical terms."[1] Jewish Hellenistic thought did accept Platonic dualism about the body and the soul, but it did not reject the body, instead considering it a valuable house for the spirit. "For Philo, it is as wrong to abandon the letter of the Torah for a 'purely spiritual religion' that imagines it can dispense with the outward observance, as it would be for a man to imagine that he can live purely in the soul while abandoning the body."[2] In Ruether's view, it is when this Platonic dualism is "fused" with another sort of dualism that everything associated with the body is dismissed:

This Platonic dualism between the body and the soul, the material and spiritual "worlds," had governed Philonic exegesis. However, when this spiritualizing exegesis is fused with the messianic dualism between "this age" and the "age to come," identifying the Church with the eschatological community of the Resurrection, Philo's spiritualizing exegesis, intended to vindicate the inward meaning of Jewish law, is now used to "prove" the radical supersession of Jewish law. Judaism is identified with all that is "old" and "carnal," while Christianity is spiritual and eschatological "newness." Judaism is the outward, temporal, and perishable which existed only as a shadow of the inward and eternal covenant of true Being that has now dawned through the power of the Resurrection.[3]

These overlaid dualistic systems of belief render everything associated with the body unnecessary and everything associated with the past obsolete. After all, if the "age to come" will be or has already been ushered in by Christ Jesus, everything that allegedly foretold this age is rendered irrelevant except *as* signs.

Paul of Tarsus explored this strain of thought most fully, theorizing the relation of the Jews to Christianity and to redemption. One of the things he stressed was that Jews affirm their commitment to God through physical rites (especially circumcision and Kashrut) and believe that their genealogy, their biological heritage as the "children of Israel," is an important source of their relationship to God. Christians would replace those physical rites with metaphoric rituals like baptism ("circumcision of the heart") and substitute spiritual for biological descent. In emphasizing this contrast, Paul made explicit what would become an ongoing Christian tradition that associated Jews with bodiliness, materiality, and biology. Daniel Boyarin traces Paul's contribution to this tradition in *A Radical Jew* (1994), having approached this view from another perspective in his previous book. In *Carnal Israel* (1993) he interprets rabbinic texts to argue that there is, in fact, an "essential descriptive accuracy" in the claim by Paul, Augustine, and others that Judaism is connected to the body more fundamentally than is Christianity.[4] Boyarin distinguishes between investing significance in the body and being unspiritual or "carnal."[5] The kind of doubly dualistic Christian thought Ruether describes, however, degrades the body and denies it any positive role in human spiritual life.

Steeped in this dualistic tradition, modernist writers inherited the notion that Jews were more bodily and therefore less spiritual than Christians. Even Matthew Arnold's influential conceptions of Hebraism and Hellenism participated in this dualism and brought it to the attention of late nineteenth- and early twentieth-century writers. Although he viewed both as "spiritual disciplines," Arnold described Hellenism as "spontaneity of consciousness" driven by a desire to "see things as they really are," while asserting that Hebraism is preoccupied with "conduct," with "right acting."[6] Hellenism is, then, more closely related to the mind – seeing – while Hebraism is more closely related to the body – doing. An article in the *Times Literary Supplement* of 1927 draws upon this distinction without mentioning Arnold. It ascribes antisemitism to the conflict between the same two ways of being in the world that Arnold described:

If in the ancient world the opposition to the ethical attitude was mainly aesthetic, and in the medieval world philosophic, it is nowadays scientific, and anti-Semitism itself is but a by-product of this interaction between European logic and Jewish ethic. Their opposition affected even the religious antagonism which developed so soon as the civilized world became Christian; for while the Church, proceeding intellectually, laid its emphasis on belief, Judaism, still dominated by its moral concepts, was chiefly concerned with conduct.[7]

This distinction served Christian culture as a way of disavowing its Jewish origins through a variety of supersession: Christians are superior to Jews as the spirit or mind is superior to the body.

Race science solidified the view that Jews were more bodily than Christians – and not only Jews but all its "others." Anyone "different" was embodied in ways the white, Christian heterosexual male was not. Just as it transformed the residue of supersessionism, then, race science also adopted the embodiment of Jews from Christian theological discourse. Sander Gilman describes the use by science and medicine of this Christian image:

The difference of the Jewish body is absolute within the Western tradition; its counterimage (from the comments of Paul, Eusebius, and Origen on the "meaning" of circumcision) is the "Christian" body which eventually becomes secularized into the "German" or "English" body with the rise of the modern body politic. Thus it is of little surprise that the image of the Jewish body shifts from the rhetoric of religious anti-Judaism to the rhetoric of the pseudoscience of anti-Semitism.[8]

Gilman describes this embodiment in detail in *The Jew's Body* (1991), showing that Jews were nearly always ascribed various physical characteristics within both popular and medical discourses, especially "Jewish" noses, dark, curly hair, flat feet, and a distinctive way of speaking.

An example of this preoccupation with the Jewish body can be found in a 1926 English review of *Are the Jews a Race?* by the German socialist Karl Kautsky. The reviewer in the *Times Literary Supplement* summarizes Kautsky's argument that Jews are not a race because "less than 15 percent" of the Jews in New York "have Jewish noses and little more than half are dark"; their narrow chests are attributable to their urban lifestyle.[9] Even in arguing against the racialization of Jews, Kautsky accepts the stereotype of the narrow-chested Jew and seems content to label hooked noses "Jewish" in spite of his contention that only 15 percent of Jews actually have them. Sexology, too, added its voice to the discourses that linked Jews to the body. As Gilman has also shown, sexologists and psychiatrists such as Jean-Martin Charcot and Richard Von Kraft-Ebing believed Jews were prone to various nervous disorders, and explained this through reference to the supposed inbreeding and other deviant sexual practices of Jews.[10]

Women, of course, were associated with the body even more strongly than Jews and other racialized "others." But, not surprisingly given the power of race science in the early twentieth century, most women modernists did not protest racialization or embodiment *per se*. Instead, they enlisted Jews, multiply embodied by Christianity, race science, and sexology, to distance themselves from such embodiment. Jews represent the force of biology that threatens the protagonists of the feminist novels I consider in this chapter. The protagonists escape that force, engaging in lesbian romance or romantic friendship rather than letting themselves be trapped by Jewish men. The novels thus endorse lesbianism in part by defining Jewishness in negative terms.

To be embodied – particularly in the modern period, when race thinking was establishment science and gender roles were in unprecedented flux – meant to be embodied *as* a member of a particular sex and race. When feminist writers such as Djuna Barnes and Dorothy Richardson used Jews to reject embodiment, therefore, they were chiefly protesting the strictures of gender and the burdens of procreation. In *Nightwood* (1936) and *Pilgrimage* (1915–1967) respectively, they portray Jewishness as a racialized force threatening to domesticate desire, entrapping women through false biological imperatives.

It is not unusual in modernism for Jewish men either to threaten women's independence or at least obsessively to desire racial continuity. In Edith Wharton's *The House of Mirth* (1905), Simon Rosedale wants to own Lily Bart as one of his possessions, not to know her as a human being; the novel's momentum depends on its readers wanting Lily to remain free from Rosedale's clutches, to refuse to become an object for him to adorn and display. In Ernest Hemingway's *The Sun Also Rises* (1926), Jake Barnes accepts Brett Ashley's sexual and emotional freedom, loving her deeply without trying to control her; but Robert Cohn attempts to possess her, following her around and beating up her fiancé in a jealous rage. In James Joyce's *Ulysses* (1922), however, Leopold Bloom does not entrap Molly. Some readers are appalled, on the contrary, by his apparent complicity with her extramarital affair. This aspect of the plot draws upon stereotypes of Jewish masochism, but Joyce does not seem to view Jewishness as a force that entraps women. Nevertheless, Bloom *is* obsessed, eleven years after his son Rudy's death, with his lack of a male heir. When he imagines Rudy in a crucial scene in "Circe," reading "from right to left . . . kissing the page," he emphasizes the Jewish aspect of his desire for a son: someone to carry on Jewish tradition, to provide racial and religious continuity.[11] An antisemitic comment in "Cyclops" highlights the connection between Bloom's desire for a son and his Jewishness. In that scene J. J. O'Molloy says that Jews wonder whether every male child born will be the messiah, and so "'every Jew is in a tall state of excitement, I believe, till he knows if he's a father or a mother.'"[12] This humorous gender-twisting – a man is a mother if he fathers a daughter – implies that Bloom is womanly because he only has a daughter, adding to the theme running throughout *Ulysses* that Jewish men are feminine, that Bloom is the "new womanly man."[13]

On the face of it, the assertion that Jewish men are feminine contradicts the concomitant assertion that Jewish men are especially patriarchal, enforcing biological necessity and using women as tools for that end. Considering the contradictory nature of antisemitic stereotypes, the charge that Jewish men are at once too masculine and too feminine is unsurprising. Each side of this dyad can be historicized. Matthew Biberman argues that the stereotype of the hypermasculine Jew, or the "Jew-Devil" dominates in the early modern period, only gradually giving way to the image of the feminine Jew, or the "Jew-Sissy," which comes to dominate by the nineteenth century.[14] The hypermasculine Jew, however, clearly does not simply dissolve when the emasculated Shylock rather than the devilish Barabbas becomes the prototype of the Jew for modern English culture, as Biberman implies.[15] Instead, the two opposing categorizations of Jewish men linger into the nineteenth and twentieth centuries, both often used together to depict Jewishness within a single text. In *Dracula* (1897), for example, as Judith Halberstam's reading shows, devilishness and femininity coincide in Bram Stoker's antisemitic representation of otherness and monstrosity.[16] In this chapter I trace some of the ways the incompatibly gendered depictions of Jewish men dovetail in *Nightwood* and *Pilgrimage*.

Analyzing the complex genderings of Barnes's and Richardson's fictional Jewish men highlights some of the ways gender and race were mutually constitutive. In *Nightwood* and *Pilgrimage* the Jewish male characters are feminized, while at the same time they espouse chauvinist attitudes, play masculinist roles, and pose threats to the protagonists' freedom. They do not seek to ensnare the women out of brutality, however, or simply to dominate them. Their larger aim is continuity. The texts portray their Jewishness as inexorably leading them, as it does Leopold Bloom, to desire sons to carry on that genealogical line so integral to Paul's critique of Judaism.

In *Nightwood* "Baron" Felix Volkbein's attraction to Robin Vote is selfish and instrumental. When he first meets her in Paris, he finds her incomprehensible because he is "racially incapable of abandon" (*N* 38). But he feels she represents "the converging halves of a broken fate" (*N* 38). When Matthew O'Connor sees that Felix "had experienced something unusual" in meeting Robin, he asks him whether he has considered marriage. "The Baron admitted that he had; he wished a son who would feel as he felt about the 'great past'" (*N* 38). His desire for Robin is explicitly for a vessel who might provide him a son – and not just any son, but narcissistically a son who feels as he does about the past. Matthew next asks Felix "of what nation he would choose the boy's mother," to which Felix replies "'The American . . . With an American anything can be done'" (*N* 39). Robin fits his image of a woman with whom "'anything can be done'" because of her apparent malleability – they first encounter her when she has fainted, when "Doctor" O'Connor has been summoned to her side – and because she is American. Felix's attitudes about her suggest that what he means by the "converging halves of a broken fate" is that through her biology, Robin would be able to repair his own broken fate, recreating the continuity whose importance the novel emphasizes in its opening description of its Jewish characters.

The novel begins by describing Felix's parents, the Jewish Guido Volkbein and his Viennese wife Hedvig. The theme of Jewish procreation is introduced in an opening sentence that includes an ambiguous use of the word "sanction": "Early in 1880, in spite of a well-founded suspicion as to the advisability of perpetuating that race which has the sanction of the Lord and the disapproval of the people, Hedvig Volkbein . . . gave birth, at the age of forty-five, to an only child, a son, seven days after her physician predicted she would be taken" (*N* 1). Except for its timing "early" in the year, everything about this birth is late: the mother is not far from menopause and, we learn in the next paragraph, dies just after naming the baby. Felix's father Guido has died six months earlier. And the "race" is viewed over a long historical period, as the reference to the "sanction of the Lord" conveys. Whether "sanction" implies chosenness by the Jewish God or criticism by a rejected Jesus, Hedvig's 1880 childbirth is presented by the text as an act with strong historical resonance. The past is heavily present in this event, which is viewed not as an individual birth but an inadvisable act of racial perpetuation.

When the text next describes Felix's dead father Guido, it continues to emphasize continuity with the past, even attributing to him a racial memory that dates to the Middle Ages. He was, we learn, most conscious of this memory in the autumn, a season that reinforces the sense of lateness in his son's birth:

The autumn, binding him about, as no other season, with racial memories, a season of longing and of horror, he had called his weather. Then walking in the Prater he had been seen carrying in a conspicuously clenched fist the exquisite handkerchief of yellow and black linen that cried aloud of the ordinance of 1468, demanded by one Pietro Barbo, demanding that, with a rope about its neck, Guido's race should run in the Corso for the amusement of the Christian populace. (*N* 2)

Jewishness is here defined as a sense of history so strong that symbols of the past "cry aloud" of oppressions hundreds of years old. The singular pronoun referring to the neck of "Guido's race" contributes to the emphasis on racial uniformity and continuity: Jews were one then, and they are one now, having passed their memories down through the generations undimmed (as the vivid colors of the handkerchief signal). As if to keep his sense of the past collected and intact, Guido manages to buy for himself and Hedvig a house that "became a fantastic museum of their encounter" (*N* 5).

Guido's son Felix inherits from the father he never meets this powerful awareness of the past. He worships aristocratic lineage, bowing down to whomever is graced with a title, and fervently believes the story his aunt repeats for him about his family's history. The story was created by Guido, who, like Ralph Manresa in *Between the Acts* (1941), had assumed an aristocratic identity that was not his. The only objects that link Felix to his father are two portraits Guido bought to provide an "alibi for the blood" (*N* 7). Felix accepts the "actors" in the paintings as his aristocratic ancestors and goes by the title "Baron." Guido and Felix's family history comprises most of the first chapter of *Nightwood*. When we meet the characters who displace them to become the novel's most important figures – Nora Flood, Robin Vote, and Matthew O'Connor – we do not find comparable background information. This omission may be part of the novel's thematization of sterility, which is analyzed by Erin Carlston; the homosexual characters need no backstories just as they will leave no heirs. Carlston writes: "Seizing on one of the aspects of homosexuality most threatening to dominant organicist discourses, its non(re)productivity, Barnes inverts it and raises it, not only to an aesthetic principle but perhaps even to a claim for lesbianism as a privileged attitude in the face of the 'universal maladies' of loss, suffering, and death."[17] The Jewish characters are, on the contrary, exemplars of the suffering that attends generation, so it is their past that must be emphasized and analyzed – and carried forward. When Felix wants a son to feel as he feels about the past, he attempts to link past and future in a way that, in this novel, is unique to Jews. Felix confirms his belief in continuity when he explains to Matthew: "To pay homage to our past is the only gesture that also includes the future" (*N* 39).

This preoccupation with continuity is suspect not only because Felix's personal history is false (the ancestors are actors, the title is assumed) but because continuity in *Nightwood* is a patriarchal force, legitimating only lines of fathers and sons. Felix wants a son, not a daughter, to feel as he does about the past. So he marries Robin, seeking to turn her into a tool of this continuity. He later describes his decision to marry in terms of gaining immortality, another version of continuity. "'It is the motivation of marriage. No man really wants his freedom. He gets a habit as quickly as possible – it is a form of immortality'" (*N* 112). Moreover, Robin's peculiar fluidity makes him feel that "[he] would not only be able to achieve immortality, but be free to choose [his] own kind" (*N* 112).

Felix is disappointed. Robin remains slippery and he lacks the force necessary to entrap her. He sees this as a weakness in himself: "he knew that he was not sufficient to make her what he had hoped" (*N* 44). Although Robin does give birth to a son, whom Felix names Guido after his father,[18] she resists Felix's use of her as a vessel for his beloved continuity, refusing the role of wife and mother. She begins to wander, staying away for days at a time (*N* 45). Once, he finds her holding the baby aloft as if she would dash him to the ground (*N* 48). Later, she slaps Felix, crying "'I didn't want him!'" (*N* 49). And after this, she leaves Felix and the baby for good: she disappears for months, finally returning to the Quarter as Nora's lover.

Felix raises his son alone, but young Guido is weak-minded, timid, and drawn to the Catholic church. He is "[m]entally deficient and emotionally excessive, an addict to death; at ten, barely as tall as a child of six, wearing spectacles, stumbling when he tried to run, with cold hands and anxious face, he followed his father, trembling with an excitement that was a precocious ecstasy" (*N* 107). He speaks of wanting to enter the Church, so Felix writes a long letter to the Pope to try to secure this and decides to return from Paris to Austria so that, should his son be "chosen" as a priest, it would be in the country he considers home (*N* 109). The word "chosen" stresses ironically the shift Guido has made in the family's history. He has reversed the direction of the line of Jewish fathers and sons, both by wishing to become a Christian and by wishing to live a celibate life – not to procreate. This is a disaster for Felix: "In accepting his son the Baron saw that he must accept a demolition of his own life" (*N* 108). Continuity fails, finally, in *Nightwood*; like the other characters, Felix does not find what he seeks. But the narrative makes clear what redemption would have meant for the Jewish line of fathers and sons. As Judith Lee puts it, for Felix, "'redemption' would be the recuperation of a sense of teleology, a triumph of the masculine over the feminine."[19]

Richardson's *Pilgrimage* is dramatically different from *Nightwood*: its emotional lows almost innocent, its style – dense as it is – almost sunny in comparison. Yet its Jewish character is portrayed in strikingly similar ways. Like Felix, Miriam Henderson's love interest Michael Shatov holds chauvinistic views about women's roles and strongly desires a masculinist continuity. Michael is Russian, learning English from Miriam, and she attributes various qualities to his being Russian, European, and Jewish in turn. His desire for traditional family life is linked explicitly to his Jewishness.

The text first suggests that an impassioned interest in fatherhood is a feature of Jewish men when it describes another Jewish character, Rodkin, who unintentionally impregnated Miriam's friend Eleanor Dear. About Rodkin, Miriam muses:

It was wonderful the way the original Jewish spirit came out in him, at every step. His loose life was not Jewish. And it was really comic that he should have been trapped by a girl pretending to be an adventuress. Poor Eleanor, with all her English dreams; just *Rodkin*. But he was a Jew when he hesitated to marry a consumptive, and perfectly a Jew when he decided not to see the child lest he should love it; and also when he hurried down into Sussex the moment it came, to see it, with a huge armful of flowers, for her. (*P* III, 284)

Jewishness here is portrayed as a drive toward family life that makes Rodkin hesitate to marry someone who is likely to die young, know he would be unable to resist loving his child, and finally give in to the force of biology, marrying Eleanor and caring for their child.

The question of biology structures the most important argument between Miriam and Michael. When Michael mentions the "peril" of being cut off from one's fellow creatures, she asks him if he is a socialist:

"No, I would call myself rather one who believes in the race."
"What race? The race is nothing without individuals."

"What is an individual without the race?"

"An individual, with a consciousness; or a soul, whatever you like to call it. The race, apart from individuals, is nothing at all . . . The biggest thing a race does is to produce a few big individualities."

"The biggest thing that the race does is that it goes on. Individuals perish." (*P* III, 150)

Michael's faith in "the race" means that he sees procreation as a solemn duty. But Miriam knows what role women must play if supreme importance is granted to the simple act of "going on." She ends the discussion by saying, "'I don't care a button for the race, and I'd rather kill myself than serve its purposes. Besides, the instincts of self-preservation and reproduction are not the only human motives. They are not human at all'" (*P* III, 152).

This argument between a Jew and a Christian about the relative value of the body and the soul ties their positions to the philosophical debates described at the beginning of this chapter. Michael's Jewishness, as Richardson portrays it, leads him to value genealogical continuity, while the Christian Miriam focuses on the individual soul as the crucial unit. And Miriam, influenced by the dualistic tradition with which Pauline Christianity is infused, refuses to acknowledge the humanity of the procreative drive. To her, such motives are animalistic, "'not human at all.'" When she says she would rather kill herself than serve the purposes of the race, she implies that Michael's interest in racial continuity poses a dire threat to women's liberty. As Jacqueline Rose points out, "by calling this version of maternal sacrificial-cum-racial destiny Jewish, Dorothy Richardson . . . runs Miriam's emancipation straight into some of the most vicious anti-Jewish representations of her time."[20] One of those representations came, as she points out, from the philosopher Otto Weininger, who argued that humanity had to choose between "Judaism and Christianity . . . between male and female, between the race and the individual, between unworthiness and worth, between the earthly and the high life, between negation and the God-like."[21]

Michael's casually misogynist comments seem to validate Miriam's worry. When a woman collides with Miriam as they cross the road, he makes a disparaging remark about women that the narrative does not immediately convey. Horrified, she asks him what he means. He replies, "'I speak only of women in the mass. There are of course exceptions'" (*P* III, 214). Miriam is enraged, seeing that Michael is unaware "that [this argument] was a matter of life and death. He could go on serenely living in an idea, that turned life into a nightmare" (*P* III 214). In response to her anger, Michael suddenly claims to be a feminist:

Miriam pondered. The word was new to her. But how could any one be a feminist and still think women most certainly inferior beings? "Ah," she cried, "you are one of the Huxleys."
"I don't follow you."
"Oh well. He, impertinent schoolboy, graciously suggested that women should be given every possible kind of advantage, educational and otherwise; saying almost in the same breath that they could never reach the highest places in civilization." (*P* III, 216)

This argument feels definitive for Miriam. If Michael is a feminist, it is only of the most patronizing kind. Although he urges her to tell him her thoughts so that his might be modified, Miriam claims not to believe in changes that might result from conversation: "it is the conclusions [people] come to, instinctively, by themselves" that count (*P* III, 217). The penultimate chapter of *Deadlock* (1921) ends with Michael asking Miriam whether she believes "'that wife and mother is the highest position of women.'" Miriam's response is of a piece with her individualist bent: "'It is neither high nor low. It may be anything. If you define life for women, as husbands and children, it means that you have no consciousness at all where women are concerned'" (*P* III, 222).

Deadlock is set at the turn of the century, and so, of course, much of Michael's sexism is typical of other men Miriam meets. But Miriam attributes important aspects of it to his Jewishness. She extends her critique of his sexism to Jewish religion when she visits Mrs. Bergstein, an English woman who has married a Jew. Here Miriam wonders whether Mrs. Bergstein "had anticipated, before she married, what it would be . . . to breathe always the atmosphere of the Jewish religious and social oblivion of women?" (*P* III, 224). In her continued musings Miriam wonders what Mrs. Bergstein may have known about Jewish women:

Had she had any experience of Jewesses, their sultry conscious femineity [*sic*], their dreadful acceptance of being admitted to a synagogue on sufferance, crowded away upstairs in a stuffy gallery, while the men downstairs, bathed in light, draped in the symbolic shawl, thanked God aloud for making them men and not women? Had she thought what it must be to have always at her side a Jewish consciousness, unconscious of her actuality, believing in its own positive existence, seeing her as human only in her consecration to relationships? (*P* III, 224–225)

Miriam's scathing dismissal of Jewish life displaces her fears of entrapment onto Jewish women, whom she describes in racialist terms as "sultry" and overly feminine. She criticizes the Orthodox synagogue and insists on the picture of women crowded into a balcony, even though she tells Mrs. Bergstein, "'Of course I have heard of the reform movement'" (*P* III, 227). She objects to Reform synagogues because "[t]o enter a synagogue that made special arrangements for the recognition of women was to admit that women were dependent on recognition" (*P* III, 227). Miriam thus places Judaism in a double bind. By changing its customs, it not only admits that the previous customs were sexist, she thinks, but takes the same paternalistic attitude toward women that she has encountered in Thomas Henry Huxley's writings and in Michael Shatov. Most important, Miriam attributes a particular sexist attitude to Jewish men: they see women as human only in relation to men or children, not as individuals in their own right.

This feminist antisemitism was common in nineteenth-century conversion novels and invented "memoirs" of converted Jewish women, as Michael Ragussis demonstrates. Participating in the literary tradition initiated by *The Jew of Malta* and *The Merchant of Venice*, in which the only daughter of a Jewish father converts to Christianity, many of these texts focused on Jewish daughters:

> [T]he location of the Jewish daughter at the center of these novelistic plots also points to a central feature of the missionary efforts to the Jews in the nineteenth century. First, it reveals the conversionists' view of the docility of the (Jewish) woman, her special vulnerability to Christian proselytism... Second, it underlines the conversionists' claim that the Jewish woman is a particularly oppressed member of the Jewish community, in need of special liberation. This oppression is consistently recorded through a kind of shorthand by quoting a specific prayer spoken by the Jewish man.[22]

The prayer is the same one Miriam refers to, in which the (Orthodox) man thanks God for not making him a woman. Ragussis points out that this prayer is cited in John Mills's *The British Jews* (1853) and in revisionist novels like Maria Edgeworth's *Harrington* (1817) and George Eliot's *Daniel Deronda* (1876) as well as in missionary texts. The prayer does indicate an attitude of male supremacy, but it does not express the whole of Judaism's attitudes toward women. Miriam's refusal to consider Reform Judaism (in which that prayer has no place) demonstrates that her objection to Judaism is disingenuous. She needs to attribute Michael's sexism to his Jewishness in order to create an apparently legitimate feminist excuse for her antisemitic responses to him.

A comparable attitude can be glimpsed in a passage from Sylvia Townsend Warner's *Lolly Willowes* (1926). In this novel Laura Willowes considers forgiving her family for helping to keep her unfree and unhappy for most of her life. But if "she were to start forgiving she must needs forgive Society, the Law, the Church, the History of Europe, the Old Testament, . . . and half a dozen other useful props of civilisation."[23] While Laura includes "the Church" in her list of destructive forces, she also singles out the "Old Testament" rather than "the Bible." This blames the *Hebrew* Bible for a particular oppressiveness, and suggests that the negative force of the Church comes especially from that source. Such an attitude recalls Miriam's obtuse comment in *Deadlock* that "Christ was the first man to see women as individuals" (*P* III, 221). As I demonstrate in chapter 2, this belief forms part of *Pilgrimage*'s supersessionist use of Jewishness.

Miriam finally rejects Michael, in scenes we do not see, somewhere between the end of *Deadlock* and the beginning of the next novel-chapter, *Revolving Lights* (1923). But he remains in her life, and in *Clear Horizon* (1935) she introduces him to Amabel, with whom she herself has been romantically involved. In the next novel-chapter, *Dimple Hill* (1938), Miriam leaves London for a Quaker farm and waits for Michael to fall in love with Amabel. She knows he loves her – Miriam – but is confident that his biological drive will overcome his resistance to Amabel's charms. And she continues to believe that it is his Jewishness that causes him to see women as vessels for racial continuity:

The Russian in him . . . knew, in spite of his Jewish philosophy, something of the unfathomable depths in each individual . . . And the Jew in him so far saw Amabel only as charmingly qualified to fulfil what he still regarded as the larger aspect, the only continuing aspect of himself, his destiny as a part of his "race," the abstraction he and his like so strangely conceived as alive, immortal, sacred, and at the same time as consisting of dead and dying particles with no depth of life in them, mere husks. (*P* IV, 427)

Here it is apparently not so much a racial trait as a "Jewish" *conception* of racial destiny that makes Michael view women in these terms. Yet the text, in portraying its Jewish characters as so intensely interested in procreation, suggests a racialized representation of Jewish men as inherently valuing biology over against the individual spirit.

In the final novel-chapter, *March Moonlight* (published posthumously in 1967), Michael and Amabel have indeed married, she has created a Jewish home for him, and they have a baby named Paul (whose allegorical significance I describe in chapter 2). In this family atmosphere Michael has become more Jewish. He can now "conform to the pattern of his beloved ritual"; he wears a "sabbath frock-coat topped by a deep crimson tie visible, when he raised his head, beneath the beard no longer trimmed to a worldly point and already on the way to becoming an oblong bush, rabbinical, the massed fine strands of his grandfather's pale gold watch-chain garlanding his breast" (*P* IV, 597). The grandfather's watch emphasizes the continuity with the past that Michael has achieved in creating this Jewish life. As in *Nightwood*, where Felix names his son after his father, here, too, the Jewish man is enamored of a masculinist view of cultural inheritance. Michael's new life leaves little room for either his Russian or his European facets: "[t]he remembered Russian in him . . . and the middle-European intellectual . . . are either in abeyance or, with his new growth toward his own roots, being gradually shed" (*P* IV, 598). Now that Michael is "a man taking his ease at home" (*P* IV, 604), he is at his most Jewish.

In both *Pilgrimage* and *Nightwood*, then, Jewishness means men desiring sons to carry on the line and using women as means to that end, not recognizing their essential individuality. Felix cannot understand Robin because he sees her only as potentially mending his broken fate. Michael cannot understand anything about women, according to Miriam, because he sees them from the outside, as bearers of racial continuity rather than containers of particular souls. The two characters are paternalistic and chauvinistic. So it may seem incongruous that they are also described in rather feminine terms.

In *Nightwood* Felix's father Guido is described through imagery of fruit, fruitfulness, and flowers. Immediately after the narrator's description of Felix's Viennese mother dying in childbirth, we learn that her late husband Guido was "small, rotund, and haughtily timid, his stomach protruding slightly in an upward jutting slope that brought into prominence the buttons of his waistcoat and trousers, marking the exact centre of his body with the obstetric line seen on fruits" (*N* 1). The round belly and the word "obstetric" playfully assign the pregnancy to Guido instead of the masculine Hedvig. His small stature and timidity contrast with the large size and courage of the stereotypically masculine Austrian man. The narrative continues to describe Guido, Jewish history, and the yellow handkerchief, comparing Guido to a flower: "This memory and the handkerchief that accompanied it had wrought in Guido (as certain flowers brought to a pitch of florid ecstasy no sooner attain their specific type than they fall into its decay) the sum total of what is a Jew" (*N* 2). Guido and Jewishness generally are here described as a flower that blooms and decays all at once. When Guido tries to walk alongside Hedvig's "goosestep of a stride," the step becomes "dislocated and comic" (*N* 3). He is intimidated by military men and by his wife with her military bearing (*N* 4).

Guido's son Felix is not described with the same overtly feminine imagery, but the description of his father encourages readers to note Felix's unmasculine traits as well. Paralleling his father's exaggerated respect for military men, Felix puts himself in a subordinate role vis-à-vis "Old Europe: aristocracy, nobility, royalty" (*N* 9). He bows down to nobility, listening to them in an "unbecoming" way, and feeling that "the great past might mend a little if he bowed low enough, if he succumbed and gave homage" (*N* 9). Moreover, Felix is blind in one eye, which has kept him out of the Great War (*N* 9). He is thus removed from the ultimate proving-ground of masculinity, while his blind eye may also symbolize deficient masculinity through its association with castration. When Felix decides he is "not sufficient to make [Robin] what he had hoped," he acknowledges his inability to play a male-dominant role.

Michael Shatov, too, is described in feminine terms. He has a rich beauty and small stature; he is childlike, wide-eyed, and kind. When she first meets him, Miriam sees "his lifted head, the extraordinary gentleness of the white, tremulous, determined features, the child-like openness of the broad forehead, the brilliant gentle deprecating eyes, familiar handsome unknown kindliness gleaming out between the high arch of rich black hair" (*P* III, 22). His eyes are "wide and beautiful with youth" (*P* III, 24). Much later, he is still described as having a "rich Hebrew beauty" (*P* IV, 300), his "Eastern beauty" "blossoming" even in his "ill-chosen clothes" (*P* IV, 288–289). Miriam finds his gentle childishness appealing. She refers to him repeatedly as "little Mr. Shatov" (*P* III, 199), and as a "dear funny little man" (*P* III, 202). Miriam's mother had used the same words to describe the "dear funny little O.M.'s [Old Maids]" for whom Miriam worked in the second novel-chapter, *Backwater* (1916) (*P* I, 193). Miriam remembers the phrase later in that novel (*P* I, 241), so that her application of it to Michael emphasizes his likeness to the mild, harmless women of *Backwater*.

These features are initially positive for Miriam and for readers following her into her first serious romance. And for the feminist novel *Nightwood*, Felix's femininity, especially his inability to control Robin, would seem to be a redeeming feature as well. It may at first seem that this femininity *is* thoroughly positive, but that it gives way, at least in Michael's case, to arrogant masculinity. Jane Garrity, for instance, writes that Miriam's "feminization of [Michael] – often referring to him as childlike, delicate, and little – is superseded by her repudiation of his relentless masculinity... Miriam's resistance to Michael is not only a rejection of his alternate world of Zionists and Russian revolutionaries, but a condemnation of his masculine privilege."[24] I argue, by contrast, that it is this very femininity – or at least one aspect of it – that Miriam most crucially rejects. Neither Michael's nor Felix's femininity is restricted to his gentleness. They are also feminine insofar as they accept for themselves the very status they (in their simultaneous role as agents of patriarchy) impose upon women: they allow themselves to be used as tools of biology. Their obsession with carrying on "the race" means they are willing to subordinate themselves to the larger aim of procreation: Felix marrying Robin for her malleability instead of any appealing individuality, and Michael settling for the fickle Amabel rather than Miriam, whose vivid personality has so impressed him.

Felix's answer to Matthew's question about whether he wants to get married, then, gains additional meaning. It shows that he views Robin as a means only, but also that he sees his *own* purpose not in finding romantic happiness but in achieving an end: having a son. When the narrator tells us that Felix is "racially incapable of abandon" (*N* 38), she implies that Felix will not be driven by sexual desire but by an instrumental view of humanity and of his own life. One of Matthew's cryptic descriptions of Felix resonates in this context. He compares Felix to a woman with no legs, whom he describes as "damned from the waist down," commenting that Felix is "damned from the waist up" (*N* 26). If the woman is damned where she is missing part of her body, then Felix must be metaphorically missing his chest, arms, and head, but retaining his procreative organs. Here the upper-body/lower-body dichotomy takes the place of soul/body dualism. Since he views himself merely as an agent of procreation, Felix is left with a lower-body only – which is to say a body only – because a tool of biology does not need a soul. From this angle, Felix's hope that Robin, through a future son, will repair his broken fate becomes evidence of his lack, his essential unfulfillment if he remains childless. And this portrait of the Jewish man is akin to the portrait of "woman" in the intertwined discourses of medicine, psychoanalysis, and race science.

In *Pilgrimage*, too, an important part of Miriam's problem with Michael is that he views himself as well as women as agents of biology, while she wants to believe, as we saw, that procreation is irrelevant to one's humanity. But her anxiety about serving biology is expressed through displacement: she claims that she cannot marry Michael because she cannot stand Jewish women. As I quote in chapter 3, she tells him that she "'can't bear Jewesses, not because they are not really like other women, but because they reflect the limitations of the Jewish male'" (*P* III, 221). She mentions this aversion to Mrs. Bergstein, whose response brings back the positive feelings that had receded when Miriam learned she had been a Unitarian before embracing Judaism:

"I think I should find it impossible to associate with Jewish women."
"*That* is a point you must consider very carefully indeed."
The room leapt into glowing reality. They *were* at one; Englishwomen with a common incommunicable sense. (*P* III, 228)

Since Miriam has just described Jewish women as having a "sultry, conscious femineity," this assertion suggests that Miriam has ascribed to them a sexual role that she herself fears. Miriam has, after all, recoiled from Michael's touch (she subsequently attributes this to an uncanny knowledge of what he has not yet told her: that he is not a virgin) and later has several false starts in her sexual relationship with Hypo Wilson. She seems here to be projecting her own fears of the body and (hetero)sexuality onto Jewish women.

But it is not only *Jewish* women she dislikes. Miriam has within her a strain of misogyny that diminishes in later volumes (in part because when she rejects Michael, she distances herself from the aspects of femininity she fears). For example, in the eighth novel-chapter, *The Trap* (1925), Miriam finds herself siding with Arthur Schopenhauer, "fearing and hating the mere semblance of woman. Its soft feebleness, its helpless blind strength in keeping life going. Felt again all her old horror and loathing of femininity, still faintly persisting" (*P* III, 462). This description of the "blind strength" of women in "keeping life going" marks exactly the role Michael wants her to play – and to which he is willing to devote himself. So as *Pilgrimage* proceeds, the image of a sexist man who relegates women to the sphere of procreation reveals itself as a cover for the image of a feminine man who also sees *himself* as an agent of biology. His Jewishness connects Michael to the very aspects of femininity Miriam fears and disdains.

This association between Michael and feminine devotion to procreation helps to explain Miriam's startling comment to Hypo in *Revolving Lights*, the novel-chapter that follows *Deadlock*. She tells him that she has ended her romance with Michael, claiming that she "couldn't have Jewish children." Hypo replies that Michael's Jewishness is incidental.

"No, the wrong material. I, being myself, couldn't do anything with it; couldn't be anything in relationship to it."
"You'd be, through seeing its possibilities and making an atmosphere."
"I've told you I'm not one of those stupendous women [who can create atmospheres]."
"What are you?"
"Well, now here's something you will like. If I were to marry a Jew, I should feel that all my male relatives would have the right to beat me." (P III, 260)

In this answer, which is not an answer to the question "'What are you?,'" Miriam of course indicates a racial betrayal: her male relatives have a stake in carrying on the Henderson stock, English and unadulterated. But her response also suggests that she cannot place herself because her gender identity is too ambiguous. Here she distinguishes herself from what she has described as the feminine art of making atmospheres (P III, 257). Earlier, she has remarked that perhaps she "'can't stand women because [she's] a sort of horrid man'" (P I, 404), and at another point, describes herself as "something between a man and a woman; looking both ways" (P II, 187). In relation to a feminine man, her masculinity would presumably come to the fore, much as *Nightwood*'s Hedvig seems especially masculine alongside her husband Guido. There is therefore a sense in which, by beating her, her male relatives would be righting the gender imbalance, forcing Miriam into a subordinate feminine role. Although Miriam lives and works against female subordination, she reveals here that she nevertheless fears her own power. A projection of that fear would explain her claim that "it was impossible to acknowledge the power of a woman, of any woman she had ever known, without becoming a slave" (P III, 37).

Miriam's confused misogyny and fears of sexuality and power infuse her reactions to Michael's sexism, complicating what at first seems merely a story of a feminist woman rejecting a sexist man. Michael's similarity to women who accept a life of sacrifice to larger biological aims provides Miriam with grist to work confusedly through her own ambivalence about gender and sexuality. In *Nightwood* Robin's rejection of Felix, and the text's as it turns to the stories of Robin, Nora, and Matthew, may work in similar ways. Felix represents both a patriarchal arrogance that expects women to serve as means for men's fulfillment and a sort of femininity the novel rejects: a femininity lodged firmly in biology and procreation. Turning to the lesbian love between Nora and Robin, *Nightwood* explores the depth of nonprocreative desire, the opposite of Felix's interest in Robin. And in *Pilgrimage*, too, Miriam moves on from her relationship with Michael to a romance with Amabel; and when she has succeeded in freeing herself from them both by encouraging them to marry, she enters a deeply romantic friendship with the devoutly Christian Jean. Both Robin and Miriam, then, escape the trap represented by Jewish men. Their interest in other women is stronger than the pull of Jewishness-as-biology.

But Amabel is not as able as Miriam to resist this pull. So while lesbian desire triumphs over Jewishness in *Nightwood*, and in *Pilgrimage* Miriam's trajectory ends not with marriage to Michael but communion with Jean, there remains a strand of *Pilgrimage* in which Jewishness succeeds in domesticating lesbian desire. By opposing Michael and Amabel, the novel sets up an additional struggle between women's independence and "Jewish" traditionalism.

The bulk of the relationship between Amabel and Miriam is narrated in *Dawn's Left Hand* (1931); its working title was *Amabel*. Besides opposing Michael and Amabel to each other as distinct romantic possibilities for Miriam, the text also opposes them in terms of their relations to race, sexuality, and gender. Michael's racial and sexual identities, as we have seen, are fixed. He is firmly Jewish, with his Russianness hovering in the background, and he is firmly heterosexual, placing procreation above individual happiness. Amabel, on the other hand, is described as racially "unlocated," unmoored, flexible (*P* IV, 292). Her accent leads Miriam to assume she is French, but it turns out that her background is "partly Irish and partly Welsh." Miriam later describes her as "more Celtic than English," and as having "no sense of nationality" (*P* IV, 242).

Likewise, Amabel's sexual interests are multiple. She pursues Miriam frankly, writing "I love you" with soap on Miriam's mirror, and sending her a letter that reads, "Forgive – I watched you – in your little English clothes – go across the square – oh, my lady – my little – you terrified my heart – I hold it out to you – my terrified heart – in my two hands – ' (*P* IV, 217). But she also tells Miriam of her entanglements with men, opening their first in-depth conversation by hinting that she is not a virgin. Her face, she says, has become less like a "'peach . . . since Basil'" (*P* IV, 188). She asks Miriam, "'This makes a difference? You are repelled?'" (*P* IV, 189). Part of Amabel's charm for Miriam is how difficult she is to pin down, either racially or sexually. But at the same time, Amabel's "unlocated, half-foreign being," her lack of a sense of nationality, creates a "fundamental separation" between the two women that leaves Miriam feeling stifled by their closeness (*P* IV, 292).

The text opposes the Jewish suitor and the lesbian partner by marking the one as rigidly located and showing the other occupying variable sexual and racial/national positions – thus tightly intertwining the categories of race and sexuality. But Michael's and Amabel's gender positions do not line up along this axis of opposition. Probably influenced by sexology, Richardson portrays sexuality and gender as separable categories.[25] In the case of gender, it is Michael's identity that is complex and ambiguous, as this discussion has shown, while Amabel's gender identity is fixed. As Garrity puts it, Amabel has an "excess of femininity."[26] Perhaps paradoxically, it is because the text defines femininity as performance, as a self-conscious fluidity, that Amabel is portrayed as unambiguously feminine. She is described repeatedly as posing, and Miriam understands the poses to be "second nature" to her (*P* IV, 240). Amabel's performance of her femininity perfectly instantiates Judith Butler's description of gender as "a kind of becoming or activity."[27] Miriam describes her: "First silence and a fresh pose of her whole person, a plastic pose, studied and graceful, and a careful conscious management of the accompanying facial effects that preceded her answer . . . contributing to her effect of being critically aloof from everything but her own power to charm" (*P* IV, 191).

When Michael and Amabel first marry, the fluid Amabel is very unhappy. Her variable sexual and national identities have been squeezed into the confining new role of the Jewish wife. Miriam describes her as "caught, for life, in a continuously revolving machinery" of domesticity (*P* IV, 602). When the couple asks her advice, she thinks with pity, "And the state of these two is the worst of all. Far worse than the normal incompatibility of man and woman is the absence in their daily life of a common heritage, stating itself at every turn. Amabel, freer than most, more genuinely catholic, could not foresee this and now pays the price. In misery" (*P* IV, 605).

After a while, however, the anchoring force of Jewishness (as *Pilgrimage* defines it) prevails, and the birth of a baby boy brings "all of bliss" to Amabel and Michael (*P* IV, 636). Amabel becomes content with her new position as Jewish wife and mother. She keeps sabbath on Saturdays, and decorates their house without any "graven images" (*P* IV, 596). She tells Miriam that she and Michael are no longer interested in Ralph Waldo Emerson, a figure who encapsulates their past common intellectual and political strivings: they find him "trite" (*P* IV, 658). And in spite of having previously gone proudly to jail for advocating women's suffrage, Amabel now announces, "'Marriage, and Paul, have swept away all my interest in votes for women'" (*P* IV, 658). Garrity describes the marriage as disastrous, "depoliticizing Amabel and domesticating her to such a degree that, for the first time, she is not an 'audience for her own performance.'"[28] Michael's Jewishness has tethered Amabel. Her national and sexual identities have become fixed, and her gender identity has become appropriately linked to her new role as "Mrs. Michael Shatov" (*P* IV, 658).

Miriam tries to convince herself that the essence of her relationship with Amabel is unchanged: "Still we remain what we were to each other when first we met" (*P* IV, 658). But she acknowledges feeling an "immortal desolation" when Amabel declares that she has abandoned their shared, passionately held points of view (*P* IV, 658). The possibility for ongoing intimacy between them has been subverted by the biological force with which Jewishness is invested. As a result, Miriam's love for Amabel can find expression only when it is transferred to the baby Paul:

Something of the inexpressible quality of our relationship revealed itself in that moment she did not share, the moment of finding the baby Paul lying asleep ... gathering him up, and being astonished to feel, as soon as he lay folded, still asleep, against my body, the complete stilling of every one of my competing urgencies. Freedom. (*P* IV, 658)

The novel ends a few lines later, so that its resolution is tied tightly to the domestication of lesbian intimacy. Moreover, Miriam's reluctance to marry Michael – though informed by both misogyny and antisemitism – is retroactively validated when we see Amabel's fluid charms and multiple identities constricted by a new, more acceptable configuration of the categories of race, gender, and sexuality. In this strand of *Pilgrimage*, the domesticating force of Jewishness helps to protect the text from the destabilizing disjunction between gender and sexuality.

For Miriam, on the other hand, Jewishness was a pitfall she was able to avoid as she journeyed on her pilgrimage. Her love for Jean in *March Moonlight* fulfils her in ways her relationships with men have not. Even without knowing when they will meet again, Miriam is confident of a closeness with Jean: whereas separations from Amabel used to bring "both regret and relief," the "thought of leaving Jean was promise as well as pain, carrying me forward across a future that held no assurance of a fresh meeting and yet promised reunion" (*P* IV, 566). When she returns to Jean after an absence, Miriam finds herself "at an unchanging centre"

(*P* IV, 566). But the intimacy of this relationship is not without its sexual charge, as Joanne Winning points out. Reading tropes of silence and voice in the relationships with Amabel and Jean, Winning reminds us that Miriam's feelings for Jean are not otherworldly, but link the spiritual and the sexual in an intense attraction.[29] So perhaps it is not surprising that in spite of the transcendence of Miriam's communion with Jean, the text expresses discomfort with this partnership as a resolution. It performs this discomfort in two ways. First, without explanation, Jean calls Miriam "Dick" throughout the novel-chapter. With this masculine, even phallic, name, the text gestures toward the "proper" heterosexual balance achieved in Amabel and Michael's marriage and Miriam and Amabel's domesticated friendship.

Second, the novel ends not with a scene between Miriam and Jean, but with the scene in which Miriam remembers holding Amabel's baby. After the one-word sentence, "Freedom," Miriam wonders why it is *this* baby who has "still[ed] her competing urgencies." "Often I had held babes in my arms: Harriet's, Sally's, and many others. But never with that sense of perfect serenity. If Jean's marriage to Joe Davenport brought her a child, should I feel, in holding it, that same sense of fulfilment?" These final words of the final novel-chapter signal something particularly satisfying about the offspring of Michael and Amabel's marriage. In chapter 2 I describe an allegorical reason the baby calls forth this feeling in Miriam. In this context I want to suggest an additional possibility: that validating the union of Michael and Amabel – the symbols of the biological drive – helps the text to relieve some anxiety about the fact that Miriam has found a spiritually and emotionally fulfilling love with another woman.

In *Nightwood* Jewishness and biology have been more thoroughly left behind by both Robin and the text. Felix leaves Paris and the text with Guido. Robin's choice after she leaves Felix (if it can be called a choice, given her eerie lack of agency) is not between Nora Flood and a man, but between Nora and Jenny Petherbridge. Although lesbian love in *Nightwood* is not characterized as healthier than heterosexual love, it is far more mysterious, compelling, and deep. In *Pilgrimage* the forces of procreation and biological continuity retain more power. Even though Miriam herself remains free from these threatening forces at the novel's end, the text demonstrates its allegiance to heteronormativity in its final scene.

All this intricate interplay among race, gender, sex, and sexuality creates multifaceted portraits of the Jewish male characters. Analyzing the representations, it may seem as though the racial antisemitism can be reduced to anxieties about gender and sexuality. After all, what the texts really seem to object to in Felix and Michael is their indeterminate gender identity – they are at once too feminine and too masculine, and their heterosexual drive threatens the independence of our female protagonists even as the men's willingness to serve biology undermines their own. But race prejudice carries its own independent weight; it is not reducible to gender or sexual prejudices, but rather inextricably intertwined with them. Their interdependence is confirmed when we look further into Richardson's engagement with her representation of Michael. Having become aware of the potential destructive power of antisemitism in the early 1930s, Richardson alters both her representation of Michael and Miriam's responses to him. In *Clear Horizon* Miriam believes she is pregnant with Hypo Wilson's baby (Hypo is based on H. G. Wells, with whom Richardson had a long friendship and a brief affair). She tells Michael, who offers again to marry her. Richardson makes it clear here that race prejudice, more than issues of gender, underlies Miriam's reiterated rejection. Yet the terms through which Miriam thinks about Michael as a racial other conjure the same biological continuity that girded her gendered responses to him in the earlier volumes.

Between the writing of *Deadlock* and *Revolving Lights* in the early 1920s and *Clear Horizon* in 1932–1935, circumstances of course worsened sharply for Central European Jews. Richardson had spent six months in Germany in 1891 as a pupil-teacher in a Hanoverian finishing school. She describes this period of her life in the first novel-chapter of *Pilgrimage*, *Pointed Roofs* (1915). Because she remained interested in Germany and followed German current events, Richardson was aware of the climate for German and Austrian Jews after Hitler became Chancellor in 1933. She wrote to Bryher early that year:

No one on earth can arrest the process going forward in Germany, nor its inevitable accompaniments. Political & racial passions unchained. The victims helpless. One longs to evacuate all the Jews & the intelligentsia of the Left.

When Germany is once more neat and tidy, and 100% Deutsch, and without unemployment, and the grosser forms of profiteering, & possibly fitted up with a dummy Emperor & certainly blessed by an obedient church, nearly everyone will have forgotten the cost. (*W* 240)

Partly in response to these protective feelings, in 1933 and 1934 Richardson translated two books on Jewish topics.

The first was the novel *Mammon*, by the Viennese Jew Robert Neumann. Of her work on this translation she wrote to her friend Ogden Heath:

> A year has vanished. Lost? Gained? I don't regret the time spent in helping to broadcast the message of Israel to a defaulting "Christianity." (Dr. Neumann is a Viennese Jew & like all the Jewish intelligentsia in central Europe at the present time, is living, together with his brethren of all sorts, amidst the menaces of a ferocious hostility. Monstrous, seen from England. But we can no more judge of their Jewish problem than of the American negro-problem.) (*W* 243)

Until its last two sentences, this passage demonstrates sympathy with Jews and a critical attitude toward "defaulting" Christians. But then Richardson backs away from her condemnation and takes an irresponsible relativist stance. This stance can be explained by other comments in her letters, which indicate that she may feel unable to judge because she believes Jews are difficult to assimilate. In *Pilgrimage* Miriam says that "'England can assimilate anything'"; but Michael replies, "'No nation can assimilate the Jew'" (*P* III, 167). In her letters Richardson often describes Jews as linguistic parvenus, ill at ease in European languages. In evaluating a novel by Jacob Wasserman, for instance, she writes, "It is the reservation I am forced to make in the case of all Jewish work & I will drown myself in my inkpot if the man is not a Jew. It is the too clever conscious grasp of everything that is being done" (*W* 56). The next book she translates, by the German-Jewish Zionist Josef Kastein, reinforces her prejudiced assumption that European Jews are foreigners by arguing that Jews must return to the Land of Israel in order to become truly native to any place.

Richardson translated Kastein's book, *Jews in Germany*, in 1934. In her introduction she writes that the translator

> shares [the reader's] horror and dismay, his shame and grief in contemplating the European centuries, the history of State and Church, from the Jewish angle. He . . . recognise[s] the vital presence of Judaism, as interpreted by Dr. Kastein, of the element missing from the Councils of Europe today, missing throughout the youth and adolescence of the Christian church.[30]

Sparking feelings of "horror and dismay," "shame and grief," Kastein's book was an important moral landmark in Richardson's life. But it did not change her view that Jews, no matter where they were born, were foreigners in European languages. In 1941, for instance, she wrote the letter to Bryher I quote in the introduction:

> Zeitung of course is mostly composed of Jewish contributions, & the Jews using German very much as Zangwill used English, are the worst offenders. They

positively revel in all these trimmings, roll them on the tongue, exploit with unction all the worst possibilities of the language, & contribute thereto their own peculiar, funny & pitiful, solecisms. (*W* 428)

Richardson may have absorbed this view (that even London-born Jews would speak English like foreigners) from Germany, where Jews were often thought to be incapable of speaking authentic German.[31] And her work on Kastein, who held that Jews ought never to have abandoned the idea of Jewish "nationality," has only slightly modulated her assumption that Jews fall into linguistic excess. Influenced by his Zionism, Richardson makes a less sweeping claim than she made about Wasserman. I give her response to Adrian Allinson's autobiography in the introduction: she writes that he is "pirouetting, with an only too obvious delight into the solecisms so very very few Jews, (of those divorced from their own tradition & unable to do more than skate along the surface of any other; as distinct from the genuine Hebrew) ever escape" (*W* 473). Accepting a tenet of Kastein's Zionism, that Jews in the Land of Israel are "genuine," Richardson is now willing to allow that only Jews living and writing in European languages would display alienation in their writing. She can now imagine authentic Jews in their own land, but still views European Jews as foreigners in their own countries. Incidentally, she accepts here about Jews the same argument she rejects about women: that they are damaged by their circumstances and need social and political changes to become whole and healthy.

Although the influence of Kastein's book only slightly altered her views about Jewish writing, it nevertheless made a strong impression on Richardson, causing her to rethink her representation of Michael. After finishing the translation, she wrote a striking letter to her new friend S. S. Koteliansky ("Kot"), himself a Russian Jew: "For one Gentile, at least, it has been, in certain respects, a life-divider. Before, & after, Kastein. It is a visit to an ethical nursing-home for a major operation. It has made me think, & feel, as much as any book I have ever read" (*W* 259). This ethical "operation" has real consequences for her fiction, visible in her portrayal of Michael's renewed proposal in *Clear Horizon*, a novel-chapter dedicated to Kot.

In this novel-chapter Richardson brings Miriam's race thinking to the fore, apparently attempting to disentangle her antisemitism from the confused misogyny that conceals it from many readers in earlier volumes (this concealment results in several critics replicating that antisemitism).[32] Now Miriam's racialist thoughts about Michael are dominated by the idea of the antiquity or timelessness of the Jews. Counterpart to the view that Jews were quintessentially modern, the idea that living Jews were also ancient formed a prominent strand of race science.

The antiquity of Jews was so commonplace a notion in the early twentieth century that Louis Golding, writing in the *Fortnightly Review* in 1927, called himself a "humble Jewish wanderer," and could unselfconsciously describe a young Jewish mother from Djerba in these paradoxical terms: "She . . . seemed less like a living woman of the people, despite the child at her breast, than the queen of some race that has ceased to exist."[33] Similarly, a review in the *Times Literary Supplement* describes Eastern European Jewry as portrayed in *La Rose de Saron* (1927) by Jérome and Jean Tharaud: "Later he and his brother visited these inquiring scholars in their Carpathian homes, and were enchanted to find . . . a way of living as simple, yet as engrossed by dogma, rite and ritual, as the life of some Judean village years before the birth of Christ. [These people are] englobed in their Orient, as though the Jews had never left Palestine."[34] In *Pilgrimage*, although Michael is a young, vibrant man, Miriam intermittently sees him as "an old old, Jew, immeasurably old" (*P* III, 168).

In accordance with this metaphoric ancientness, which pervades *Clear Horizon*, Miriam describes Michael when he arrives at her boarding house to meet Amabel: "The heavy white lids came down over his eyes and for a moment his face, with its slumbering vitality, at once venerable and insolent, was like a death-mask, a Jewish death-mask" (*P* IV, 288). Michael's deathlike face, with its "slumbering vitality," represents the Jews as an inexplicably living remnant of an extinct people. As he gets up to leave the room, Miriam sees him as a "modest, proud ambassador of his race, going through the ceremonial of farewell" (*P* IV, 289).

At a concert they attend after parting from Amabel, Miriam tells Michael that she thinks she is pregnant with Hypo's child. He is sympathetic, even awed, as he listens. "In a moment he would turn and pay tribute, from the depth of his Jewish being to the central fact, for him the fact of facts; and to herself as its privileged consecrated victim. What else could he do? What had it to do with him, or with any man on earth?" (*P* IV, 301–302). Although Miriam still connects Michael's Jewishness to his veneration of pregnancy as "the fact of facts," her comment that her pregnancy has nothing to do with him or any other man removes him somewhat from the link to femininity that his interest in procreation had created.

More important, Miriam's response to his proposal is more straightforward than it was in *Deadlock* when she claimed she could not marry him because she could not associate with Jewish women. Although Michael does not quite believe that she is pregnant, he pleads with her anyway: "'Oh, Miriam, now, at last, marry me. As brother. At once'" (*P* IV, 302). Miriam is touched by his offer, but

> even while this revelation of the essential Michael struck at her heart, the muscles of her lips were uncontrollably twisted by amusement over his failure to recognize that the refuge he offered from what indeed might be a temporary embarrassment as well as a triumphant social gesture, was a permanent prison; over his assumption that she might be scared into flight, disguised as a Jewess, from the open road, down into Judea. (*P* IV, 302–303)

To marry a Jew, for Miriam, would be to adopt another identity (or at least a disguise), and more strikingly, to move into another time and place: the ancient kingdom of Judea. As in *Nightwood*, where Guido's handkerchief cries aloud of the Middle Ages, here, too, Jewish history is preternaturally present. The "slumbering vitality" Miriam noted in Michael's face seems also to describe Jewish history for *Clear Horizon*. Rather than being inaccessible, ancient Jewish history is available as a possible fork in the road of Miriam's pilgrimage.

Miriam has finally admitted to herself, the same day of the concert, that it is "nationality" that has prevented her from marrying Michael. Before the concert, Amabel, impressed with Michael, tells her, "'You MUST marry him!'" (*P* IV, 291). It is then that Miriam feels the "fundamental separation" between herself and Amabel mentioned earlier:

> And here indeed was thought, a tide flowing freely from an immovable deep certainty which for Amabel had no existence. This certainty stood between them, marking ... a fundamental separation. And there was no one alive who could decide, in this strange difference, where lay right and wrong. Why should it be right to have no sense of nationality? Why should it be wrong to feel this sense as something whose violation would be a base betrayal? Much more than that. Something that could not be. Not merely difficult and sacrificial and yet possible. Simply impossible. With her unlocated, half-foreign being, Amabel could see nothing of the impossibility of spending one's life in Jewry. (*P* IV, 292)

This kind of frank acknowledgment was absent from *Deadlock*, when except for the reference to Michael's Jewishness as a "hidden flaw" (*P* III, 193), Miriam's reluctance to marry Michael was always expressed in gendered terms. Now Miriam is able to question her sense of nationality, asking why it should be wrong. Although she is expressing the same sentiment, she has lost the flippant certainty with which she told Hypo in

Revolving Lights that Jewishness was the wrong material for her. Her vague assertion that there is "no one alive" who can decide what is right suggests guilt for her inalienable commitment to Englishness. Together with Richardson's letter stating that Kastein's book was a "life-divider" and *Clear Horizon*'s dedication to Koteliansky, this change indicates Richardson actively working to admit, and to some degree apologize for, Miriam's inability to be other than England has made her.

Richardson's new awareness of antisemitism in her culture, her novel, and herself prompted her to shift the terms through which she represented Michael, displaying Miriam's racialist responses to him through images of Jewish antiquity. And it prompted her to revisit Michael's marriage proposal and present a more forthright version of Miriam's reasons for rejecting him. One of the most interesting things about this shift is that it highlights the deep interfusion of gendered and raced discourses. It was because of Miriam's racist assumptions about Jewish men (that they would, for example, see "women as human only in consecration to relationships") that she found Michael especially sexist. It was because of Richardson's racist assumptions that she *portrayed* Michael as believing in the sanctity of race, and therefore willing to use women as means toward biological continuity and to submit himself to the power of biology as well. So it was always already race that created the gendered problems that Michael represented.

Now, as the terms shift in *Clear Horizon*, these gendered issues seem to be cast aside. But the emphasis on the antiquity of the Jews merely presents another facet of "Jewish" continuity. The scene I describe in chapter 2, where Miriam imagines Michael dancing "with the tablets of the Law invisibly held within his swaying arms," caps the portrait of a present-day conduit to a much earlier time (*P* IV, 521). But what links Michael to Moses, who received the tablets, and David, who danced before the Lord? Genealogy, of course; and biological continuity is thus sacred, as Michael believes, and must not be broken. Michael must marry and procreate – and have a son. And for that he needs a woman. The very idea of racial continuity, that is, necessitates the procreative role. So the representation comes full circle, arriving again at the Jewish man's potential oppression of women in service of "the abstraction he and his like so strangely conceived as alive, immortal, sacred" (*P* IV, 427). The gendered and racial representations of Jewishness in *Pilgrimage* provide a compelling example of the mutually constitutive nature of gender and race.

Nightwood, too, makes visible this interdependence. Felix, like Michael, is an "ambassador" of his race, worshiping the past in order to gesture toward the future. His misuse of Robin and his willingness to see himself as a tool of the race are functions of his role as healer of the broken past, a role dictated, as far as the novel is concerned, by his Jewish racial identity. Considering the intricate relationship between the constructions of gender and race, it is, finally, only to be expected that Jewish men should be viewed in gendered terms. That they are seen as both too feminine (gentle, small, and willing to accept a role as tools of biology) and too masculine (arrogant, sexist, insisting that women serve as means to their own biological continuation) is confusing only until we look more deeply into the ways race and gender intertwine. And the apparent contradiction further dissipates when we remember that antisemitic discourses are not rational, but simply harness available discourses so as to project onto Jews various anxieties of dominant groups. For feminist modernism, one of the crucial webs of anxiety surrounded gender identity, changing sex roles, and the power of biology over women. Richardson and Barnes grappled with some of these anxieties by imagining sympathetic but chauvinistic Jewish male characters. And as though issues of gender were not freighted enough, feminist modernism also used Jews to think about the phenomenon of timelessness, a sense resulting from traumatic breaks in the psyche's experience of passing time.

5

The "No time region": time, trauma, and Jewishness in Barnes and Rhys

Imagined Jewishness sustains an elastic relationship to time. Within feminist modernism it can represent modernity, as it does in *Summer Will Show* (1936) and *Between the Acts* (1941); it can represent the past, and continuity with that past, as it does in *Nightwood* (1936) and *Pilgrimage* (1915–1967). And it can serve a further kind of temporal inquiry, as when Djuna Barnes and Jean Rhys use Jewishness to explore the phenomenology of timelessness. As I demonstrate in this chapter, Jewishness in *Nightwood* and in both *Voyage in the Dark* (1934) and *Good Morning, Midnight* (1939) comes to signal the timelessness attendant on psychological trauma.[1]

Trauma gives rise to a sense of timelessness by distorting people's perception of time and continuity. A traumatic experience is "remembered" differently from ordinary events, in that it cannot be placed in time or located within a coherent sequence. One distinctive and defining quality of traumatic memories, therefore, is that they are temporally elusive. Cathy Caruth describes their position outside of time: "The history that a flashback tells – as psychiatry, psychoanalysis, and neurobiology equally suggest – is, therefore, a history that literally *has no place*, neither in the past, in which it was not fully experienced, nor in the present, in which its precise images and enactments are not fully understood."[2] Recent biopsychological research suggests that the parts of the brain that handle chronology may be inactivated in times of overwhelming stress, so that the "memory" of a traumatic event leaves what the psychologists Bessel van der Kolk and Onno van der Hart call "context-free fearful associations, which are hard to locate in space and time."[3]

Readers of *Nightwood* have noticed its preoccupation with time and history – and its odd invocation of timelessness and the absence of history. Robin Vote lives in an endless present, continually repeating, wandering without arriving, and drawing her lover Nora Flood into a similar series of repetitive and never-satisfying quests. The text replicates this sense of never arriving with its succession of images that seem "to point to nothing, to be an elaborate tapestry . . . which does not signify anything beyond the fact of its own existence."[4] Rhys's texts approach issues of timelessness as well, not via Barnesian strings of images, but through fragmented, nonlinear narrative. One of Rhys's goals for *Good Morning, Midnight* and *Voyage in the Dark* was to address questions of time in her characters' mental lives. In a letter about the last chapters of *Good Morning, Midnight*, Rhys wrote, "I wanted Sasha to enter the No time region there. 'Everything is on the same plane.'"[5] She described *Voyage in the Dark* in similar terms, and with deceptive humility. "It's written almost entirely in words of one syllable. Like a kitten mewing perhaps. The big idea – well I'm blowed if I can be sure what it is. Something to do with time being an illusion I think. I mean that the past exists – side by side with the present, not behind it; that what was – is."[6] Both writers explore this sense of temporal discontinuity, employing fragmentation and repetition as at once formal, thematic, and psychological strategies.

Without a sense of temporal continuity, a sufferer of trauma lacks a coherent identity. As Lynne Layton points out, cultural and feminist criticism that "denigrates" the desire for a stable identity, viewing it merely as a phallocentric illusion, is not mindful of the difference in *degree* of coherence between a traumatized and nontraumatized psyche.[7] While ontological coherence may never be attainable, its approximation is necessary for a victimized person to heal from the devastating effects of trauma. In their novels Barnes and Rhys both present characters whose identities have been fragmented or diffused by trauma, contributing insightful portrayals to the body of research on the psychological effects of traumatic experience. They treat trauma and timelessness quite differently, of course. Rhys's work could be said to analyze the fragmentation of time and identity, portraying traumatized psyches in painful and vivid detail, demonstrating how the parts (dissociation, fragmented memory, a sense of timelessness) make up the whole (overwhelmingly helpless characters who periodically erupt into rage). Barnes, on the other hand, performs more of a philosophical meditation on the structures of trauma, its confusing interventions into identity, memory, and time.

Both Barnes and Rhys suffered sexual traumas in their early lives. Barnes was almost certainly seduced into a sexual relationship with her grandmother, in a family where the boundaries between sexual and familial relations were porous at best. She said she was forced by her father into a sexual relationship with an older man when she was sixteen, and her father may also have attempted to rape her.[8] Rhys, at the age of fourteen, was molested by an older man who then told her a "serial story" over several occasions about her sexual humiliation by and submission to him.[9] The two authors wrote out and wrote through their pain, in the process documenting some of the most complex and fascinating – and terrible – psychic responses to trauma. These responses are important because they help to motivate the writers' formal experimentation with fragmentation and temporal uncertainty, and, further, because they demonstrate a deeper meaning of what critics sometimes take for granted as modernist alienation and inadvertently dismiss.

Although I link aspects of the novels to Barnes's and Rhys's personal histories, my readings do not suggest that their narratives emerged unbidden or unmediated from their traumatized psyches. On the contrary, I emphasize the highly crafted, purposeful, modernist project of Barnes's and Rhys's texts, which, like the treatment of the thought processes of Stephen Dedalus and Leopold Bloom in *Ulysses* (1922), lay bare in brilliantly sketched detail their characters' mental lives. Their narratives are formally innovative because the authors were seeking literary means by which to represent particular mental processes (even if those processes were similar to their own). Barnes, for her part, disregards multiple kinds of unity and clarity; depends on long series of juxtaposed, contradictory images; and keeps her character Robin Vote just outside the bounds of her readers' grasp. These qualities further her effort to consider history and identity from the point of view of those who are expelled from them by their nonnormative gender and sexuality, as well as by trauma. And Rhys "breaks the sequence" (*Room* 81) in order incisively to portray her protagonists' fragmented minds.

Jewishness gets bound up with their explorations of trauma for multiple reasons. The confused and complex relationships of Jewishness to time which I have been exploring in the modern literary imagination could make Jewishness seem paradoxically outside of time. The well-known myth of the eternally Wandering Jew conveyed timelessness, claiming, as Mr. Deasy puts it in *Ulysses*, that the Jews are "wanderers on the earth to this day."[10] Race science's claim that the Jewish race had "retarded or stopped" progressing added its suggestion that Jews existed on a unique temporal plane.[11] In addition, Barnes and Rhys seem to link Jews to timelessness because of their belief that Jewish history resembles their personal traumatic histories. In this sense the prototypical use of an imagined Jew to reflect an author's own emotional state takes on additional complexity: it is not just that "the Jew" is alienated like the personae of the authors, but that he is similarly outside of history, exiled, like the traumatized characters, from the ordinary sense of personal continuity that precedes any larger relation to a social group. The liminality of "the Jew" with regard to the categories of history, race, nation, and gender contributes to his usefulness as a reflection of the liminal temporal existence of traumatized psyches.[12]

Links between Jews, timelessness, and trauma are sprinkled through *Nightwood*'s descriptions of its Jewish characters. Judaism is shown to have a fragmented and traumatic past that lingers no matter how much the Jewish characters worship the idea of seamless continuity. Jewish history is marked by discrete traumatic events that leave their trace in the characters' responses hundreds of years later. Guido Volkbein, who dies before the narrative opens, remembered the degradation of Jewish history most in autumn, that "season of longing and of horror" filled with "racial memories" (*N* 2). In autumn, as I describe in chapter 4, Guido could be seen carrying the yellow and black handkerchief "that cried aloud of the ordinance of 1468, issued by one Pietro Barbo, demanding that, with a rope about its neck, Guido's race should run in the Corso for the amusement of the Christian populace" (*N* 2). With this reference to an edict by Pope Paul II (Pietro Barbo), Barnes establishes the connection between Jewish history and pain, degradation, and victimization. "He had walked, hot, incautious and damned, his eyelids quivering over the thick eyeballs, black with the pain of a participation that, four centuries later, made him a victim, as he felt the echo in his own throat of that cry running the *Piazza Montanara* long ago, '*Roba vecchia!*' – the degradation by which his people had survived" (*N* 2).

This description of medieval abuse and Guido's response to it depends on the idea of racial uniformity and inherited racial memory: the history of the Jews runs in Guido's blood. As Meryl Altman points out, even writers who identified with the marginality of Jews "inescapably participated in an ongoing European discourse about 'race,' 'heritage,' 'heredity,' 'degeneracy,' which was entirely legitimated, even by those who were called degenerate by it."[13] But more important here is the timelessness that such a racial memory implies. The concept of racial identity itself erases time. Guido feels in his own throat the cry of the peddler of old clothes; the past is present not just in an abstract notion of his "blood" but concretely in his very throat. Clutching the handkerchief, Guido iterates past trauma – trauma that can only be said to be *his* if one accepts race thinking's telescoping time. As Victoria L. Smith argues, Barnes's choice of Guido's story to open the novel "signals an analogical mode of narrative" that "provides a pattern for understanding the rest of the novel."[14] The opening descriptions of the Volkbeins help set the stage for the text's exploration of trauma, which is patterned after Jewish history.

In *Nightwood* trauma is specifically incest. This links Jewishness even more strongly to the text's thematics, because Jews were associated with the continuum between exogamy and incest by late nineteenth- and early twentieth-century race science and sexology. Within these discourses, Jews were considered a mongrel race who had long ago lost the homogeneity necessary for health, and at the same time, said to be prone to unhealthy inbreeding.[15] In *James Joyce's Judaic Other* (1999), Marilyn Reizbaum describes how important the theme of Jewish mongrelization is to *Ulysses*, whose portrait of a "deracinated" Jew seems to have influenced Barnes's use of Jewishness.[16] As Reizbaum notes, Otto Weininger helped popularize the view of Jews as mongrels; he viewed Jews as related to "both negroes and Mongolians" and found the "question of the origin of the Jewish race . . . insoluble."[17] On the other hand, in *Difference and Pathology* (1985) Sander L. Gilman discusses the charge, found within the same "scientific" discourses, that Jews were overly pure, an inbred race disposed toward incest. From Gilman's reading of medical and anthropological journals, I gather that the accusation of sexual perversion directed at all "others" was combined with anthropological descriptions of Jewish endogamy to produce the specter of incest. Gilman writes, "The confusion of endogamous marriage with incestuous inbreeding was a result both of the level of late nineteenth-century science and of the desire for categories with which to define the explicit nature of the Other."[18]

Such an incompatible pair of descriptors (Jews are mongrels, Jews are inbred) is, as we have seen, typical of antisemitic discourse. And in *Nightwood* just as in racial and sexological discourses, when Jews occupy one endpoint of the continuum between incest and exogamy, they also help to define the other. This continuum comes to structure the novel, and Jewishness, aligned most strongly with exogamy, works also to describe its opposite. Jewishness in this text is associated with the alienation of exogamy, thereby helping to frame the trauma of incest.

Nightwood presents three generations of Jewish men who become less Jewish with each exogamous marriage, until the third-generation boy, Guido, named after his Jewish grandfather, becomes devoted to the Catholic Church. As Lara Trubowitz points out, Jewishness in *Nightwood* is defined by its disappearance.[19] The novel opens with a description of the first Guido Volkbein and his Viennese wife Hedvig. Hedvig is a masculine, soldierly woman: she has a "goose-step of a stride" (*N* 3) and when she dances, "the dance floor [becomes] a tactical manoeuvre" (*N* 4). Her masculinity complements her husband's femininity. As I note in the previous chapter, Guido is described in terms that conjure femininity and fecundity. By contrasting this feminine Jewish man with the militaristic Austrian Hedvig, Barnes stresses the mongrelization of this family along lines of gender as well as race. To emphasize the link between Jewishness and exogamy, the text also describes their son Felix in terms of "the mingled passions that make up his past," and alerts us to his "diversity of bloods" (*N* 8).

After giving a detailed description of this Jewish family's history and meditating on Jewish history more broadly throughout the opening chapter, *Nightwood* turns to the relations of its main characters, Nora, Robin, and Matthew. Critics have speculated about the relevance of the opening section to the rest of the novel, some suggesting that it was simply a distraction, perhaps a ruse to throw off the censors from its real subject, the lives and sufferings of "inverts."[20] Others have proposed that the Jewish characters are necessary to establish the themes of marginality on which the novel depends. In her influential article "Laughing at Leviticus: *Nightwood* as Woman's Circus Epic," Jane Marcus asserts that *Nightwood* makes a "modernism of marginality" and focuses on the abjection of the characters as politically efficacious.[21] Julie Abraham similarly argues that the "history of social marginality and its accompaniment of persecution that Barnes invokes at the beginning of *Nightwood* provide a framework within which the social positions of all the characters in the book are circumscribed."[22]

I agree with Abraham that insofar as Jewish history is the story of *not* being part of "the history of the official record," it serves as an analogue to the nonhistory of lesbian desire.[23] And as Abraham further implies, this expulsion from history is authorized by racial and sexological discourses. "Felix Volkbein, with his 'impermissible blood,' provides a paradigm for the relation of the author, as well as her characters, to the official record."[24] But further, I believe, *Nightwood* needs Jewishness because of its specific – and specifically contradictory – relationship to the question of incest. In its emphasis on exogamy and difference, on mixtures and contrasts, the Jewish content of the novel establishes a counterweight to the relationship of Nora and Robin, a pairing that erases difference and collapses identity and time.

Before she meets Nora, Robin has married Felix Volkbein. Like Felix's parents Guido and Hedvig, Felix and Robin are opposites. Even their similarities, such as their common wandering and lack of identity, seem to stem from opposing conditions. Felix, like his father, is a "wandering Jew" (*N* 7) and while she is married to him, Robin begins her chronic wandering, "aware of some lost land in herself" (*N* 45). But Felix wanders, as it were, in spite of himself, compelled by race and fate to wander even though it thwarts his longing for stability and a clear relation to the past. He is trying desperately to locate himself and his family, to remember. Robin, on the other hand, wanders because it frees her from remembering. She wanders both because she forgets and in order to forget. For her, remembering is associated with staying put, and wandering not with finding herself but with losing herself, traveling to and from the "lost land" within her.

Moreover, because he is a Jew, in the world of this text Felix's identity is precarious. The narrator claims that Jews are "everywhere from nowhere" (*N* 7), and as if to declare his unfitness for the society in which he lives, Felix is never dressed appropriately for any occasion (*N* 8). As Mairéad Hanrahan puts it, "the Barnesian Jew suffers from so total a lack of identity, so unredeemable a confusion that any attempt to redeem his condition only aggravates it."[25] Matthew sums up Felix's ambiguous identity when he remarks that "there's something missing and whole about the Baron Felix" (*N* 26). This makes him an appropriate analogue for Robin, who is always on the verge of forgetting herself (*N* 121). When she agrees to marry Felix, it is "as if Robin's life held no volition for refusal" (*N* 43). Even her suffering is indeterminate: her face has the look of an "incurable yet to be stricken with its malady" (*N* 41).

As this brief description suggests, both characters have difficult relationships to time, to the past. Felix single-mindedly seeks contact with the past, wanting a son to feel as he does about the "great past" (*N* 38). But because what he has learned about his family's aristocratic origins was invented by his father in an attempt to assimilate into Christian culture, Felix does not really have a past. Robin, on the other hand, has a past but seems not to realize it, or know that she could continue it into the future: she can only indirectly convey to Nora that she wishes for a home, "as if she were aware . . . that she belonged to Nora, and that if Nora did not make it permanent by her own strength, she would forget" (*N* 55). Matthew describes her as having a "sort of fluid blue under her skin, as if the hide of time had been stripped from her, and with it, all transactions with knowledge" (*N* 134). And later, Nora complains to Matthew, "Robin can go anywhere, do anything . . . because she forgets, and I nowhere because I remember" (*N* 152). As James B. Scott puts it, "nature has wronged [Robin] by misplacing her in time."[26] Felix focuses on continuity with the past, though that continuity is compromised; Robin utterly lacks continuity, and instead seems to exist on a timeless plane.

The past Felix comes to represent, through his unwavering attachment to it, is a patriarchal one, as I describe in chapter 4. In contrast with this patriarchal past, Robin is associated in Nora's mind with her grandmother. This link is established most plainly by a sad and disturbing dream Nora has about her grandmother's room – a room that does not resemble any of her grandmother's actual rooms when she was alive, but, like Nora herself, is "nevertheless saturated with the lost presence of her grandmother, who seemed in the continual process of leaving it" (*N* 63). Nora has had this dream before, but it never felt complete until now, "with the entry of Robin" (*N* 62). Robin seems lit by a source outside herself: "A disc of light, which seemed to come from someone or thing standing behind her and which was yet a shadow, shed a faintly luminous glow upon the upturned still face of Robin" (*N* 62). The light suggests the "lost presence" of the grandmother, herself "yet a shadow"; this light shines through Robin as though it is the source of her animation. Robin becomes a shadow of a shadow, glowing faintly like a memory within Nora's dream.

Nora tries to invite Robin into the grandmother's room, "knowing it was impossible because the room was taboo" (*N* 62). When she thinks about this dream, Nora remembers encountering her grandmother in a corner of their house. The grandmother was "[d]ressed as a man, wearing a billycock and a corked moustache, ridiculous and plump in tight trousers and a red waistcoat, her arms spread saying with a leer of love, 'My little sweetheart!'" (*N* 63). She realizes that to create the dream, she has "drawn upon" her grandmother – presumably this aspect of her grandmother, masculine, leering, and sexualized. And this image now appears to Nora as "something being done to Robin, Robin disfigured and eternalized by the hieroglyphics of sleep and pain" (*N* 63).[27] The link to Nora's grandmother adds meaning to Felix's comment about Robin, that she "had an undefinable disorder, a sort of 'odour of memory' like a person who has come from some place that we have forgotten and would give our life to recall" (*N* 118). In her timelessness Robin comes to stand for other people's semi-forgotten pasts.

The association with the grandmother might seem simply to oppose a matriarchal past to the patriarchal past that Felix worships. But again, Robin seems to exist in a continual present, lacking any kind of continuity. Her association with Nora's grandmother compounds that sense of timelessness because of the suggestion of incest. The grandmother's room in the dream is a taboo space; the childhood image of which it reminds Nora is her grandmother leering, loving, both ridiculous and seductive. Robin stands both in and as the grandmother's shadow. As Karen Kaivola points out, "Nora's love is both homoerotic and incestuous: Robin – the forbidden whom she can't understand and who thus has the power to produce terror – is to Nora at once lover, mother, and child. Unable to admit the incestuous element in her love or determined to forget it, Nora represses it from consciousness but dreams it in the form of her grandmother."[28] Later in the novel, however, Nora *is* able to "admit the incestuous element in her love." She addresses the topic directly, saying to Matthew:

"For Robin is incest too; that is one of her powers. In her, past-time records, and past time is relative to us all. Yet not being the family she is more present than the family. A relative is in the foreground only when it is born, when it suffers and when it dies, unless it becomes one's lover, then it must be everything, as Robin was; yet not as much as she, for she was like a relative found in another generation." (*N* 156–157)

Punning on the word "relative," Nora comments on the eerie ability of time to shift its meaning, to appear to adapt to the needs of individual psyches. She describes Robin as like a relative who becomes a lover. Their relationship, she implies, stands in for, in a sense replicates, intergenerational incest: incest with the grandmother. Barnes used the word "relative" similarly outside of fiction. Phillip Herring and Mary Lynn Broe both quote a letter from Emily Coleman in which she writes, "Why did you say he [Scudder Middleton, a former lover] was a 'relative' – does relative mean *sex?* If not, why should you have felt such a sex-passion for Scudder, and also for Thelma who was also 'your family.' *Family means sex. I suddenly knew it.*"[29] The repetition of the word "relative" in reference to a sexual partner returns us to Barnes's own sexual relationship with her grandmother. She is clearly addressing that experience – only somewhat obliquely – in *Nightwood*.

Incest, particularly incest with a member of an earlier generation, collapses that which ought to be distinct. It erases boundaries, collapses time, and blurs identity. Barnes signaled this blurring when she wrote to

Coleman, "I always thought I *was* my grandmother."[30] And Nora echoes Barnes's comment, defining lesbian love as in some sense narcissistic: "A man is another person – a woman is yourself, caught as you turn in panic; on her mouth you kiss your own" (*N* 143). This narcissistic element, though, stems not from the lesbianism as Nora suggests, but from the incest this particular lesbian relationship is recapitulating, from the broken boundaries between grandmother and granddaughter such incest entails. Herring points out that "[a]ll desire in *Nightwood* is insatiable and ultimately narcissistic."[31] Nora reiterates the theme of collapsing identity when she says to Matthew, "She is myself. What am I to do?" (*N* 127) and later, "Have you ever loved someone and it became yourself?" (*N* 152).

Matthew seems to comprehend Robin's place in Nora's psyche. Even before she has told him that "Robin is incest too" he has described her predicament in terms of inbreeding:

"You are . . . experiencing the inbreeding of pain. Most of us do not dare it. We wed a stranger, and so 'solve' our problem. But when you inbreed with suffering . . . you are destroyed back to your structure as an old master disappears beneath the knife of the scientist who would know how it was painted . . . Time is a great conference planning our end, and youth is only the past putting a leg forward." (*N* 129–130)

Through inbreeding – uniting with the self rather than the other – Nora is living her present through her past (which puts a "leg forward" into the present). When he compares Nora to a scientist who scrapes away at an old painting, Matthew implies that her love is a sort of exploration, a return to origins in an effort to understand them. And she inbreeds not with a person, exactly, but with "suffering." If Nora was "endlessly embroiled in a preoccupation without a problem" (*N* 53) before she met Robin, Robin has provided the problem; if Robin's face was that of an "incurable yet to be stricken with its malady," Nora writes the malady across her face when she awakens her and watches her "turn befouled before me, she who had managed in that sleep to keep whole" (*N* 145).

In the context of inbreeding with suffering, Robin's existence outside of time resonates strongly: she acts within – even represents – the temporal uncertainty and confusion created by the trauma of incest. When Nora feels that her dream has "disfigured and eternalized" Robin through "the hieroglyphics of sleep and pain," she means that her semi-conscious associations between Robin and her grandmother do violence to Robin, turn her into a sign for something that has been lost. Nora's relationship with Robin performs a violence similar to Felix's. Both Nora and Felix render Robin a container for their own desires; neither recognizes nor makes room for Robin's own identity, which the text, too, hides from view, and which is hidden, it seems, from Robin herself. Matthew's comment about those we murder or have sex with in dreams seems also to reflect upon Nora's use of Robin in this sense. He tells Nora that the dream figures' "very lack of identity makes them ourselves" (*N* 88).

The lack of identity common to Felix and Robin, it seems to me, extends to the impossibility of telling trauma. Hanrahan proposes a link between the Jew's lack of identity and the failure of representation. She describes the Jew's "condition" in *Nightwood*:

While Barnes adopts the classic image of the Jew as Other, outcast, pariah, she adds a twist in that this image does not suffice to provide him with a distinct identity; the Jew features only in his relationship to the Other, his relationship *as* Other, so Other that even his Otherness does not belong to him . . . For Barnes, the Jew's condition crystallizes a predicament she considers general: the failure of representation itself.[32]

The failures of both identity and representation suggest the failure to narrate trauma. Caught within trauma, one cannot quite name it, identify it, or represent it; one can hardly name, identify, or represent oneself. One can only defer the telling through dreams, substitutes, half-comprehensible images. On this level, too, then, Jewishness relates to one of the deepest themes of the novel: the hole in identity and representation created by the trauma of incest.

To approach this constellation of subjects, Barnes structures her novel around opposed sets of elements: on the one hand are Felix, Jews, patriarchy, exogamy, and the past. On the other are Robin, Christians, the grandmother, incest, and timelessness. The choice for women in this text is not, as it is sometimes described, between a threatening patriarchy and a liberating lesbian sexuality. Instead, the novel offers patriarchal entrapment, which turns women into pawns for continuity, as opposed to a total enmeshment or melding that leaves them without continuity: a double bind if ever there was one. Lacking continuity altogether means living with trauma, within a realm where past and present are indistinguishable, where the past seems instead to repeat itself again and again in the present. Robin, who is described as "a catastrophe that had yet no beginning" (*N* 48), conjures and represents the traumatic fragmentation of experienced time.

Robin's associations with timelessness and incest help to clarify a few of the more enigmatic passages about her. When we first meet her, she is described as childlike and vibrant, with legs "looking too lively" for her prone pose, and yet decaying, akin to the cut (dying) flowers that surround her, to fungi, and to "an inner malady of the sea" (*N* 34). Through this imagery Robin is further linked to Felix, whose Jewishness, as I mention earlier, is compared to flowers that "brought to a pitch of florid ecstasy no sooner attain their specific type than they fall into its decay" (*N* 2). Both these descriptions can be read as gesturing toward an overlapping past and present. In her timelessness Robin serves as a window onto Nora's submerged past, associated by the text with "evil and degradation" (*N* 135). And as her "lively" legs suggest, she makes that past preternaturally alive. Robin's function as a cipher of past incest also helps to explain the description of her as an "infected carrier of the past: before her the structure of our head and jaws ache – we feel that we could eat her, she who is eaten death returning, for only then do we put our face close to the blood on the lips of our forefathers" (*N* 37). Much as Guido felt the cry of "*Roba vecchia*" in his throat, here "we" feel the ache in our jaws of a buried past (savage, degraded). The specific incest that Robin comes to represent is enfolded within a larger realm of degradation that includes cannibalism as a sign of that which is disavowed by day, and only "remembered" in the world of the night.[33]

When she searches for the wandering Robin, Nora is periodically drawn into a timeless state similar to that which Robin represents. A particularly acute instance occurs when she sees Robin embracing another woman. Her jealousy is so strong that she is "incapable of speech" and experiences "a sensation of evil, complete and dismembering" (*N* 64). This feeling of being dismembered suggests the overwhelming fear of losing the attention and protection that can accompany incest with a familial authority. But Nora feels a simultaneous "awful happiness" when she closes her eyes – she is in another sense relieved to find the past repeating itself. This is the known, finally; what she has feared has happened. She feels an "intolerable automatism" as she plays her part in the predetermined script that calls for her abandonment. Automatism, a motif in Rhys's work as well, conjures the eerie feeling Freud describes trauma victims experiencing, of playing out a fated future which is really the past. Tyrus Miller identifies automatism as a theme of late modernism, noting that late modernist writers

perceived as a general state of affairs a kind of all-pervasive, collective, and incurable shell-shock, from which all suffer and which need not have trench experience as its precondition (though for many, of course, it did). Everyone, they suggest, has a bit of the automaton about him or her; it follows from the conditions of history within which we must make our selves, our lives, our cities.[34]

For Nora, the fated future entails the grandmother's betrayal: she has slept with others, has withheld protection, has gone away, has (finally) died. Nora stresses this concurrent relief and horror when she describes her life as "what I hoped Robin was – the secure torment" (*N* 151).

The theme of betrayal, in the context of an incestuous fusion of identity, becomes indistinguishable from self-betrayal. Nora is described at the beginning of the "Night Watch" chapter as defined by the past, as lacking privacy, and as courting betrayal. Her skin reveals patterns of past and future: "there could be seen coming, early in her life, the design that was to be the weather-beaten grain of her face, that wood in the work; the tree coming forward in her, an undocumented record of time" (*N* 50). Her "descent," which is in part this tree, this past patterning, coming forward to define her, is, the text says, always "observable." Nora, a "singular," is "deprived of the privacy of disappearance; as if privacy, moving relentlessly away, by the very sustaining power of its withdrawal kept the body eternally moving downward, but in one place, and perpetually before the eye" (*N* 51). Although this is one of the cryptic images for which *Nightwood* is notorious, it suggests another aspect of the intertwined themes of time, identity, and trauma. Nora can never have privacy because her identity is always already dependent on fusion with the loved one, the grandmother and her substitutes. The continual withdrawal of privacy is destructive as much as it is sustaining, since privacy would cut Nora back to only part of a self. At the same time, however, the fusion is an invasion and privacy something to be sought, so Nora sabotages her relationships by seeking honesty "at the liar's door" (*N* 135).

Courting betrayal, she courts the privacy which, when achieved, breaks her. Betrayal is one of Nora's characteristics: "Wandering people the world over found her profitable in that she could be sold for a price forever, for she carried her betrayal money in her own pocket" (*N* 52). Nora is described as "by temperament . . . an early Christian" (*N* 51) and here the money for betrayal reminds us of Jesus and the thirty pieces of silver. But unlike Jesus, Nora offers the betrayal money herself. In Barnes's late play *The Antiphon* (1958), the daughter Miranda, a victim of sexual violence within her family, is described similarly as courting her own betrayal. Her mother accuses her of giving "her weapons to the enemy."[35] And when her brother Jeremy is asked if he will betray her, he answers, "It won't be necessary; she is her own collision. / . . . / She has rash fortitude; she will undo herself."[36] In *Nightwood* the assertion that Nora carries her own betrayal money returns the description to its beginning, to the image of the tree coming forward. To be betrayed is to repeat the past: the incest and the end of the incest. The privacy continually withdraws, the betrayal money is continually proffered, the past continues to repeat itself.

This sense of Nora repeating her painful past interacts ironically with Robin's failure to remember. Nora knows that Robin combines in herself all of Nora's own confused and partial remembering. "Everything we can't bear in this world, some day we find in one person, and love it all at once," she tells Matthew (*N* 135). And this painful love is linked precisely to Robin's diffuse identity, because that is what allows her to function as a vehicle, to re-present Nora's grandmother. In fact, immediately after this assertion, Nora describes Robin as having too little identity: "A strong sense of identity gives man an idea he can do no wrong; too little accomplishes the same. Some natures cannot appreciate, only regret" (*N* 135). Robin's weak sense of self signals the collapse of identity that forms the core of the experience of incest.

Robin's lack of identity is reflected by Felix's false personal history. Jewishness frames the motif of incest both through its extratextual association with incest and through its opposing link, stressed by the novel, with exogamy. Felix's isolation and lack of a genuine past, as well as his obsession with the past, resonate against the continual present of trauma, where trauma is the enmeshment of incest. Representing one endpoint of the continuum between exogamy and incest, Jewishness helps *Nightwood* to highlight the other. Between embeddedness in history and expulsion from history, between exogamy and incest, between patriarchy and the incestuous grandmother are the continuums that link them as much as they divide. In his introduction to *Nightwood*, T. S. Eliot describes *Nightwood* as akin to an Elizabethan tragedy (*N* xvi). It bears comparison, too, to the earlier tragedy of Oedipus. Both Robin and Felix are associated with imagery of blindness.[37] Nora is drawn to, we might even say fated to find, her own torment, and that torment is incest. These echoes of the Greek tragedy mark another layer of this multiply tragic novel.

Although they are much less grotesque and dramatic than *Nightwood*, Rhys's novels also lean toward the tragic. Her characters are unable to help or defend themselves. They periodically imagine or commit violent acts – Anna Morgan burns Walter Jeffries's hand with a cigarette (*V* 86); Sasha Jansen fantasizes about using a hammer to crack a woman's skull "like an egg-shell" (*GM, M* 52) – but these bursts of rage are brief and ineffective. The characters are caught in the tragedy of repetition, helplessly recapitulating self-destructive scenarios. This form of tragedy is conveyed most strongly through polyvocal, nonlinear narration and fragmented interior monologues. Although critics such as Elaine Savory, Coral Ann Howells, Teresa O'Connor, and Sue Thomas have insightfully discussed Rhys's personal history of sexual trauma, Rhys criticism lacks an account of how trauma informs her textual strategies.[38]

Perspectives provided by the burgeoning field of trauma studies allow us to see in Rhys's fragmented narratives negotiations with what Judith Herman, in her pioneering theorization of trauma, calls trauma's "central dialectic": a knowledge so partial that it borders on denial, a revelation so incomplete that it obscures. Like Barnes, Rhys analyzes these fragmented and traumatized minds in part through presenting their associations with and responses to Jewish figures. The sense of indeterminacy, of liminality, that attached to the imagined Jew made it possible for Rhys to use her Jewish characters, especially Serge Rubin, as vehicles for exploring the temporal and conceptual uncertainty that attends memory of trauma.

Critics have debated whether Rhys's characters are inherently passive and masochistic, or only socially marginalized and disempowered. Trauma studies offers a nuanced response to this debate, acknowledging the characters' passivity without locating it in masochistic personalities, but also without implying that such psychological helplessness is attributable solely to social factors. Helplessness is a condition of trauma, in that the fewer means a victim has to attempt to save herself from a life- or body-threatening experience, the more likely she is to be traumatized by that experience. And it is a result of trauma, in that a *sense* of helplessness lingers in people (and animals) who have been *actually* helpless in the face of previous threats.[39]

Anna Morgan in *Voyage in the Dark* appears to have survived an unnarrated, largely inaccessible sexual trauma. Sasha Jansen, the protagonist of *Good Morning, Midnight*, also shows signs of having survived some sort of sexual violation and perhaps a suicide attempt.[40] And she has had a baby who died within weeks of his birth. Sasha's occasional bursts of self-protection and hope for change alternate with numb capitulation to new dangers. This alternating set of responses creates a split self-image, prompting Sasha to feel as though she is "a bit of an automaton" (*GM, M* 10) and at the same time worry constantly about her emotions overflowing into tears. In her astute portrait of traumatized characters, Rhys represents the defining phenomena of the traumatic double bind, all of which can be viewed as types of fragmentation: dissociation (fragmentation of the psyche), traumatic "memory" (fragmented, often incoherent images or intuitions that bear only faint resemblance to ordinary memories), and a discomfiting sense of timelessness (fragmentation of one's experience of continuity).

Herman explains how dissociation may arise from states of helpless passivity: "When a person is completely powerless, and any form of resistance is futile, she may go into a state of surrender ... The helpless person escapes from her situation not by action in the real world but rather by altering her state of consciousness." These alterations "combine with a feeling of indifference, emotional detachment, and profound passivity in which the person relinquishes all initiative and struggle."[41] To the extent, then, that a traumatized person resists her victimization, she often does it by removing herself mentally from the situation, leaving her body to suffer the trauma.

Many readers have noticed that Rhys's protagonists dissociate, usually in sexual situations. In her autobiography Rhys describes telling a Frenchman, "'I can abstract myself from my body.' He looked so shocked that I asked if I was speaking bad French. He said, '*Oh non, mais ... c'est horrible.*' And yet for so long that was what I did."[42] As Herman's discussion suggests, this dissociation, or splitting, both contributes to a subject's passivity and protects her emotionally from her own helplessness. In *Good Morning, Midnight* Sasha describes a brief experience of splitting in a scene she remembers from her life with her former husband Enno. When they were stranded in Brussels, she went to visit a Mr. Lawson to borrow money. "I am standing there with the note in my hand, when he comes up and kisses me. I am hating him more than I have ever hated anyone in my life, yet I feel my mouth go soft under his, and my arms go limp" (*GM, M* 119). Although she has the money in her hand, Sasha's body responds to the advance from the man she so intensely resents. This response is a trace of sexual trauma, with Sasha split between a yielding body and a repulsed mind.

Sasha uses the defense of splitting more clearly to carry her through her experiences with the gigolo, René, in the narrative present.[43] Although when she first finds he has followed her up to her room, she hugs him happily, she very quickly moves into a state of detachment. "We kiss each other fervently, but already something has gone wrong. I am uneasy, half of myself somewhere else" (*GM, M* 177). Soon, in fact, the encounter becomes violent, as René describes gang rapes he has enjoyed in Morocco and begins to force his knee between her knees. When he reduces her to tears, he is satisfied, saying, "'That's better, that's better'" (*GM, M* 182).[44] In her description of Sasha's response to his cruelty, however, Rhys complicates the story of how splitting functions: in some cases, she shows, a victim may reverse the typical roles of the two selves. Instead of submitting to abuse while inwardly resisting by imagining another self, a victim may at times protect herself in the real world while another part of her is content to continue with the dangerous encounter.

Through her ambivalent pain, Sasha tells René to take her money and go, to save himself the "trouble" of raping her. She tells him that she is not "vexed," that "everybody's got their living to earn" and that she's "just trying to save [him] a lot of trouble." With this sarcasm she manages to convince him to leave, successfully defending herself from the assault. But part of her dissociates from the self that is protecting her body, and she thinks, "Don't listen, that's not me speaking. Don't listen. Nothing to do with me – I swear it" (*GM, M* 183). Here Rhys demonstrates a more disturbing reason why someone accustomed to victimization might dissociate: part of her is unsure it wants to protect itself.

The most vivid of Sasha's dissociative episodes occurs when René has finally left her alone in her room. She is crying, while an ironic voice mocks her and the whole situation:

I cry in the way that hurts right down, that hurts your heart and your stomach. Who is this crying? The same one who laughed on the landing, kissed him, and was happy. This is me, myself, who is crying. The other – how do I know who the other is? She isn't me.

Her voice in my head: "Well, well, well, just think of that now. What an amusing ten days! Positively packed with thrills. The last performance of What's-her-name And Her Boys or It Was All Due To An Old Fur Coat." (*GM, M* 185–186)

The mocking voice goes on for several paragraphs until she stops it by having another drink: "Damned voice in my head, I'll stop you talking . . . " (*GM, M* 187). Sasha's multivoiced interior monologue, laden with "hum[s] of voices," a train saying "Paris, Paris, Paris, Paris," a joke she remembers reading on a bathroom wall, and references to Venus and Apollo, delineates two rigidly opposed fragments of self: one who feels pain, and another who mocks it. After the drink, Sasha is "walking up and down the room. She has gone. I am alone." The dissociative episode is over, but now Sasha begins to fantasize that she can communicate with René and make him turn back. The scene is painful, raw: Sasha has broken down under the pressures of René's brutality, as she experiences the repetition of trauma.

In *Unclaimed Experience* (1996) Cathy Caruth describes Freud's observation that traumatic repetition seems to trail people as if it were their fate. "In some cases, Freud points out, these repetitions are particularly striking because they seem not to be initiated by the individual's own acts but rather appear as the possession of some people by a sort of fate, a series of painful events to which they are subjected, and which seem to be entirely outside their wish or control."[45] This possession by her "fate" haunts Sasha throughout *Good Morning, Midnight*. One of her nightmares features a Tube station with signs pointing "This Way to the Exhibition"; but Sasha wants the way out. She asks a man how to exit, but he "points to the placards and his hand is made of steel" (*GM, M* 13). Moreover, one of the important motifs of the novel, one which ties together imagery and plot (as I discuss below), is Sasha's vision of being alone in a room, waiting fatalistically for the door to open: "And the dreams that you have, alone in an empty room, waiting for the door that will open, the thing that is bound to happen . . ." (*GM, M* 100). These images, of a crowd drawing one along, of a steel hand pointing the way, of a door opening, figure Sasha's sense of helplessness, her difficulty even imagining agency.

Helplessness can spark dissociation, a splintering of the experiencing self. But even when they are not dissociating, Rhys's characters are troubled by another kind of fragment: bits of images or memories that erupt inexplicably into consciousness. Herman writes that traumatic memories "are not encoded like the ordinary memories of adults in a verbal, linear narrative that is assimilated into an ongoing life story."[46] Caruth's description of trauma coincides with this view of memories out of time: trauma is "the breach in the mind's experience of time, self, and the world."[47] Traumatic memories, that is, are images, scenes, or sensations *without context*.

Rhys worked into *Good Morning, Midnight* one of her own traumatic memories – a scene which Sasha imagines but does not own as a memory. As Sasha is arriving at her hotel with René, who is whistling a tune, there is a break in the text marked by white space and a bibliographic separator, and then Sasha imagines the following scene:

I am in a little whitewashed room. The sun is hot outside. A man is standing with his back to me, whistling that tune and cleaning his shoes. I am wearing a black dress, very short, and heel-less slippers. My legs are bare. I am watching for the expression on the man's face when he turns round. Now he ill-treats me, now he betrays me. He often brings home other women and I have to wait on them, and I don't like that. But as long as he is alive and near me I am not unhappy. If he were to die I should kill myself.
   My film mind . . . ("For God's sake watch out for your film mind . . . ") (*GM, M* 176)

By referring to this negative fantasy as emerging from her "film mind," Sasha distances it from her own psyche, implicitly echoing her interior assertion as she talks René into leaving her room that it is "[n]othing to do with me – I swear it" (*GM, M* 183). But her metaphor of the film is nevertheless apt, since Sasha is indeed projecting her fantasy outward, imagining it on a movie screen in some separable part of her mind.

In this passage Rhys has given Sasha a vision of a story of submission and humiliation she herself was told as a young teenager by Mr. Howard, the elderly man who molested her.[48] Rhys seems to have recovered the memory of this experience in 1938 just when she was working on this novel.[49] Although the event had until then gone "out of [her] memory like a stone," she woke up one morning to find her novel-in-progress "wiped clean out" of her mind.[50] She took up a notebook and wrote instead a narrative about Mr. Howard, a friend of her mother. According to this narrative, the fourteen-year-old Rhys had gone with Mr. Howard on an outing to a botanical garden, where he molested her on a secluded bench and then began to tell her what she later called a "serial story," which he continued on subsequent outings. In these stories Rhys would go with him to another island and belong to him, wait on his guests, seldom wear clothes, have her hands tied by ropes covered with flowers, and be punished for "the slightest mistake."[51]

Although the scene in *Good Morning, Midnight* is set off from the rest of the narrative both on the page and in terms of setting and plot, only linked through the tune whistled by both René and the man in the fantasy, it bears a thematic relationship to Sasha's situation in that it shows a self clinging to its own subordination. It may be that Rhys added it to (or left it in) this part of the novel – just before Sasha will wish for the abusive gigolo to stay – in part to explain the origin of Sasha's ambivalent willingness to be humiliated. Although Rhys did not use this terminology, she was aware that her early traumas had shaped her. She wrote in the same notebook that the experience with Mr. Howard "formed me made me as I am."[52] With the heartbreaking internalization of guilt characteristic of those abused in childhood, she blamed herself for not struggling enough against Mr. Howard. Although she attempted to refuse to go with him on a second outing, she gave into her mother's admonishments not to be rude and continued to meet him.[53] About this surrender she wrote, "Oh I agree. I only struggled feebly[.] What he had seen in me was there all right."[54] In this notebook Rhys also describes being beaten by her mother, astutely surmising that that may have damaged her earlier on, contributing to her failure to protect herself from Mr. Howard.[55]

Even before she was able to write the "film mind" version of Mr. Howard's story and the narrative of her own abuse, Rhys portrayed Anna Morgan in *Voyage in the Dark* as haunted by fragmentary images and memories. Again, these fragments often erupt during memories or experiences of sexuality. In the original ending to the novel (published in Bonnie Kime Scott's *The Gender of Modernism* [1990]), Anna is remembering her time with Walter Jeffries, a lover who has in effect pensioned her off; then she switches scenes, thinking, "And another clock was ticking." In the published novel this scene seems more coherent, distinguishing what appear to be two time-frames with the line "And the clock was ticking loud, like that time when I lay looking at the dog in the picture *Loyal Heart* . . . " (*V* 184). This picture hung in the room in the flat she rented from Ethel Matthews. So when Anna remembers, "I kept saying, 'Stop, stop,' so that Ethel wouldn't hear" (*V* 184), it seems as though the whole scene, introduced by the reference to the other clock, refers to a scene in Ethel's flat. But there are indications that Anna may be half-hiding additional layers.

In the original version Anna is remembering a time when someone said to her "well I told you I would didn't I I always told you I would didn't I and you never believed that I really would did you."[56] The "always" and "never" suggest a long acquaintance, excluding from possible speakers all the men she has had up to her room in Ethel's flat except for Carl Redman. But the narration continues in both the draft and published versions with the man saying, "I'm too old for this sort of thing . . . it's bad for the heart he laughed and it sounded funny les emotions fortes."[57] (The lines are punctuated in the published text.) As Carl is presented in *Voyage*, he is unlikely to have used French or worried about his heart. It seems more likely that a memory of telling Carl to "stop" triggers in Anna an older memory of someone else, an older man who would not stop.[58] The French suggests the West Indies as a plausible setting for the partially obscured scene, and points to a blurring between Rhys and her character that may have produced the layered memory.

Both the content of this image, a rape, and its lack of context indicate the presence of trauma. But by entwining what may be her own partial memory within Anna's more recent, conscious one, Rhys protects Anna – and perhaps herself – from actually having to think about the trauma. Readers of the text are not sure exactly what happened, but neither does Anna have to be sure. This half-telling illustrates the fundamental dynamic of trauma: "The conflict between the will to deny horrible events and the will to proclaim them aloud is the central dialectic of psychological trauma. People who have survived atrocities often tell their stories in a highly emotional, contradictory, and fragmented manner which undermines their credibility and thereby serves the twin imperatives of truth-telling and secrecy."[59] Since the survivor often finds secrecy necessary even from herself, the traces she leaves may be largely metaphoric, or they may be layered within other scenes and stories, as here where the room in Ethel's flat provides a cover for the emotional core of the half-remembered scene.

The fragmentation of Anna's memory is necessarily entwined with a sense of her past as discontinuous, an inability to order her memories. At times Anna wonders explicitly about her past. Once, as she walks through the London streets, a man speaks to her "out of the side of his mouth" and she wants to hit him. She moves to follow him, but a policeman at the corner stares at her "like a damned baboon – a fair baboon, too, worse than a dark one every time." Along with its awareness of the policeman's racist expectations, this reaction can be read as one of shame at being looked at by him, or guilt for her violent impulse, or both. Immediately after this, Anna's thoughts are enclosed in parentheses: "(What happened to me then? Something happened to me then?)" (*V* 148). This "then" is ambiguous: it is unclear whether it indicates time (i.e., what happened to me at some particular time?) or cause (i.e., if I react like this, then what happened to me?). The ambiguity demonstrates Rhys's understanding that unresolved trauma distorts one's emotional development; and it highlights the temporal undecidability of traumatic memory.

The text addresses the temporal indeterminacy of such shadowy memories even more directly when Anna is with Walter, early in the novel. As they approach a sexual encounter, Walter "start[s] talking about [her] being a virgin" and Anna loses her "feeling of being on fire" and becomes cold. "'Why did you start about that?' I said. 'What's it matter? Besides, I'm not a virgin if that's what's worrying you'" (*V* 36). Soon she begins to cry, and Walter wipes her eyes but continues to coax her upstairs. Although she keeps saying "I must go," she follows him upstairs, entering a dreamlike state in which her sense of time becomes nebulous and vague fragments of memory seep through her cracking defenses:

I stopped. I wanted to say, "No, I've changed my mind." But he laughed and squeezed my hand and said, "What's the matter? Come on, be brave," and I didn't say anything, but I felt cold and as if I were dreaming.

When I got into bed there was warmth coming from him and I got close to him. *Of course you've always known, always remembered, and then you forget so utterly, except that you've always known it. Always – how long is always?* (*V* 37)[60]

The cold and dreamlike feeling recalls the "trance" days Rhys wrote that she herself experienced. She described the state as "the unreal feeling which is I suppose kindly Nature's way when complete catastrophe arrives." In the same letter she explains that "[s]ometimes it's pure panic – other times my mind goes blank which is a mercy."[61] Here Anna's mind is blank enough that she cannot articulate even to herself what "it" is (she omits the direct object in the first two clauses), nor can she place it in time. "It" may well be her belief that she is not a virgin, considering her disturbed reaction to the conversation about whether virginity matters. The warmth of Walter's body sparks this vague memory, but its difference from ordinary memories, its lack of context and of any specific content, suggests an eruption of trauma.[62] Wondering "how long is always?" is appropriately muddled, accentuating the sense of timelessness that prevents traumatic memories from being incorporated into a life story, from being fully comprehended by their subjects.

One result of the chronological confusion that attends trauma is that the subject can be said to have in a sense *missed* the traumatic event. Caruth, reading Freud's *Beyond the Pleasure Principle* (1920), discusses the eerie sense in which the subject is compelled to repeat the trauma, sometimes in new experiences, sometimes in nightmare or flashback, in order to experience it at all. As Caruth describes it,

[i]t is not simply, that is, the literal threatening of bodily life, but the fact that the threat is recognized as such by the mind one moment too late. The shock of the mind's relation to the threat of death is thus not the direct experience of the threat, but precisely the missing of this experience, the fact that, not being experienced in time, it has not yet been fully known. And it is this lack of direct experience that, paradoxically, becomes the basis of the repetition of the nightmare.[63]

In *Good Morning, Midnight* Rhys conveys this feeling of missing the experience in her shadowy portrayal of Sasha's baby's death. The death itself is not narrated, it is simply stated in the past tense: "And there he is, lying with a ticket tied round his wrist because he died in a hospital" (*GM, M* 61). Although Sasha narrates various painful experiences from her past, Rhys implies that she cannot bring herself to describe bringing the baby to the hospital or learning of his death. Rhys herself lost a baby boy before she give birth to her daughter Maryvonne, and she and her first husband Jean Lenglet literally missed his death. They were drinking champagne at home with a friend, trying to cheer themselves up.[64]

In her novel Rhys treats the sense of missing the experience more symbolically. The woman who runs the house where Sasha goes to have her baby ("There is no doctor to give chloroform here. This is a place for poor people" [*GM, M* 58]) promises that by wrapping her tightly in bandages for a week, she will ensure that Sasha bears "no trace, no mark" of having borne a child.

> And it is true. When she takes them off there is not one line, not one wrinkle, not one crease.
> And five weeks afterwards there I am, with not one line, not one wrinkle, not one crease.
> And there he is, lying in a hospital with a ticket tied round his wrist because he died in a hospital. And there I am looking down at him, without one line, without one wrinkle, without one crease . . . (*GM, M* 61)

The fact of the baby's death is given as a past event; we have no indication that Sasha has seen him in the hospital prior to this scene. This suggests a missed, an incomprehensible event. And more symbolically, with her unmarked, uncreased body, Sasha has no tangible evidence that the birth ever happened. It is as if the baby himself were erased, pressed out of existence like the wrinkles. Sasha mentions the death only once more, later in the novel, repeating the same words: "He has a ticket tied round his wrist because he died. Lying so cold and still with a ticket round his wrist because he died" (*GM, M* 139). The raw sadness of the event for readers of the novel is compounded by an echoing sense of not comprehending, of having missed it too.[65]

Considering Rhys's characters in the context of trauma highlights issues of pain and alienation, feelings of helplessness and (often sexual) exposure, and temporal uncertainty. In *Voyage in the Dark* and *Good Morning, Midnight*, this constellation of affective and conceptual states is both reflected and condensed by the figure of a Jew. Rhys's Jews, like those in *Nightwood*, mirror the pain of other alienated characters. But like Barnes's Jewish characters, they serve more complex and interesting functions as well. Taken together, the Jews in these two Rhys novels gather to themselves crucial social and psychological questions: questions about the nature of being when being is always nationalized, racialized, and gendered, and questions about knowing oneself through the traumas that have hidden pieces of oneself from one's own view.

Jewishness plays a small but significant role in *Voyage in the Dark*. In part because Anna Morgan finds racial identity that can be pinned down less compelling than the liminal identity she associates with Jewishness (but not all Jews), Jewishness becomes for the novel a continual possibility, something to seek but not necessarily to find. In the second section of the novel, Anna meets her old friend Laurie with two American men: "The big one was Carl – Carl Redman – and the other one's name was Adler. Joe, she called him. He was the younger, and very Jewish-looking. You would have known he was a Jew wherever you saw him, but I wasn't sure about Carl" (*V* 113). In spite of the fair bit of time given to Joe in the narrative, he scarcely makes any impression on Anna. He is uninteresting to her because his identity as an American and a Jew is plain. His Jewishness casts a shadow onto Carl, however, causing Anna to wonder whether he is Jewish as well. Alongside the hint of possible Jewishness, Rhys enlists the image of the American Indian (Redman) to stress Carl's ambiguous foreignness.[66]

Jewishness in *Voyage in the Dark* is most powerful when most uncertain. Much as she is drawn to wonder about her own past, Anna is also drawn toward Carl, around whom Jewishness lingers as a possibility but not a fact. Toward the beginning of the novel, she asks a friend whether the man she is dating is Jewish:

"Viv gave me that coat," Maudie said. "He's like that. He doesn't give much but what he gives is good stuff, not shoddy."
"Like a Jew," I said. "Is he a Jew?"
"Of course he isn't. I told you." (*V* 16)

This exchange, of course, contains the stereotyped notion that Jews have the money to buy good things and the taste to choose them, but are stingy all the same. But more interesting is Maudie's statement, "I told you." With this sentence Rhys indicates that Anna has asked this question before, and yet feels the need to ask it again. Just as the truth about one's own past is unstable, so the truth about racial or ethnic identity must continually be sought, and negative answers never quite accepted.

After all, Anna is uncertain not only about her personal history but also about her placement within national categories. She is a white Creole from a "little" island in the West Indies (*V* 124), unhappy and always cold in England, and passing for English without quite intending to. When Joe teases her about her claim that she is from the West Indies, and pretends to have known her father, whom he calls "Old Taffy Morgan," she retracts her claim, telling him that she was born in Manchester (*V* 125). When Ethel Matthews asks her "'don't you hate foreigners?'" she replies, "'I don't think I do; but, you see, I don't know many'" (*V* 110). The complicated status of Jewishness – is it a matter of nation, race, religion, or some combination of these? Are Jews Europeans or foreigners? – mirrors Anna's own, helping to make it a focal point for all the forms of uncertainty that haunt her. Anna's repeated question to Maudie bears a suggestive parallel to her own question, "What happened to me then? Something happened to me then?" In *Voyage in the Dark* the truth about race and nation, about who belongs and who remains outside, can never be fully apprehended.

In *Good Morning, Midnight* the Jew is labeled as such, but the various forms of uncertainty that attach to him nevertheless make him a rich field for Sasha's projections. Critics have noted that Serge Rubin, who occupies the physical center of the novel and to whose painting Sasha returns at the end, is important because with him and in the presence of his paintings Sasha feels temporarily happy and free.[67] As I mention in chapter 1, when Delmar props up Serge's paintings around his studio, Sasha reacts as if to a "miracle." "Now the room expands and the iron band round my heart loosens. The miracle has happened. I am happy" (*GM, M* 99). As she parts from him, Sasha thinks, "When he shakes my hand like that and says 'Amis' I feel very happy . . . " (*GM, M* 101). Serge is one of the few men in any Rhys novel who neither condescends to the protagonist nor treats her as a sexual object. This in itself would be enough to make him stand out as a friendly force; yet Sasha's process of identification with him and disavowal of that identification indicates that Serge plays a more significant role in the novel.

Serge's national identity is ambiguous: since he is living in Paris but is introduced to Sasha by Delmar (who Sasha thinks is Russian but who turns out to be Ukrainian), we assume that he is either French or Russian (or perhaps he, too, is Ukrainian). We learn his first name shortly after Sasha meets him, but by leaving his national background unstated, Rhys also leaves us uncertain how to pronounce it (with two syllables as in the Russian, or with one as in the French?). Toward the end of the scene, Serge has to go out for an hour, and addresses Delmar in a language that Sasha does not recognize: "He turns at the door and, with the mocking expression very apparent, says something in Russian. At least, I suppose it's Russian" (*GM, M* 98). Finally providing us with Sasha's guess, Rhys never does fill in the gaps in this story. Serge has no definite national history; his exile, like Sasha's implied displacement, remains vague enough to serve double duty as a metaphor for his emotional state.

Sasha's own nationality is obscure as well. She has come to Paris from London, and Rhys omits mention of any previous home. But her nationality is suspect, so that the hotel staff wants to take a second look at her passport (*GM, M* 14). She makes nonspecific references to her own exile. For example, she remarks that she has "no pride – no pride, no name, no face, no country. I don't belong anywhere. Too sad, too sad" (*GM, M* 44). And when she mentally combines comments about her by two strangers, she imagines them saying, "What the devil (translating it politely) is she doing here, that old woman? What is she doing here, the stranger, the alien, the old one?" (*GM, M* 54). Her exiled status seems to her analogous to her age and her lack of pride: all remove her from the status of the proper, beautiful, rooted young woman who would have the only kind of power Sasha has ever been able to approximate.

Without giving Sasha a particular place of origin, Rhys nevertheless suggests that she is in exile and can relate to Serge on that basis. But in another sense, Sasha's exile has already been implied in part by the very presence of the Jewish Serge. Having chosen not to give Sasha the explicit West Indian past she gives to other protagonists, including Anna Morgan, Rhys uses the quintessential figure of exile to conjure physical and emotional displacement.

The issue of race is only nominally clearer. What follows Sasha's assertion that Serge "is a Jew of about forty" (*GM, M* 91) is as jumbled as late nineteenth- and early twentieth-century race science itself, which could not decide where on various branches of racial "family trees" to place Jews. Entering his studio, Sasha asks, "'West African masks?'" and he answers, "'Yes, straight from the Congo . . . . I made them'" (*GM, M* 91). In this odd pair of sentences, Serge calls into question his racial identity as well as his works' cultural authenticity, yet paradoxically lays claim to a modernist authenticity that depended on the "primitive." Here the text seems satirically to play upon racialist classifications that aligned and sometimes conflated Jews and blacks, undermining notions of authenticity in artistic discourses and of nativeness in nationalist discourses. The uncertainty implicit in Serge's description of his masks echoes for the novel as a whole, questioning Sasha's national identities and personal authenticity and signaling the deep divisions within her, the split between a Sasha who mocks and a Sasha who cries, an alien and a native.

When she first meets him, as I note in chapter 1, Sasha describes Serge: "He has that mocking look of the Jew, the look that can be so hateful, that can be so attractive, that can be so sad" (*GM, M* 91). The mocking, hateful look gives Serge an affinity with the sarcastic side of Sasha, who exhibits these traits as protective gestures whenever she finds herself sad, the other aspect of "the Jew's" look. Sasha's description emphasizes that it is not just *this* Jew whose look is mocking, hateful, and sad, but *"the* Jew." We are left to infer that this combination of expressions originates in the national and racial nonbelonging of European Jews; and we also conclude that Sasha's awareness of and identification with that nonbelonging enables the projective aspect of her impression.

What completes her ability to identify with him, however, is the ambiguity of his gender performance. Serge is positioned as feminine first by his willingness to dance for Sasha:

Serge puts some béguine music, Martinique music, on an old gramophone in the corner and asks whether I'd like to dance.
"No, I'd rather watch you."
He holds the mask over his face and dances. "To make you laugh," he says. He dances very well. His thin, nervous body looks strange, surmounted by the hideous mask. (*GM, M* 92)

Watching Serge dance, Sasha relaxes into the unusual role of spectator and judge.[68] The West African mask Serge holds in front of his face partly protects him from that judgment, and yet contributes to his vulnerability as a spectacle. He is racialized by this display, rendered exotic. And he is feminized by his willingness to accept her gaze, by his dancing, and by his "nervous" body. Moreover, Serge freely admits to being moved by art to the point of weeping: when they "seriously discuss the subject of weeping," he says that he cries about Van Gogh. "When he gives me a cigarette his hand is shaking. He isn't lying. I think he has really cried over Van Gogh" (*GM, M* 94). Both Jewish men and artists were so often feminized in fiction and popular discourses of the early twentieth century that these signs only confirm the association with femininity created by the label "Jewish painter."

Sasha's response to his dance is to embark on a peaceful tropical fantasy: "I am lying in a hammock looking up into the branches of a tree. The sound of the sea advances and retreats as if a door were being opened and shut. All day there has been a fierce wind blowing, but at sunset it drops. The hills look like clouds and the clouds like fantastic hills" (*GM, M* 92). This is one of the most tranquil images that occurs to Sasha during the course of the novel. But the song that is playing on the gramophone highlights the pain she is always keeping at bay: "Pain of love, / Pain of youth, / Walk away from me, / Keep away from me, / Don't want to see you / No more, no more . . . " (*GM, M* 93). Just as the fantastic clouds and hills of her fantasy succeed a day of fierce wind, this pain is never far from Sasha's mind. But Serge enables her to project her negative feelings outward so that she gets a respite from them. It is as if by taking on the gendered roles within which Sasha usually finds herself caught – to be exposed and watched, to be masked and even grotesque – Serge has enabled her to externalize and disavow them. She sympathizes with him, but feels shielded by the mask. And his otherness (his racialization as a Jew and his association with the African) protects her from identifying too strongly with him, from knowing too much. This set of simultaneous identifications and distancings frees her, albeit temporarily, from the expectation and fear of exposure and mockery.

The painting she chooses to buy from him sparks in her a similar dynamic of sympathy and distancing, and becomes a locus for Rhys's exploration of time as it is filtered through Sasha's consciousness. "It is an old Jew with a red nose, playing the banjo" (*GM, M* 100). Although Serge does not believe she can pay him (as described in chapter 1), he gives her the picture, asking only that she "find some other idiots who'll buy [his] paintings" (*GM, M* 100). "Exalted" by his kindness and the power of his art, she leaves his studio without dwelling, as she has these several days in Paris, on the humiliations of the past: "Now I am not thinking of the past at all. I am well in the present" (*GM, M* 101).

Sasha's positive feeling about Serge and his paintings is renewed when she receives a letter from him, apologizing for not turning up to collect the money. Her paraphrase of the letter ends, "and he is my friend, Serge Rubin. Well, I'll have a whiskey on that" (*GM, M* 109). In its offer to exchange the painting for a more cheerful one, the letter emphasizes Serge's sympathy with Sasha's emotional state. This understanding has a fuller expression in a letter Rhys received from Serge's original, Simon Segal, a Russian Jewish painter Rhys met in Paris (a portrait by Segal appears on the cover of this book).[69] In Segal's letter to Rhys, however, he does not offer to change the painting; instead, he encourages her to use her pain in the service of her art.

He writes:

I hope you will enjoy my little man playing the banjo. He's unhappy, dignified, and uncomplaining, like wise men, artists and madmen. Maybe he will give you strength. Do not despair. I know pain is the "unique nobility," as Baudelaire said. And it is from the depths of our terrible grief that the spark and creative flow finally shoot forth. Believe me, I too often suffer – always, deeply. But I like this suffering because it alone never betrays me, and gives me courage and a beautiful fury.[70]

This letter puts beautifully what Rhys seems to have lived and written, even providing a rationale for clinging to one's suffering. It shows a respect for Rhys as a writer that, since Sasha is not an artist, can only be faintly echoed in the fictional letter. Segal's descriptions of the man as "dignified and uncomplaining" and like a "madman" seem to spur Sasha's characterization of the man in the painting as "gentle, humble, resigned, mocking, a little mad" (*GM, M* 109). But perhaps the most important trace of Segal's letter, which so sympathetically acknowledges Rhys's anguish, is that Serge's letter seems to bring Sasha closer to her traumatic past. She approaches it not by remembering anything in particular, but by being drawn into a different sense of time. From being "well in the present," she seems to verge upon the "No time region" that Rhys wanted her to enter.

After reading Serge's letter, Sasha takes out the painting.

I unroll the picture and the man standing in the gutter, playing his banjo, stares at me. He is gentle, humble, resigned, mocking, a little mad. He stares at me. He is double-headed, double-faced. He is singing "It has been," singing "It will be." Double-headed and with four arms . . . I stare back at him and think about being hungry, being cold, being hurt, being ridiculed, as if it were in another life than this. (*GM, M* 19)

Here Rhys uses the painting as an *ekphrastic* device that "tells in full" what Sasha can only vaguely apprehend.[71] The man in the painting conjures her sense of loss ("being cold, being hurt") and exposure ("being ridiculed"). Sasha's repeated statement that he stares at her evokes a sense of being drawn in by his powerful gaze, of being unable to avoid her own troubled past even when faced with this marker of one of her happiest moments. His doubled quality, with his two heads and four arms, seems to account for the song Sasha imagines him singing, a song of both the past and the future. The song is even a bit menacing, suggesting that what has been (hunger, cold, mockery), will continue to be.

This threat recalls the *ekphrasis* in *After Leaving Mr. Mackenzie* (1931) that Mary Lou Emery has discussed in her article "Refiguring the Postcolonial Imagination." In that scene the woman in the Modigliani painting says to Julia Martin, "I am more real than you. But at the same time I *am* you. I am all that matters of you."[72] Here, too, the man in the painting seems to make visible, or narratable, the pain and repetition that define Sasha's life. Through Sasha's description of the painting, Rhys anchors the narrative to the underlying trauma.

This propulsion into the past is part of a larger propulsion into timelessness. When Sasha sees her pain made visible in the painting, she disowns it. And her disavowal is crucially nontemporal. She distances herself from trauma not by situating it in the distant past, but by feeling "as if it were in another life than this." (Given the constant threat that the past will repeat itself, this is perhaps the only way Sasha can distance herself from the pain.) It is as if the moments of pain and of serenity exist side by side rather than in any chronological order. The painting of the Jew has become a key site through which the narrative conveys the timelessness Rhys envisioned as crucial to the novel.

Part II ends with Sasha looking at the painting and finding her room "saturated with the past." With the pun on "saturated" (Serge's paintings are "vivid" even in "dim light"), Rhys suggests that the painting and the room are both alive with memory. The letter (its original hovering behind it) and the painting prompt Sasha to sink into her past, seeing it again as if it were projected onto a movie screen. "Now the whole thing moves in an ordered, undulating procession past my eyes. Rooms, streets, streets, rooms . . . " (*GM, M* 109). This serves as an introduction to Sasha's immersion in memories narrated as though they were present in part III.

Sasha returns to the painting at the end of the novel, when René has left and she is crying "in the way that hurts right down." "Don't forget the picture, to remind you of – what was it to remind you of? Oh, I know – of human misery" (*GM, M* 185). She has been catapulted by René's cruelty into a traumatic episode – it is in the midst of her split between a wounded and a sarcastic response – and her reaction to the painting contains both identification and hostility:

And I'll look back at him because I shan't be able to help it, remembering about being young, and about being made love to and making love, about pain and dancing and not being afraid of death, about all the music I've ever loved, and every time I've been happy. I'll look back at him and I'll say: "I know the words to the tune you're playing. I know the words to every tune you've ever played on your bloody banjo." (*GM, M* 185)

Sue Thomas astutely notes the temporal complexity of this scene: "Under the pressure of his gaze Sasha relives her past (given the immediacy of present-tense narration) and imagines a future in which she *remembers* 'about being young . . . .' "[73] I would go further and say that under the compulsion of the Jew's eyes, past and present become indistinguishable, as do pleasure and pain. From within her traumatic dissociation, Sasha no longer needs the Jew to create a sense of timelessness with his imagined music. She knows the words to the song in which past and future mingle; she will embrace the end of time by reenacting the sexual trauma that has haunted her, as she lies and waits for "the thing that is bound to happen."

These issues of trauma and timelessness help to contextualize the much-debated end of the novel, in which Sasha accepts into her bed the menacing figure of the man in the white dressing-gown whom she has labeled a *commis voyageur*. While she is still in Serge's flat, Sasha thinks about living in an empty room like it, and about "the dreams that you have, alone in an empty room, waiting for the door that will open, the thing that is bound to happen" (*GM, M* 100). In this fantasy the subject imagines leaving herself physically vulnerable and conceives such vulnerability as fate. At the end of the novel, Sasha plays out this fantasy by unlocking the door and lying down naked on her bed, willing René to return, but accepting her ghostly neighbor when he comes instead.

Some Rhys critics read this acceptance as redemptive.[74] But there is nothing in the novel to suggest that Sasha's reaction to the *commis* changes from one of horror. This man has knocked on her door earlier in the week, in his "beautiful dressing-gown, immaculately white, with long wide, hanging sleeves . . . He looks like a priest, the priest of some obscene, half-understood religion" (*GM, M* 35). She asks him what he wants but he only says "nothing" and continues to stand there, smiling.

I put my hand on his chest, push him backwards and bang the door. It's quite easy. It's like pushing a paper man, a ghost, something that doesn't exist.
And there I am in this dim room with the bed for madame and the bed for monsieur and the narrow street outside (what they call an impasse), thinking of that white dressing-gown, like a priest's robes. Frightened as hell. A nightmare feeling . . . (*GM, M* 35)

When the *commis* comes into her room later, she knows without looking that it is he and not René. She feels that she needs to know which dressing-gown he is wearing:

I think: "Is it the blue dressing-gown, or the white one? That's very important. I must find that out – it's very important."
I take my arm away from my eyes. It is the white dressing-gown.
He stands there, looking down at me. Not sure of himself, his mean eyes flickering.

Since his white dressing-gown reminded her of a priest of some "obscene" religion, it seems that Sasha is interested not in humanizing the neighbor, but rather in enduring the horror he represents. The "nightmare feeling" he sparks in her overwhelms the spin Sasha puts on her submission to this dread-inspiring figure when she says, "I look straight into his eyes and despise another poor devil of a human being for the last time. For the last time . . . " (*GM, M* 190).

In my view, what happens at the end of the novel is that Sasha is unable to continue her project of "arrang[ing] her little life" so as to suppress her painful memories: conscious ones of losing her baby, and of other losses, as well as repressed ones that half-surface in moments of fragmented memory and dissociation. Her defenses have been temporarily shredded by the incident with René, and the unraveling process carries her along even when he fails to return. She begins to relive the traumatic past she has been dodging throughout the novel. Releasing her hold on the boundaries that are supposed to keep her safe but continually break down anyway, Sasha submits to the repetitive character of trauma.

Against René's brutality in the earlier scene, she felt as "strong as the dead." "I lie very still, I don't move." Keeping still is just what the young and powerless Rhys did when Mr. Howard touched her on the bench: "I sit perfectly still staring at the branch of the tree which hangs over the bench thinking this is a mistake a mistake doesnt know if I sit quite still & dont move he take his hand away and wont know realize that he has touched me."[75] Rhys, obviously writing quickly and freely, omits the pronoun before the phrase "doesnt know," suggesting not only that Mr. Howard does not realize what he is doing, but also that her girl-self may have refused to "know" what was happening to her, or that the adult Rhys was still protecting herself against full knowledge. In Sasha, stillness and passivity are the nonactions of the traumatized self. Now when she waits for René to return but accepts the *commis* who gives her the "nightmare feeling", she has ceased struggling to keep the victim-self represented by the "film mind" at bay. She accepts the return of trauma with the triple "yes" at the novel's end.

Several critics have read this final " 'Yes – yes – yes' " of the novel as an ironic, mocking version of Molly Bloom's affirmative cry. Certainly this allusion signifies a response to and revision of Joyce's version of "woman." But the contrast with Molly's stereotypically earthy sexuality makes Sasha's yeses more disturbing than such a reading acknowledges. Sasha's yeses go beyond irony to invert and even pervert the affirmation that Joyce imagined for Molly. Rhys described her own abuse as "cruelty submission utter submission."[76] Sasha's submission to the *commis* is akin to the reluctance to resist humiliation that we find in the dissociated "film mind" and in Rhys's account of her abuse. The repeated yeses indicate most meaningfully a helpless acceptance of the repetition of trauma.

It is the projection of the mental states intrinsic to trauma that defines Jewishness in *Voyage in the Dark* and *Good Morning, Midnight*. Rhys's protagonists view the figure of the Jew as an emblem of their own uncertainties. They find in him a reflection and embodiment of their alienation and pain; they see him as situated in the liminal space in which their own psyches reside. Displaced by exile and split by trauma, these Rhys women identify with and distance themselves from the figure of the Jew who echoes those conditions. Anna Morgan views Jewishness as a continual possibility, something like her own past, lingering within the present. Sasha Jansen sees both pain and timelessness in the painting of the "Jew with the red nose," but moves away from her identification with the painting, retreating into a hostility that in the end she turns back onto herself. When Sasha imagines the Jew in the painting singing "It has been . . . . It will be," she echoes the sense of stasis, of time folding in on itself, given first in the paradoxical title, *Good Morning, Midnight*. The Jew's song intimates the doomed sense of repetition around which Rhys has crafted her disquieting novel.

Nightwood, too, is haunted by a sense of doom, of past pain repeating itself, which is conjured by Jewish history. The "degradation" of the Jewish past lives in Guido's throat; the grandmother's abandonment lives in Robin's wandering. Jewishness and its accompanying themes – continuity, patriarchy, exogamy – help the text to establish their opposing counterparts in the story of Nora and Robin. Felix's obsession with continuity underscores Robin's utter lack of it, highlighting the eerie sense of timelessness that clings to her. His worship of patriarchy contrasts Robin's association with Nora's grandmother, establishing a strong opposition between heterosexual and homosexual love and aligning heterosexual mating with women's oppression (though homosexual love does not turn out to be a healthier alternative). And finally, Felix's desire to marry "out" opposes and emphasizes Nora's and Robin's identity or sameness, making room for the text to meditate on the meaning of enmeshment and incest. Like *Voyage in the Dark* and *Good Morning, Midnight*, *Nightwood* constructs Jewishness as a kind of scaffolding that allows the text to approach its most painful and important subjects.[77]

6
Metatextual Jewishness: shaping feminist modernism

In the previous chapters I have focused on the thematic and political functions of Jewishness in key modernist texts. In this concluding chapter I describe additional functions of Jewishness that occur on a metatextual level as the authors enlist their representations of Jews to shape their particular versions of modernism. The Jews in these texts serve as models, foils, and scapegoats for aspects of the authors' artistic approaches. Focusing on these metatextual processes reinforces and sharpens the argument, conveyed throughout this study, that feminist modernism relies on Jewishness for its own self-fashioning.

For Jean Rhys and Sylvia Townsend Warner, the metatextual functions of Jewishness arise more or less directly from their sympathetic thematic enlistment of their Jewish figures. For Djuna Barnes, *Nightwood*'s somewhat grotesque evocation of Jewishness serves as a ground for an ambivalent metatextual response. For Dorothy Richardson and Virginia Woolf, a metatextual Jewishness that is distinct from their thematic treatment of Jews gathers powerful implications for their modernist projects. This chapter briefly revisits the work of Rhys, Warner, and Barnes before teasing out these implications in Richardson and Woolf.

As I argue in chapter 1, Rhys and Warner use their Jewish characters as models for disinterested art, opposing them to the financial interest that dominates the commercialized world of publishing. These *characters* are not idealized: Serge arrogantly assumes the Martiniquean woman wants sex and later he fails to show up to bid Sasha farewell; Minna is greedy for attention and unscrupulous in her revolutionary activities. Yet what they represent on a metatextual level is an idealized artistic sphere, an arena in which artistic integrity takes priority over money and power. These two authors use Jewishness against the grain to signal their longing for a space where art can flourish outside of commodity exchange. This imagining of an idealized realm allows them to criticize mass-market control of literary production. It also, by implication, associates their own art with such an idealized realm. Although the novels' protagonists are Sasha and Sophia, Serge and Minna can be seen as their authors' immodest doppelgangers. Their art is disinterested and yet compelling, and it compels only to freedom. Like Serge's paintings and Minna's narrative, Rhys's and Warner's writings convey a sense of wonder and expansion: "Now the room expands and the iron band around my heart loosens. The miracle has happened" (*V* 99).

Through their fictional Jewish presences, Rhys and Warner position their own art as superior to that made on the basis of economic exchange or any other use-value. For Warner, this includes the usefulness of art to Communism. Minna's narrative, useless as propaganda because of her delight in her own effectiveness (as Ingelbrecht points out in the novel), serves as a model for the kind of art that a just society must protect. In a move diametrically opposed to Woolf's use of the Jew in *The Years* (1937), Rhys and Warner invert antisemitic discourses in order to align themselves with a disinterested sphere of artistic creation.[1]

Jewishness functions metatextually in more contradictory ways in *Nightwood* (1936). Barnes uses Jewishness as both a model and a foil for her modernist aesthetic. Lara Trubowitz argues persuasively that Jewishness becomes a sign of the fragmentation and dissolution – the wandering – that Barnes draws upon to compose her elusive narrative. Analyzing the link between Jewishness and the "flowers brought to a pitch of florid ecstasy [that] no sooner attain their specific type than they fall into its decay," Trubowitz asserts that "both the flower and the Jewish Guido become nothing more than an integral analogy for the inevitably linked 'blooming' and 'decay' of the narration of *Nightwood* itself."[2] She reads the novel's final chapter not as "a failure of narrative but, quite the contrary, the novel's natural progression and triumph – the ecstasy of the text's 'florid' style 'naturally' followed by its 'wilting.'"[3] In this reading *Nightwood* uses Jewishness as a model for narration, employing its burgeoning and disappearance as a template for its own dynamic structure.

In addition, when Barnes uses Felix's false past to signal a psychological breach or emptiness, as I describe in chapter 5, she is using him as a mirror for the mystery and psychological confusion that makes her narrative so compelling. Mairéad Hanrahan's claim, which I quote in that chapter, reinforces this sense that Jewishness functions as an exemplar of lack or emptiness. When Hanrahan writes that "For Barnes, the Jew's condition crystallizes a predicament she considers general: the failure of representation itself," she suggests that the Jewishness Barnes imagines is intimately related to her modernist project.[4] In these ways Barnes uses Jewishness – though it is defined negatively – as a productive model for the modernism she is creating.

But Barnes also uses Jewishness as a foil against which she can define her modernist style when she represents it as a racialized past and the source of Felix's homage to continuity, whether that continuity takes the form of aristocracy, individual identity, or communal history. With his belief in and longing for the fullness of identity, Felix stands for a kind of oneness that contrasts with the multiplicity of the narrative. Andrea L. Harris writes:

In *Nightwood* identity, meaning the sameness and oneness of the self, is repeatedly undone and erased by the force of the night and the anonymity that is associated with it. Barnes's text is the opposite of the discourse of sameness: with otherness and multiplicity as its key terms, it works at undoing sameness. In *Nightwood*, coherent identity is a fiction that only comes to be through a repression of otherness.[5]

It is ironic that in this novel of multiplicity and difference, Jewishness, elsewhere treated as difference *par excellence*, comes to represent sameness, a patriarchal oneness and sign of continuity that functions as a foil for the narrative's "undoing" of sameness.

Jewishness works as a foil for Barnes in another way as well. Felix's nature is to "bow down" to anyone or anything sanctioned by high society. He has inherited this obsession from his father Guido, who "had prepared out of his own heart for his coming child a heart, fashioned on his own preoccupation, the remorseless homage to nobility, the genuflexion the hunted body makes from muscular contraction, going down before the impending and inaccessible" (*N* 2–3). Such a conformist bent opposes Barnes's relentlessly individual modernism. Discussing this individuality in the context of French symbolism, Cheryl J. Plumb stresses the opposition of conformity versus individuality:

Once Barnes's work is set against a background of symbolist assumptions and methods, it becomes clear that her work consistently focuses on consciousness and moral integrity and on the superior sensibility, represented in her work by artist figures . . . Within this context her art, rich in its complexity, is discovered to be centrally related to a dialogue that had dominated American literature, a dialogue between individual values and identity and social conformity.[6]

In these terms Felix's conformity defines by contrast the superior sensibility of Nora and Matthew, and by implication Barnes's own art.

Plumb also stresses a closely related aspect of Barnes's aesthetic: her valorization of the idiosyncratic. "In addition, fiction that focuses on 'characteristic detail,' or the 'act by which a man distinguishes himself from other men' [the words are Rémy de Gourmont's], exploits not social conditions but the individual, the idiosyncratic, the unusual."[7] Felix and his family stand not for the individual but for the collective. As I describe in chapter 4, the history of Felix's family and indeed his "race" is stressed by the narrative, as if without it the Jewish characters would be meaningless. Robin and Nora, on the other hand, seem to emerge from nowhere. Although Felix is described as being "everywhere from nowhere," it is the women characters who are without histories. The familial, social, and racial identities of the Jews in the novel contrast with and again highlight the individual and idiosyncratic identities of Nora, Robin, and the novel itself.

While Barnes's depiction of Jews is unflattering on the level of both character and theme, her metatextual use of Jewishness is ambivalent, in that she enlists Jewishness as both model and foil for her aesthetic aims. Dorothy Richardson's use of Jewishness is, we might say, the inverse of Barnes's. *Pilgrimage*'s relatively unambiguous disavowal of the elements it associates with Jewishness contrasts with its sympathetic portrait of its Jewish character. In spite of her generally positive portrayal of Michael Shatov – Miriam Henderson values his friendship, comes alive intellectually through conversations with him, begins translating literature because of his encouragement, and seriously considers marrying him – Richardson uses Jewishness to define her artistic goals by contrasting her modernism with Shatov's linearity and generality.

Because the novel is a *Künstlerroman*, Miriam's observations about literature, writing, and perception represent the development of what Lynette Felber calls Richardson's "femimodernist" aesthetic.[8] It is through Miriam's interest in and subsequent frustration with Michael that she realizes the extent to which she values individual perceptions, even when they turn out to be mistaken. In *Dawn's Left Hand* (1931), for example, Miriam meets a woman on the train, comes to various conclusions about her which are described at length, and then realizes they were all misperceptions. Miriam never meets the woman again, and readers may wonder why her wrongheaded assumptions were given so much time in the narrative. But this emphasis on her character's peculiar responses for their own sake, rather than for their accuracy, is one of the key elements of Richardson's modernism.

Indeed, one of the most striking things about *Pilgrimage* is its sheer bulk of detail – detail always filtered through Miriam's consciousness. Miriam meticulously describes her thoughts, her responses to people she meets, her surroundings. As Jean Radford puts it, there is "an excessive proliferation of elements whose function seems purely referential."[9] That is, although many thematic elements function on the allegorical level, the great mass of details in *Pilgrimage* is *not* symbolic, *not* resonant with thematic concerns. Radford discusses this piling up of observation, differentiating it from nineteenth-century realist detail:

Pilgrimage breaks with the nineteenth-century contract described by [Roland] Barthes. It uses physical description, descriptive detail, repeatedly and at great length, not to produce the "reality effect" but to produce a resistance to meaning. Richardson's use of detail is a device to delay or impede meaning-construction, to slow up the reading and "hold up the development of the whole" (I, 11) which Richardson thought desirable in the novel . . . In other words, the particularism of *Pilgrimage* is a reaction to master narratives, to the conviction that all the major discursive modes – "history, literature, the way of stating records" – were "on a false foundation."[10]

Radford quotes here from the foreword to *Pilgrimage*, written in 1938, where Richardson agrees with Goethe that the "thought-processes of the principal figure must, by one device or another, hold up the development of the whole." This slow and roundabout progression prevents the narrative from becoming what Richardson views as a masculine, linear, plot-driven novel.

In *March Moonlight* (1967), as Miriam becomes the woman who will write *Pilgrimage*, she reflects on the verbal habits of village people:

But the best and, for me, the most searching moment of the afternoon was the sudden perception of what lies behind the "simple" person's inability to summarize, behind the obvious deep enjoyment, particularly remarkable in women, of the utmost possible elaboration of a narrative, of what is evoked in the speaker's mind, while in torment one waits for the emergent data: "Well now, let me think. It couldn't have been a *Thursday*, because I've been out working every Thursday this month . . . " (*P* IV, 569)

This kind of narrative, she realizes, actually demonstrates "the deep delight of the dancer of the interminable *pas seul* in honour of the joy of life at first hand" (*P* IV, 569). The chains of association that make up *Pilgrimage* are validated retroactively, as Miriam comes to recognize the importance of detailed perception for conveying the "joy of life." Richardson's modernism privileges particularity, interiority, and instability over summaries, fact, and linearity.

Michael, however, as I demonstrate in chapter 2, stands for the very generality and definitiveness that *Pilgrimage* works against. His focus on the letter instead of the spirit means he cannot appreciate musings that do not lead to accurate conclusions. His views about the importance of race, continuity, and procreation further oppose *Pilgrimage*'s emphasis on the particularity of a woman's perceptions: his appreciation of wholes – nations and races – prevents him from recognizing the particularity of any one member. Miriam thinks that with Michael, "There was no need to do or be anything, individual. It was too easy. It must be demoralizing" (*P* III, 151). Richardson had a similar response to Michael's original, her Jewish suitor Benjamin Grad. According to John Rosenberg, Richardson grew tired of "all this thought and these ideas that . . . stopped short of life, and distracted her from what was more important, from seeing things minutely: the streets, people's faces."[11] Readers of *Pilgrimage* cannot fail to see that Miriam's "minute" examination of her surroundings comprises the heart of the novel.

This sort of psychological particularism places great value on interiority. Richardson aimed to present Miriam's idiosyncratic perceptions without falling into egotism. She wrote to Owen Wadsworth in 1923:

Information there must be, but the moment it is given directly as information, the sense of immediate experience is gone. Yet [to present] nothing but immediate experience spells the titanic failure of Joyce. It is the great & abiding problem of all those who take the inward way, this business of getting something tremendously there as it were unawares. I haven't solved it. But a recognition of it all the time is necessary in order to avoid total wreckage of the sense of direct experience. (*W* 68)

Although Richardson was wary of what she saw as James Joyce's self-absorption, she was nevertheless committed to taking "the inward way." Miriam reflects this aesthetic desire, translating it into terms that fit her life. She wants throughout *Pilgrimage* to find the mental space to go down into her "centre of being." In *Interim* (1920) she concludes that there is only one thing that "came near and meant anything at all. It was happiness and realization" (*P* II, 322). The word "realization" marks a parallel between Miriam's life and Richardson's work: Richardson used it to describe parts of the novel that satisfied her. When a passage or novel did not, it was "imperfectly realized."[12] To find realization, to go to the center of her being, Miriam needs the practical counterpart of the aesthetic "inward way": silence.

Michael continually interjects his definite views into her attempts at silence. He looks always outward, opposing Miriam's affinity for stillness as well as Richardson's attempt to write the interior of her character's mind. In fact, in *Deadlock* (1921) Michael warns Miriam, "'Beware of solipsism'" (*P* III, 171). He threatens to undo the sense, for Miriam and for the narrative, that other minds exist only insofar as they teach her lessons and either prevent or further her journey to her center. The narrative does allow for some sympathy for Michael's view, of course. His objections to Miriam's self-absorption serve as a warning against the very egotism Richardson worries about in her letter to Wadsworth. But Michael's bias in favor of wholes is much more strongly the antithesis of Richardson's aesthetic creed than Joyce's egotistical barrage of detail.

Although Hypo Wilson is as definite and voluble as Michael, Jewishness in *Pilgrimage* seems especially opposed to silence. In *Dimple Hill* (1938) Amabel has visited Miriam at the Quaker farm and met Richard Roscorla, whom Miriam is considering marrying. Miriam asks her what she thinks of the Quaker family: "'Then they don't make you want to fly for your life?' 'No, Mira . . . There's only one thing I couldn't stand. My God, those awful silences!'" (*P* IV, 522–523). The women have just been discussing Amabel's impending marriage to Michael, so their talk implies a comparison with the world Amabel will enter with him. An opposition is established between Judaism and Quakerism, speech and silence. Miriam has been enamored of Quakerism and Richard precisely because of their silences, and Amabel's "repudiation of what most attracted" Miriam only confirms its appeal (*P* IV, 523).

Michael's volubility and definitiveness, aligned as they are with masculine norms of logic and coherence, serve as foils against which Richardson constructs her feminist modernism. Jacqueline Rose describes it this way: "Coherence, sequence, continuity, teleology – all these insignia of patriarchal language and culture, these aesthetic markers to which so much of modernist experimentation by women, although not only by women, comes as the response – are handed over to the Jewish conception of destiny."[13] They are handed over in order to sketch the outlines of that which *Pilgrimage* is not, so as more clearly to define what it is. Jewishness is productive for *Pilgrimage* in this negative way – negative in the sense of both disparaged and inverted – assisting its self-promotion as feminist, interior, meditative, and deeply particular.

Like Richardson, Woolf uses Jewishness as a foil against which she can define her own artistic approaches; but she also adds another element, that of the scapegoat, to her employment of Jewishness, placing metatextual blame on the Jewish figure for a difficult "turn" in her aesthetic aims. As I demonstrate in chapter 1, Woolf uses the figure of a Jew in *The Years* (1937) to signal the threat to imaginative autonomy and mental privacy posed by financial interest. Here I focus on the context surrounding this linkage, sketching out the connections between her use of this figure and her anxieties about an outward shift in her fiction of the middle and late 1930s. Not only does Woolf use Abrahamson to represent money interest, but she also uses the Jewishness of Leonard's family in her letters and diaries throughout the 1930s to represent bodiliness. In both cases the material element associated with Jewishness (money, the body) serves as a foil for her own modernism, as Woolf struggles to maintain the "spirituality" or "vision" of her work even while embracing a more "factual" and external world in her fiction.

Several critics have noted that in the 1930s Woolf felt public events pressing closer than ever before. As Jed Esty writes, it became urgent for Woolf, "an intellectual pacifist," to consider how she could "respond to the growing menace of fascism . . . and what stance [she could] take in relation to the wagon-circling patriotism of the late 1930s."[14] Woolf mentions Hitler's activities frequently in her diaries during the 1930s, and often comments on external pressures. For example, in March of 1938 she writes that "the public world very notably invaded the private at MH. last week end. Almost war" (*Diary* V, 131). Such external pressures weighed even more heavily on her because Leonard was Jewish, making the Woolfs obvious targets of fascist violence. When she was preparing for their trip to Germany in 1935, she was painfully aware of the threat Leonard's Jewishness posed for her, calling herself a Jew in letters to friends: "Oh so many dreary letters to dispatch – German Embassy today to get a letter out of Prince Bismarck, since our Jewishness is said to be a danger" (*Letters* V, 386).[15] Before her marriage Woolf's Englishness was already tenuous because she was a woman, as she notes in *Three Guineas* (1938) (*TG 108*), but now Leonard's Jewishness began to define her as well, requiring the protection of Prince Bismarck, and raising fears for her life should the Nazis invade England. When Woolf referred to herself as Jewish, she was acknowledging the power of external events and definitions.

Demonstrating her awareness that her identity was shifting without her consent, Woolf wrote a letter of introduction into the scene in *The Years*: Sara Pargiter needs such a letter to be admitted to the newspaper office where she goes to apply for a job. In the 1934 drafts of the scene,

Elvira does not yet have a letter of introduction; she simply tells the man at the office that her grandfather went to Eton. But as Woolf revised the scene soon after her trip to Germany, the letter of introduction she and Leonard brought to Germany seems to have worked its way in, becoming Sara's "talisman": "'But I had a talisman, a glowing gem, a lucent emerald' – she picked up an envelope that lay on the floor – 'a letter of introduction. And I said to the flunkey in the peach-blossom trousers, Admit me, sirrah'" (*Years* 341). Woolf's use of the letter of introduction points to the powerful social significance that her marriage to Leonard had assumed.

This significance was intensified by her increasing feeling of isolation from Leonard and from her friends, most of whom abandoned their pacifism to support rearmament. Alex Zwerdling notes that in her continued pacifism, "she differed from other left-wing intellectuals of her time, including her husband" and that her views "increasingly [brought] her into conflict with those on her own side."[16] Especially after 1935, Leonard's views differed significantly from Woolf's. Hermione Lee agrees with Zwerdling that this issue caused "prolonged and unresolved" tension between them.[17] This disagreement placed pressure on Woolf to "sign on" by supporting Britain's rearmament. In 1936 she wondered if she should resign from the Labour Party over its support for rearmament. "Aldous [Huxley] refuses to sign the latest manifesto because it approves sanctions. He's a pacifist. So am I. Ought I to resign [from the Labour Party]. L[eonard] says that considering Europe is now on the verge of the greatest smash for 600 years, one must sink private differences and support the League" (*Diary* V, 17). As England coalesced into an antifascist, militarized bloc that itself threatened free imagination, and in spite of her personal fears, Woolf did not yield to the pressure to support military solutions. But she did decide to expand the ways her fiction engaged with the sociopolitical world. She shifted her narrative focus, portraying characters "from every side; turn[ing] them towards society" (*Letters* VI, 116).

Although the antifascist feminist essay that would become *Three Guineas* was simmering in her head, she postponed it to write the "essay-novel" *The Pargiters/The Years*. She wanted this novel to emphasize anonymity and "facts" instead of personality and "vision" (*Diary* IV, 151). But addressing the world of facts created a new aesthetic problem, making the novel extremely difficult for Woolf to write. Her diaries of the mid-1930s keep returning to her distress, which she is sure is worse than it had been with earlier novels. "I'm worried too with my last chapters. Is it all too shrill and voluble?" (*Diary* IV, 234). "Seldom have I been more completely miserable than I was . . . reading over the last part of The Years. Such feeble twaddle . . . [Leonard] said This always happens. But I felt, no it has never been so bad as this" (*Diary* V, 8). She had been wondering since 1933 how she could include "millions of ideas [in this novel] but no preaching?" (*Diary* IV, 152). She was "doubtful of the value of those figures . . . afraid of the didactic" (*Diary* IV, 144–145).

This turn away from "vision" and toward "ideas" was an important and anxiety-provoking shift in Woolf's art. Although she had never hidden from social issues behind a cloak of hermetically beautiful language, as some early critics suggested, she had certainly emphasized, especially in *To the Lighthouse* (1927) and *The Waves* (1931), her characters' interior lives. These lives were politically inflected, and Woolf had astutely analyzed the effects of patriarchal tyranny on the psyches of both male and female characters. Now, though, she stressed social more than psychological results of oppression, refusing to allow her characters profound or even coherent meditations. As she was "breaking the mould made by The Waves" (*Diary* IV, 233), she had to "reassure herself that her studied denial of lyricism and inner life [was] not misguided."[18] She needed to reassure herself because her new focus on the visible aspects of people, on the surfaces of objects, on social, communal life, could not completely allay the loss involved in turning away from the interior life and embarking on the often painful work of her novel of "fact."

One of the ways Woolf expresses her anxieties about this shift is through the antisemitic scene in *The Years*. Sara's reaction to Abrahamson suggests an analogy between Sara's and Woolf's predicaments. Both Woolf and Sara are pressured by the proximity of a Jewish man to turn outward, to leave aside their own visions and identities in order to conform to socially sanctioned behaviors or points of view. Sara feels pressured to do this by writing for a newspaper, Woolf by supporting the use of force as a means of fighting fascism. Neither capitulates. Instead of renouncing her pacifism, Woolf decides to expand her inquiries (ongoing at least since *A Room of One's Own* [1929]) into the links between patriarchal and fascistic oppression, writing the political texts *The Pargiters/The Years* and *Three Guineas*.[19] Insofar as Woolf may have felt obliged by Leonard's status and its effects on her own identities to engage with sociopolitical realities in broader terms, we can see Sara's neighbor as an expression of Woolf's resentment about her aesthetic shift. Abrahamson is held responsible for the threat to Sara's mental freedom, but also, on a figurative level, for the threat to Woolf's. On a metatextual level he is blamed for the political and artistic pressures on

Woolf herself to give up her pacifism and to sacrifice her modernism of interiority and "vision."

In the earliest draft versions of these scenes, the threat to Sara's mental privacy came from Nicholas, who was at that stage (as I demonstrate elsewhere) her Jewish lover, and much closer to a representation of Leonard than Abrahamson could be.[20] This earlier characterization of the threat bolsters my sense that Woolf felt betrayed by Leonard's commitment to British rearmament, in spite of seeing, and feeling in her own person, the urgency of the Nazi threat. She responds to the challenge positively by committing to a new emphasis on "fact" in her work as she writes *The Pargiters/The Years*, and *Three Guineas*. (*Three Guineas* attempts to reconcile the acknowledgment of this threat with the pacifism in which Woolf still believed.) But alongside this aesthetic turn, Woolf also responds negatively, resenting the pressures pushing her in that direction: Jewishness, which she perhaps viewed as drawing her into the circle of danger, and the external itself, which was commanding her attention, "violating solitude" and "breaking into the privacy of [her] mind" (*Pargiters* 6:75). The figure of Abrahamson serves as a scapegoat on whom she can lay the blame for the difficulty involved in this artistic shift. Sara's aversion to him reveals the embittered underside of Woolf's commitment to the world of "fact."

The reasons behind this characterization include the link between Jews and financial interest which I demonstrate in chapter 1, and an additional link between Jews and the body which seems to motivate the corporeal details of the hair and grease in the bathtub that disgust Sara and North. A similar physical aversion animates Woolf's responses to Jews in her private writings. Expressing discomfort with bodiliness and sexuality, Woolf adapted for her private use a prevalent antisemitic discourse that associated Jews with the sexual, the material, the bodily. In turn, and on a broader level, this association serves a function similar to that performed by Abrahamson when he represents financial interest: it helps Woolf to differentiate herself, and implicitly her own writing, from the body, especially as her work begins to treat external reality more fully in the late 1930s.

Woolf began linking Jews to bodiliness when she was still Virginia Stephen. In an early letter to Leonard in which she details her feelings about his marriage proposal, she writes, "Then, of course, I feel angry sometimes at the strength of your desire. Possibly, your being a Jew comes in also at this point. You seem so foreign." She goes on to pinpoint his sexual interest in her as one of the chief obstacles to their marriage, writing,

"I sometimes think that if I married you, I could have everything – and then – is it the sexual side of it that comes between us?" (*Letters* I, 496). Leonard Woolf did not, objectively speaking, seem foreign in England. Born in London, educated at English public schools and continuing on to Trinity College, Cambridge, he was as English as any of Thoby Stephen's other friends, except for his self-consciousness about being a Jew. That Virginia Stephen linked his sexual desire to his Jewishness and to foreignness says more about her prejudices than about either Leonard's sexuality or his racial or national identity.

One of Woolf's early sketches, entitled "Jews," links Jews to the body via images of vulgarity, fat, food, and heat. In this 1909 sketch, Virginia Stephen describes having dinner at the house of a Mrs. Loeb. Mrs. Loeb is "kind, in her vulgar way" but "one wonders how [she] became a rich woman. It seems an accident. She might be behind a counter."[21] Both Mrs. Loeb and her food are described in terms of fat: she is a "fat Jewess" and "her food, of course, swam in oil and was nasty." Nevertheless, she "pressed everyone to eat, and feared, when she saw an empty plate, that the guest was criticising her." When Woolf describes the Loebs' house, she notes that "[t]hey had a great gas fire, burning in a florid drawing room."[22] The word "florid" is well-chosen here, since it refers both to the rosy heat cast by the fire and to the ornate, implicitly vulgar drawing room.[23] And the title of the sketch, "Jews," removes any doubt that Mrs. Loeb serves not merely as a particular human being but as a representative of Jews.

What strikes me about this brief, early piece is its similarity to Woolf's later descriptions of her mother-in-law, Marie Woolf. The same elements – a deadening middle-class vulgarity, rich, fattening food (cake in particular), and oppressive heat – link Mrs. Woolf as a Jew to the body in her daughter-in-law's diaries and letters throughout the 1930s, particularly during the period in which she was drafting and revising *The Years*. By this point, Woolf also adds an element to her Jews/body connection: she attributes to them a bodily vitality that keeps them alive in spite of all odds.

Woolf continually comments on her in-laws' middle-class vulgarity. In a letter to Ethel Smyth in 1930, she details the interruptions she has been facing:

Worst, superlatively worst, my mother in law has settled at Worthing . . . So that if she says can she come over on Friday . . . what can I do, but race off to Lewes, buy pink, red, and yellow cakes, cakes striped with sugar bars and dotted with chocolate spots, return just in time to collect chairs, light fire; and then – here they are, dressed, *like all Jews*, as if for high tea in a hotel lounge." (*Letters* IV, 222; italics added)

Even when Woolf frames her comments as positive, her view of the Woolfs as dully middle-class overwhelms the appreciative note:

Indeed, in spite of the glumness, grimness, and oh the intolerable middle class timidity respectability and lack of accent distinction adventure dash, daring colour – I cant describe to you the low level of all these childless people, with their uniformity of cars, dogs, country houses and gardens, – in spite of my damned snobbishness about them, I always feel slightly warmed and overcome by the entire absence of pretense, and the goodness, and the rightness – if it is right so to people the world – of the vast family to which as Herbert said, I have the honour to belong. (*Letters* IV, 241–242)

As Woolf makes clear in the letter about the Woolf family coming to visit, Marie Woolf had a fondness for cakes. Woolf mentions cakes many times in connection both with her mother-in-law and with boredom. One example from 1933 reads, "No, I had to go to my poor old mother in law; aged 85 ... we arrive at 5; choc cake; 'oh my dear V how you've cheered me after my dreadful day with George – ' So there I was, eating choc. cake some of which I conveyed secretly into my pocket, and not listening ... " (*Letters* V, 258). The fact that Woolf mentions her mother-in-law's fondness for cakes at regular intervals suggests that the image performs some service for her, helps her to define herself against Mrs. Woolf as one who resists indulgence, who is free from vulgar appetites. This need to distance herself from gluttony may be a result of Woolf's uneasiness about food, which intensified during her breakdowns.[24] But it also works to separate Woolf's life of the mind from the life of the body lived in the senior Woolf household. Woolf even uses cake as a metaphor to describe the dull, bourgeois atmosphere of her in-laws: "Well it was rather a glum, deliberate, middleaged assembly last night [Mrs. Woolf's birthday party] – all, oh my word, so much like cuts off one long yard of cake – slice after slice; no beauty, no eccentricity" (*Letters* IV, 241).

While Woolf consistently denies Leonard's family beauty, she does grant them a certain "vitality" to which she attributes Mrs. Woolf's longevity – which she describes as an inability to die. She writes to Ethel Smyth that "L's mother is still very ill, but at 83 she entirely refuses to die, and so they say, will persist in living" (*Letters* V, 154). She returns to this theme when she describes a romance Mrs. Woolf has been engaged in: "My mother in law, having for the past 5 years, carried on an elderly flirtation with an old man called Legge, who stood her Burgundy and took her on the pier, is now once more desolated, because the old man is naturally dying; which she cant do" (*Letters* V, 311). The paradox here is that it is "natural" to die, but Mrs. Woolf is so alive, so vital, that she, unnaturally, "cant do" it. When Mrs. Woolf is hurt by a fall, Woolf tells Smyth, "And now L's old mother has been knocked down, seriously hurt, and we have to spend hours trying to cheer her. The Jews can lament: but how they cling to life!" (*Letters* VI, 219). In her portraits of vital, vulgar Jews, Woolf recapitulates stereotypes common enough since the late nineteenth century that they also pepper Amy Levy's 1888 *Reuben Sachs*. In that novel Reuben Sachs's doctor attributes Sachs's nervous breakdown to his Jewishness, saying, "'You pay the penalty of too high a civilization.' 'On the other hand,' Reuben answered, 'we never die; so we may be said to have our compensations.'"[25]

The most elaborate version of this theme is contained in the famous letter where Woolf admits what a snob she was to "hate" marrying a Jew. As I note in chapter 1, no sooner has she admitted her snobbery than she proceeds to link Jews to physical vitality, sexuality, and money:

How I hated marrying a Jew – how I hated their nasal voices, and their oriental jewellery, and their noses and their wattles – what a snob I was: for they have immense vitality, and I think I like that quality best of all. They cant die – they exist on a handful of rice and a thimble of water – their flesh dries on their bones but still they pullulate, copulate, and amass (a Mrs Pinto, fabulously wealthy came in) millions of money. (*Letters* IV, 195–6)

The word "pullulate" sums up Woolf's view of Jews as representative of bodiliness. The OED defines it as "to sprout, to germinate; to be developed or produced as offspring, to spring up abundantly; to teem, to swarm." Woolf has associated Jews with the physical life force, in a way that she claims to admire at times but that clearly makes her uncomfortable and at times disgusted. Disgust can be seen, for example, in a letter to Clive Bell where she ends by writing "and here's Leonard come to hurry me off, to Worthing, to the aged, to the ugly. How I hate it – ugliness and age" (*Letters* IV, 64).

These letters were written nearly twenty years into Woolf's marriage. They do not demonstrate her snobbishness when she first gets to know the Woolf family, but instead offer a running refrain, one so consistent that it must serve to shore up some aspect of her identity. Leena Kore Schröder perceptively suggests that Woolf treats Jewishness as the abject, using it to help distance herself from her own fears of the body, sexuality, and death. To argue this, Schröder points to a revealing diary entry in which Woolf complains that the presence of her husband's family makes her day "cheap & ugly and commonplace," that Mrs. Woolf is "so fond

Metatextual Jewishness: shaping feminist modernism 187

of cakes, so incapable of amusing herself . . . , so vampire like & vast in her demand for my entire affection & sympathy," and ends, "Lord Lord! How many daughters have been murdered by women like this! What a net of falsity they spread over life. How it rots beneath their sweetness – goes brown & soft like a bad pear!" (*Diary* III, 320–321). As Schröder points out, "in this piece of rotting fruit is condensed Woolf's horror of corporeality itself . . . The decomposing fruit is . . . not so much an external object as it is that which determines identity from within, continually reminding her of what must be ejected or at best controlled in order to maintain the idea of self."[26] I would add that corporeality must be ejected also to maintain the ideal of Woolf's bodiless, "spiritual" modernism.

In fact, Woolf treats Leonard's family as a hindrance to her writing in her comments about the heat of her in-laws' house. The references to heat serve to compound the sense of a vulgar and oppressive vitality. She writes to Smyth, "And then my poor old mother in law gets blinder. and I get kinder Yes I'm very kind to her – but oh the heat of the room, the sweet sticky cakes (*Letters* VI, 106). Woolf's exaggerations about the number of people present at Woolf family gatherings add to the atmosphere of "teeming" Jews, heat, and oppressiveness, as when she writes to Vanessa, "On Saturday all the Wolves come – hundreds of them, and then I change my skin, and inhabit an extraordinary world. They talk incessantly. Whats it about God knows" (*Letters* VI, 58). In 1933 she describes a Woolf gathering, another birthday party for Mrs Woolf, in terms of both numbers and heat. "Tonight I slip on a magnificent dress of purple velvet and old lace and dine with 22 Jews and Jewesses to celebrate my mother in laws 84th birthday. And we shall play Bridge. And it'll be as hot as the monkey house. And tomorrow I shall have a headache and shan't be able to write" (*Letters* V, 239). In addition to the racialized comment, "hot as the monkey house," Woolf here blames the company of the Woolf family for an inevitable headache, and casts them as an obstacle to her work.

She repeats this idea in a short letter to Smyth in 1936, where she stresses the invariability of the cycle: see Woolf family, get headache, be unable to work. "No more [she writes]. The Wolves did me for the next day; but my mother in law was so delighted and so blind and so touching in her gratitude that I couldnt think my headache ill earned" (*Letters* VI, 62). The Woolf family, then, serves as an impediment to Woolf's creative force – they, too, apparently, break "into the privacy of the mind" (*Pargiters* 6: 75). This theme of blame for artistic blockage recalls the opening of the scene in

The Years. Much as North cannot overcome his disgust at the "thought of the line of grease" sufficiently to continue with the recitation, Woolf assumes that an evening with the Woolfs, in their hot house, eating cake and pretending to listen to the "hundreds" of Jews present, will similarly forestall her own imaginative autonomy and prevent her from working on her novel the next day.[27]

With her deep understanding of the ways in which material reality affects one's ability to write – expressed in *A Room of One's Own* and *Three Guineas* – and her traumatized relation to the body, Woolf seems to have been particularly aware of the dangers bodiliness posed to her work. What needs to be taken seriously is the extent to which she linked that dangerous bodily existence to Jewishness. Portraying Jews within an atmosphere of heat, food, and corporeality, Woolf associated Jewishness with a threat to mental autonomy. Over the course of the 1930s, she established a set of links between Jewishness and bodiliness that culminates in the image of the greasy Jew whose presence in Sara's building, like Leonard's family in Woolf's life, threatens mental freedom with its insistence on the animal nature of the body. Woolf thus uses Jewishness not only as a scapegoat for her outward aesthetic turn, but also as a foil for the act of writing itself. Jewishness becomes that which must be overcome to achieve artistic creation.

Woolf cast her writing, then, as spiritual as opposed to bodily through the material – financial, embodied – Jew. Her prejudices against Jews and Jewishness, while themselves conventional and unimaginative, were put in the service of her brilliant imagination until they functioned not only thematically to help shape her individual fictions, but also metatextually to help shape her modernism. Like Rhys, Warner, Barnes, and Richardson, Woolf found in the fictional Jew a floating signifier she could use to define the contours of her literary endeavors.

With the flexible and sometimes threatening power of that which crosses boundaries, Jewishness serves modernism as a sort of multipurpose tool (a Leatherman or Swiss Army knife if you will), whose components can be adapted to nearly any task. When modernists consider the possibilities for disinterested art, they think about the stereotype of the greedy Jew. When they work to create a modernism that supersedes masculine realism, they rely on the paradigm provided by the Christian supersession of Judaism. When they think about modernity, racial continuity, or timelessness, they enlist the plastic Jew to support their exploration of these temporal modes. And as they shape their modernist aesthetics, the authors use the exceptional adaptability of Jewishness to create models, foils, and scapegoats for their artistic aims.

About T. S. Eliot, Anthony Julius writes that "the exploitation of anti-Semitic discourse" is "an inseparable part of his greater literary undertaking. Exclude the anti-Semitic poems and one damages the integrity of *Ara Vos Prec*."[28] Antisemitism is integral, too, to Pound's and Lewis's conceptions of themselves and of their art.[29] And Hemingway, Lawrence, and Joyce similarly shape their modernist aesthetics in part by reference to Jewishness. In *The Sun Also Rises* (1926), Hemingway implicitly defines his modernism as deeply felt but without sentimentality, as raw, masculine, and spare, by contrast with Robert Cohn's sentimental and slobbery affections for art and for Brett Ashley. Lawrence uses Loerke in *Women in Love* (1920) as an example of a soulless and sterile artist, distinguishing his own compassionate and psychological fiction. And with happier but still mixed political results, Joyce uses Leopold Bloom in *Ulysses* (1922) to represent a bodiliness that needs to be incorporated into the sort of commodious modernism he is crafting.

I have argued in this study that Julius's assertion about Eliot applies equally well to feminist modernism. The antisemitism of Barnes, Richardson, and Woolf is milder than that of the "men of 1914" and Rhys and Warner use semitic discourse in more sympathetic ways. For this reason, and because of the lure of canonicity, it is not surprising that critics have scrutinized the allosemitism of male writers while discounting women writers' engagement with Jewishness. But the relative mildness of these women writers' treatment of Jews does not correspond to an equally mild *dependence* on Jewishness. On the contrary, feminist modernism relies on Jewishness as a shaping tool to tackle some of its most crucial thematic and structural challenges. Conceived in multivalenced ways, Jewishness bolsters and sustains the efforts of these women writers to create a feminist modernism that would surpass existing masculine models.

Notes

Introduction: imagined Jews and the shape of feminist modernism

1 Djuna Barnes insists on a reading of Jews similar to Milly's in its emphasis on atmosphere. Lara Trubowitz reproduces an exchange Barnes had with the editor Clifton Fadiman, who wrote to Barnes that "Jews are just like others – they're not haunted, superior[,] inferior, or anything else except in the proportion common to all races." Barnes wrote to her friend Emily Coleman, "[H]ow can he say that Jews are like others, not haunted or hunted. Were they neither of these then their past has not reverberated[.] The idiot man might as well say a church has no atmosphere." See Lara Trubowitz, "In Search of the Jew in Djuna Barnes's *Nightwood*: Jewishness, Antisemitism, Structure, and Style," *Modern Fiction Studies* 51.2 (2005), 313. Notice that it is Barnes who adds the word "hunted," since that fits with her conception of Jewishness in *Nightwood*.
2 Alain Finkielkraut, *The Imaginary Jew*, trans. Kevin O'Neill and David Suchoff (1983; Lincoln, NE: Bison Books, 1997).
3 Woolf calls Bennett, Galsworthy, and Wells "materialists" in "Modern Fiction." See Virginia Woolf, *The Common Reader: First Series* (London: The Hogarth Press, 1951), p. 185.
4 Zygmunt Bauman, "Allosemitism: Premodern, Modern, Postmodern," in Bryan Cheyette and Laura Marcus, eds., *Modernity, Culture and "the Jew"* (Stanford: Stanford University Press, 1998), p. 143.
5 Quoted in "The Challenge to Jewry: A Paradox of Persecution," *Times Literary Supplement*, June 13, 1936.
6 Slavoj Žižek, "'I Hear You with My Eyes'; or, The Invisible Master," in Renata Salecl and Slavoj Žižek, eds., *Gaze and Voice As Love Objects* (Durham: Duke University Press, 1996), p. 108.
7 Ibid., pp. 109–111.
8 Bauman, "Allosemitism," p. 144.
9 Ezra Pound, *The Cantos* (New York: New Directions, 1986), p. 229.
10 Maud Ellmann, "The Imaginary Jew: T. S. Eliot and Ezra Pound," in Bryan Cheyette, ed., *Between "Race" and Culture: Representations of "the Jew" in English and American Literature* (Stanford: Stanford University Press, 1996), p. 93.

11 Wyndham Lewis, *Time and Western Man* (New York: Harcourt, Brace and Co., 1928), p. 112.
12 Ibid., p. 89.
13 Ibid., p. 112.
14 In a study of Catholic educational attitudes toward Jews, Clair Bishop notes that one of the "truths" that Catholic children learned in the late nineteenth and early twentieth centuries was "[t]hat Judaism was once the best religion, but then became ossified and ceased to exist with the coming of Jesus." See Clair Huchet Bishop, *How Catholics Look at Jews: An Inquiry into Spanish, French, and Italian Teaching Materials* (New York: Paulist Press, 1974), p. 31. Quoted in Neil Davison, *James Joyce, "Ulysses," and the Construction of Jewish Identity* (New York: Cambridge University Press, 1996), p. 21.
15 The myth of the Wandering Jew has its own varied history. See Galit Hasan-Rokem and Alan Dundes, eds., *The Wandering Jew: Essays in the Interpretation of a Christian Legend* (Bloomington: Indiana University Press, 1986).
16 Jonathan Boyarin, *Storm from Paradise: The Politics of Jewish Memory* (Minneapolis: University of Minnesota Press, 1992), p. 81. Europeans did, however, add to this temporal banishment by Orientalizing Jews, insisting on their Eastern origins.
17 George Stocking, "The Turn-of-the-Century Concept of Race," *Modernism/Modernity* 1.1 (January 1994), 12, 14.
18 Zygmunt Bauman, *Modernity and the Holocaust* (1989); Matti Bunzl, *Symptoms of Modernity: Jews and Queers in late 20th-Century Vienna* (2004); Sander L. Gilman, *Difference and Pathology: Stereotypes of Sexuality, Race, and Madness* (1985) and *Jewish Self-Hatred: Anti-Semitism and the Hidden Language of the Jews* (1986); George Mosse, *Nationalism and Sexuality: Middle-Class Morality and Sexual Norms in Modern Europe* (1985); and Judith Walkowitz, *City of Dreadful Delight: Narratives of Sexual Danger in Late Victorian London* (1992).
19 Wyndham Lewis, *Hitler* (London: Chatto & Windus, 1931), p. 41.
20 Elizabeth Bowen, *The House in Paris* (New York: Anchor Books, 2002), p. 124.
21 Daniel Boyarin, *Unheroic Conduct: The Rise of Heterosexuality and the Invention of the Jewish Man* (Berkeley: University of California Press, 1997), p. 232.
22 Sander L. Gilman discusses feminized Jewish men in the context of hysteria and disease in *The Jew's Body* (New York: Routledge, 1991).
23 Ritchie Robertson, "Historicizing Weininger: The Nineteenth-Century German Image of the Feminized Jew," in Cheyette and Marcus, eds., *Modernity, Culture and "The Jew"*, p. 26.
24 Matthew Biberman, *Masculinity, Anti-Semitism, and Early Modern English Literature* (Burlington, VT: Ashgate, 2004), p. 3.
25 Boyarin, *Unheroic Conduct*, pp. xiv, 33–80.
26 Ann Pellegrini, *Performance Anxieties: Staging Psychoanalysis, Staging Race* (New York: Routledge, 1996), p. 18.
27 Ibid.

28 For example, in the past several years: on James, see Jonathan Freedman, *The Temple of Culture: Assimilation and Anti-Semitism in Literary Anglo-America* (2000); on Pound, see Leon Surette, *Pound in Purgatory: From Economic Radicalism to Anti-Semitism* (1999); on Eliot, see the revised version of Anthony Julius, *T. S. Eliot, Anti-Semitism, and Literary Form: with a preface and response to the critics* (2003); on Joyce, see Marilyn Reizbaum, *James Joyce's Judaic Other* (Stanford, 1999).
29 In fact, as Suzanne Raitt points out, "Lesbianism was not always a radical force in terms of both social and sexual roles." See Raitt, *Vita and Virginia: The Work and Friendship of Vita Sackville-West and Virginia Woolf* (New York: Oxford University Press, 1993), p. 9.
30 Erin Carlston, *Thinking Fascism: Sapphic Modernism and Fascist Modernity* (Stanford: Stanford University Press, 1998), pp. 4–5.
31 Bonnie Kime Scott, *Refiguring Modernism*, 2 vols., *Volume I: The Women of 1928* (Bloomington: Indiana University Press, 1995).
32 Quentin Bell, *Virginia Woolf: A Biography* (New York: Harcourt Brace Jovanovich, 1972), p. 23.
33 Hermione Lee, *Virginia Woolf* (New York: Vintage Books, 1999), p. 251.
34 John Whittier-Ferguson, discussing Mary Seton's narrative about Fernham, points out similarly that "We would be mistaken to hear nothing but unqualified celebration of this lack of authority at this moment in *Room*. Here, in her first extended polemical composition, speaking in the uncertain voice of Mary Seton, Woolf acknowledges her own hesitation and her anxious sense that her listeners are probably bored and skeptical." (See John Whittier-Ferguson, *Framing Pieces: Designs of the Gloss in Joyce, Woolf, and Pound* [New York: Oxford University Press, 1996], p. 79).
35 Carol Angier, *Jean Rhys: Life and Work* (Boston: Little, Brown, & Co., 1990), p. 359.
36 Jean Rhys, *Smile Please: An Unfinished Autobiography* (New York: Harper & Row, 1979), p. 20.
37 Ibid., pp. 103–104.
38 "Sylvia Townsend Warner in Conversation. An Interview with Warner conducted by Val Warner and Michael Schmidt in 1975," *PN Review 23* 8.3 (1978), 35.
39 Claire Harman, *Sylvia Townsend Warner: A Biography* (London: Minerva, 1989), pp. 53–54.
40 Gloria Fromm, *Dorothy Richardson: A Biography* (Urbana: University of Illinois Press, 1977), p. 48.
41 Ibid., p. 59.
42 Ibid., p. 61.
43 Ibid., p. 66.
44 Phillip Herring, *Djuna: The Life and Work of Djuna Barnes* (New York: Viking, 1995), pp. 1–23.
45 Virginia Woolf, *Women and Writing*, ed. Michele Barrett (New York: Harcourt Brace Jovanovich, 1979), p. 49.

46 Ibid., pp. 60–61.
47 Angier, *Jean Rhys*, p. 217.
48 Ibid., p. 178.
49 Bonnie Kime Scott, ed., *The Gender of Modernism* (Bloomington: Indiana University Press, 1990), p. 543.
50 Ibid., p. 401.
51 Ibid., p. 406.
52 Ibid., p. 413.
53 Ibid., p. 411.
54 Ibid., p. 400.
55 Carolyn Burke, "'Accidental Aloofness': Barnes, Loy, and Modernism," in Mary Lynn Broe, ed., *Silence and Power: A Reevaluation of Djuna Barnes* (Carbondale: Southern Illinois University Press, 1991), p. 69.
56 Djuna Barnes, *Ladies Almanack* (Normal, IL: Dalkey Archive Press, 1992), pp. 24–6.
57 Herring, *Djuna*, p. 209.
58 Rhys, *Smile Please*, p. 100.
59 John Efron, *Defenders of the Race: Jewish Doctors and Race Science in Fin-de-Siècle Europe* (New Haven: Yale University Press, 1994), p. 52.
60 For a thorough discussion of Jewish life in the interwar period, see chapter 5 of Todd Endelman's *The Jews of Britain, 1656 to 2000* (Berkeley: University of California Press, 2002).
61 John Vincent, *Disraeli* (New York: Oxford University Press, 1990), p. 14.
62 David Feldman, *Englishmen and Jews: Social Relations and Political Culture, 1840–1914* (New Haven: Yale University Press, 1994), p. 264.
63 Endelman, *The Jews of Britain*, p. 127.
64 Feldman, *Englishmen and Jews*, pp. 280–290.
65 Maurice Samuel, *Blood Accusation: The Strange History of the Beiliss Case* (New York: Alfred A. Knopf, 1966), p. 181.
66 James Joyce, *Ulysses*, ed. Hans Walter Gabler (New York: Random House, 1986), p. 567.
67 Sharman Kadish, *Bolsheviks and British Jews: The Anglo-Jewish Community, Britain, and the Russian Revolution* (London: Frank Cass Press, 1992), pp. 46–48.
68 Ibid., pp. 30–38.
69 Ibid., p. 10.
70 Kadish quotes Captain Peter Wright, a Foreign Office official who wrote part of *The Samuel Report on Poland* published in June 1920. Wright wrote that "Bolshevism spells business for poor Jews; innumerable posts in a huge administration... The rich bourgeois Jew also manages to get on with it in his own way, 'Judischer Weise' as the Jews call bribery. Many Jews who are by no means poor try at the present time to escape into Russia, so fine are the business prospects" (ibid., pp. 19–20).
71 Stuart Cohen traces the debates over Zionism within the British Jewish community before 1920, when Britain's Mandate for Palestine was formally

accepted. See Stuart Cohen, *English Zionists and British Jews: The Communal Politics of Anglo-Jewry, 1895–1920* (Princeton: Princeton University Press, 1982).
72 Kadish, *Bolsheviks*, pp. 138–165.
73 "About Zionism: Speeches and Letters by Professor Albert Einstein," *Times Literary Supplement*, November 27, 1930.
74 "The Jew in Europe," *Times Literary Supplement*, November 17, 1927.
75 "Jews in Babylonia," *Times Literary Supplement*, July 20, 1933.
76 "The Jews and Minority Rights," *Times Literary Supplement*, September 14, 1933.
77 "Complete Translation of Mein Kampf: Bases of Hitler's Power-Politics," *Times Literary Supplement*, March 25, 1939.
78 "In Defence of the Jews," *Times Literary Supplement*, March 25, 1939.
79 Todd Endelman, *Radical Assimilation in English Jewish History 1656–1945* (Bloomington: Indiana University Press, 1990), p. 192.
80 Ibid., p. 193.
81 Andrew Sharf, *The British Press and Jews Under Nazi Rule* (New York: Oxford University Press, 1964), pp. 78ff.
82 Practically all the debates around Barnes, Rhys, Richardson, Warner, and Woolf proceed under a feminist rubric, so it is difficult to single out those that have most shaped this study. Trauma studies, particularly work by Judith Herman and Cathy Caruth, has strongly influenced my sense of the lives of Barnes, Rhys, and Woolf, and especially bears on chapter 5. Bonnie Kime Scott's anthology *The Gender of Modernism* (1990) has long been the text to which I turn for information about and excerpts from the previously unpublished work of these and other authors.
83 Texts in queer studies that have most influenced this book include Judith Butler's *Gender Trouble* (1999), Erin Carlston's *Thinking Fascism* (1998), Terry Castle's revision of Sedgwick's model of homosociality (in *Between Men*, 1985) in her chapter in *The Apparitional Lesbian* (1993) on Sylvia Townsend Warner, Eve Kosofsky Sedgwick's *Epistemology of the Closet* (1990), readings of lesbian literature such as Patricia Juliana Smith's *Lesbian Panic* (1997), and Joanne Winning's *The Pilgrimage of Dorothy Richardson* (2000).
84 Important work in Jewish cultural studies is being conducted by Daniel Boyarin, Jonathan Boyarin, Sander L. Gilman, and, among others, those whose essays are included in two key collections: *Jews and Other Differences: The New Jewish Cultural Studies* (1997) and *Insider/Outsider: American Jews and Multiculturalism* (1998). The studies of literary Jewishness that have most influenced my thinking are Bryan Cheyette's *Constructions of "the Jew" in English Literature and Society* (1993), Cheyette's collections *Between "Race" and Culture* (1996) and (with Laura Marcus) *Modernity, Culture, and "the Jew,"* (1998), Michael Ragussis's *Figures of Conversion* (1995), and Jonathan Freedman's *The Temple of Culture* (2000).
85 Matti Bunzl, "Jews, Queers, and Other Symptoms," *GLQ: A Journal of Lesbian and Gay Studies* 6.2 (2000), 323.

1 "Strip each statement of its money motive": Jews and the ideal of disinterested art in Warner, Rhys, and Woolf

1 William I. Brustein, *Roots of Hate: Anti-Semitism in Europe Before the Holocaust* (New York: Cambridge University Press, 2003), p. 229.
2 As Ragussis argues in his study of nineteenth-century conversion narratives, "no portrait of a Jew can exist in English without reference to [*The Merchant of Venice*], and the English imagination seems unable to free itself from Shakespeare's text." See Michael Ragussis, *Figures of Conversion: "The Jewish Question" and English National Identity* (Durham: Duke University Press, 1995), pp. 58–59.
3 Brustein, *Roots of Hate*, p. 180.
4 Ibid., p. 230.
5 By starting the Hogarth Press, Leonard and Virginia Woolf were able to remove themselves from such power struggles with editors.
6 Howard Sacher writes that "[b]y the turn of the century, and especially by the end of the first World War, Jewish participation in European cultural life had assumed major dimensions... There were Jewish writers, doctors, musicians, scholars, professors – not to mention untold tens of thousands of Jewish patrons of the arts, letters, music, and humanities – in numbers far beyond the fondest hopes and dreams of Moses Mendelssohn... a century earlier." See Howard Sachar, *The Course of Modern Jewish History* (New York: Random House, 1990), p. 473.
7 An exception in British women's fiction is Nick Kralin in Mary Butts's *The Death of Felicity Taverner* (1932), one of the most antisemitic of modern novels. Kralin plans to sell his dead wife's beloved land to commercial developers. Yet even he, though he gets no pleasure from them, collects art objects and has impeccable taste.
8 Ernest Hemingway, *The Sun Also Rises* (New York: Scribner, 1970), p. 90.
9 Walter Benn Michaels, *Our America: Nativism, Modernism, and Pluralism* (Durham: Duke University Press, 1995), p. 27.
10 D. H. Lawrence, *Women in Love* (New York: The Modern Library, 2002), pp. 440, 446.
11 Ibid., pp. 446–447.
12 Ibid., pp. 444, 449.
13 Lewis, *Time and Western Man*, p. 101.
14 Mark Morrison argues that the writers he studies – Margaret Anderson, Ford Madox Ford, Dora Marsden, and Ezra Pound, among others – show, at least before the First World War, great optimism about the possibilities of adopting the methods of mass culture to promote their own work, even while they used the mass market as a "rhetorical enemy." See Mark Morrison, *The Public Face of Modernism: Little Magazines, Audiences, and Reception, 1905–1920* (Madison: University of Wisconsin Press, 2001), pp. 5ff.

15 Ibid., p. 5.
16 In addition to Morrison's study, other examples are Paul Delany's *Literature, Money and the Market: From Trollope to Amis* (2002), Kevin Dettmar and Stephen Myers Watt's collection *Marketing Modernisms: Self-Promotion, Canonization, Rereading* (1996), Sean Latham's *Am I a Snob? Modernism and the Novel* (2003), Lawrence Rainey's *Institutions of Modernism: Literary Elites and Public Culture* (1999), Michael Tratner's *Modernism and Mass Politics: Joyce, Woolf, Eliot* (1995), and Catherine Turner's *Marketing Modernism Between the Two World Wars* (2003).
17 I disagree here with Gary Martin Levine, who reads Lawrence's use of Loerke (along with T. S. Eliot's and Wyndham Lewis's use of Jews) as a symbol of the "corruption of art through commodification." While this thesis does apply to Eliot and Lewis, I am unconvinced by his brief argument about *Women in Love*. See Gary Martin Levine, *The Merchant of Modernism: The Economic Jew in Anglo-American Literature, 1864–1939* (New York: Routledge, 2003), p. 13.
18 Freedman, *The Temple of Culture: Assimilation and Anti-Semitism in Literary Anglo-America* (New York: Oxford University Press, 2000), p. 56. See also Catherine Gallagher, "George Eliot and *Daniel Deronda:* The Prostitute and the Jewish Question," in Ruth Yeazell, ed., *Sex, Politics, and Science in the Nineteenth-Century Novel* (Baltimore: Johns Hopkins University Press, 1986), pp. 39–62.
19 Freedman, *Temple of Culture*, pp. 56–57.
20 Janet Montefiore uses this phrase in her excellent description of how Sophia listens to Minna's narrative and how Minna performs her Jewishness. See Janet Montefiore, "Listening to Minna: Realism, Feminism, and the Politics of Reading," *Paragraph* 14.1 (November 1991), 203.
21 In *The Auden Generation* Samuel Hynes describes the central feature of literary criticism by left-wing writers in the 1930s: "The questions to which these critics addressed themselves were questions primarily about the social aspects of literature: what is its relation to immediate history? how does it reflect the social background? what is its function in an unstable, perhaps a revolutionary society?" See Samuel Hynes, *The Auden Generation* (New York: Viking, 1977), p. 160.
22 Terry Castle, *The Apparitional Lesbian: Female Homosexuality and Modern Culture* (New York: Columbia University Press, 1993), p. 89.
23 As Robin Hackett argues, there is also a less savory aspect to this link between Jewishness and Sophia's sexual and political transformation. This transformation may depend on Minna's exoticism: Warner's "plot turns on the stereotype of the primitive Oriental, a stereotype that says Minna's erotics will be especially powerful, compelling, and transformative even to the point of bewitchment." See Robin Hackett, *Sapphic Primitivism: Productions of Race, Class, and Sexuality in Key Works of Modern Fiction* (New Brunswick: Rutgers University Press, 2004), p. 102. While there is a Svengali-like power about Minna, especially at the women's first meeting, the text resists this

stereotype by having her ultimately *free* Sophia in ways I describe. In contrast, Svengali, the antagonist of George du Maurier's 1894 bestseller *Trilby*, mesmerizes and mentally enslaves Trilby.

24 Warner consistently has the plot refute Sophia's stereotypes about Jews: when Sophia asks the men at Minna's flat to pawn her ring so that she can buy them all dinner, they begin to discuss whose "pawn-shop technique" would get them the best price. Sophia finds it "strange that in a company where so many were Jews no Jewish candidate was proposed" (*SWS* 245).

25 Castle suggests that Warner may be gesturing toward a fantastical resurrection, a plotline in which Minna is still alive and will return to the flat where Sophia waits. See Castle, *Apparitional*, pp. 87–88. I am grateful to Erin Carlston for describing the ambiguity of Minna's death in terms of a lack of a *body*, in response to a conference paper I presented on Warner at the Modernist Studies Association meeting of 2002.

26 Catherine Vaughan, *The Money Pit: Filling the Blank Spaces in Jean Rhys's "Good Morning, Midnight,"* unpublished manuscript, p. 19. Vaughan is developing an idea of Jan Curtis: that the *commis* as "priest" serves the god of illusion in a world reduced to materialism. See Jan Curtis, "The Room and the Black Background: A Re-Interpretation of Jean Rhys's *Good Morning, Midnight*," *World Literature Written in English* 25.2 (1985), 269.

27 Vaughan, *The Money Pit*, p. 16.

28 Veronica Marie Gregg writes that Serge, in spite of his cultural uses of Africa and the West Indies, was "unable to touch a flesh-and-blood West Indian colored woman in a human way." She argues that he was unable to embrace her "because of her difference" and that he rejects Sasha's comparison of herself with this person "on the basis of race." See Veronica Marie Gregg, *Jean Rhys's Historical Imagination: Reading and Writing the Creole* (Chapel Hill: University of North Carolina Press, 1995), p. 158. Even if my reading is too optimistic, Gregg's description of the situation has no supporting evidence in the text. First, Serge *does* touch the woman "in a human way" by putting his "arm round her" (*GM, M* 96); what he does not do is make the touch sexual. Second, there is no evidence that race was the reason he could not "make love to her"; perhaps he is homosexual as Camarasana suggests, or perhaps he is just not aroused by drunken misery. At any rate, his statement "But alas, I couldn't" betrays neither disgust nor revulsion.

29 Linda Camarasana, *Exhibitions and Repetitions: Jean Rhys's "Good Morning, Midnight" and the World of Paris, 1937*, unpublished manuscript, p. 5.

30 Carole Angier points out that one reason Sasha feels safe with Serge, and with René at the beginning of their friendship, is that they do not examine her but display themselves. See Angier, *Jean Rhys*, p. 380.

31 Grace Radin, for example, in her otherwise compelling discussion of *The Years* and its draft versions, dismisses this scene with a footnote, saying that Sara's view of Abrahamson "may well have been Virginia Stephen's own attitude before she came to know Jews like Leonard Woolf and S. S. Koteliansky." See Grace Radin, *Virginia Woolf's "The Years": The Evolution of a Novel* (Knoxville: University of

Tennessee Press, 1981), pp. 94–95. Jean Moorcroft Wilson goes further, arguing that "[w]hen Virginia married a Jew in 1912, she took a daring step and one which alone might vindicate her from the charge of anti-Semitism." See Jean Moorcroft Wilson, *Virginia Woolf and Anti-Semitism* (London: Cecil Woolf, 1995), p. 12.

32 I have not corrected the punctuation or spelling in Woolf's diaries and letters; she often omits apostrophes, hyphens, and occasional periods.

33 Besides arguing that her marriage itself proves that Woolf was what she calls "pro-Semitic," Moorcroft Wilson goes to great lengths to exonerate Woolf from the charge of antisemitism. In the process she undermines her own credibility by referring to Jews' "undoubted business abilities," questioning whether we should "impose notions of 'political correctness' on writers retrospectively," and attributing Woolf's antisemitic remarks about Leonard's mother to "perfectly natural family tensions" (Wilson, *Woolf and Anti-Semitism*, pp. 13, 17, 9).

34 Lee, *Virginia Woolf*, p. 309.

35 Jane Marcus, *Virginia Woolf and the Languages of Patriarchy* (Bloomington: University of Indiana Press, 1987), p. 64.

36 Margaret Comstock, "The Loudspeaker and the Human Voice: Politics and the Form of *The Years*," *Bulletin of the New York Public Library* 80 (1977), 273.

37 Radin puts it like this: the "keystone of Elvira's [Sara's] character will be her repudiation of society's bribes and rewards" (Radin, *Virginia Woolf's "The Years"*, p. 41).

38 David Bradshaw, "Hyams Place: The Years, the Jews and the British Union of Fascists," in Maroula Joannou, ed., *Women Writers of the 1930s: Gender, Politics and History* (Edinburgh: Edinburgh University Press, 1999), p. 182.

39 Ibid., pp. 182–183.

40 Woolf succeeded in publishing the story only when she had removed the explicit references to her character's Jewishness. For analysis of this story and Woolf's revisions, see Phyllis Lassner, "The Milk of Our Mother's Kindness Has Ceased to Flow: Virginia Woolf, Stevie Smith, and the Representation of the Jew," in Cheyette, ed., *Between "Race" and Culture*, pp. 129–144, and Leena Kore Schröder "Tales of Abjection and Miscegenation: Virginia Woolf's and Leonard Woolf's 'Jewish' Stories," *Twentieth Century Literature* 49.3 (2003), 304–305.

41 Bradshaw, "Hyams Place," p. 184.

42 Dirty baths are associated with a similar sort of degradation in the 1918 section of *The Years*, where the elderly Crosby has to clean the dirty bath of the "Count" for whom she currently works. This count is a "foreigner," foreshadowing this link between the dirty bath and the Jew. "'Dirty brute, dirty brute,' she repeated . . . She saw once more the blob of spittle that the Count had left on the side of his bath – the Belgian who called himself a Count. 'I've been used to work for gentlefolk, not for dirty foreigners like you,' she told him as she hobbled" (*Years* 303–304).

43 George's musings are, in the published version, given to Eleanor, but without reference to this metaphor of grease on a tub: "When shall we be free? When shall we live adventurously, wholly, not like cripples in a cave?" (*Years* 297).
44 Schröder, "Tales of Abjection," 304–305.
45 Ibid., 308.
46 I am grateful to Anne Fernald for stressing Woolf's strong interest in her earnings at the Modernism Workshop, DePauw University, 2004.
47 Sean Latham, *Am I a Snob? Modernism and the Novel* (Ithaca: Cornell University Press, 2003), pp. 90–117.

2 Transformations of supersessionism in Woolf and Richardson

1 This is true for Woolf at least until the early 1930s when she began working on *The Years*, her novel of "fact."
2 Virginia Woolf, *The Common Reader: First Series* (London: The Hogarth Press, 1951), p. 184.
3 Ibid., p. 185.
4 Ibid.
5 Virginia Woolf, *Moments of Being* (New York: Harcourt Brace & Company, 1985), p. 72.
6 Kenneth Gentry, for example, defends Christian Reconstructionist theology from charges that its supersessionism implies antisemitism. He writes that "the idea of supersessionism is fundamental to the Christian faith itself. The basic idea of supersessionism is that Christianity has superseded Judaism as the true faith. This is heresy? Supersessionism . . . shamelessly endorses the words of Christ: 'I am the way, the truth, and the life: no man cometh unto the Father, but by me (John 14:6).'" See Kenneth Gentry, Jr., *Reformed Anti-Semitism or Dispensational Absurdity? A Consideration of Dispensational Charges Related to the Role of Israel in the Plan of God*; available at www.cmfnow.com/articles/pt567.html, visited May 24, 2004.
7 Diane Samuels, *Kindertransport* (New York: Theatre Communications Group, 2000), pp. 33–34.
8 As Ruether points out, this parable also appears in Luke 14, but in that version the invited guests are merely too busy to come; they do not murder the servants. See Rosemary Radford Ruether, *Faith and Fratricide: The Theological Roots of Anti-Semitism* (New York: Seabury Press, 1974), p. 85.
9 Ibid.
10 Ibid., p. 92.
11 This parable also appears in Mark 12:1–12 and Luke 20:9–19.
12 Peter Kreeft, *Comparing Christianity and Judaism*, May 1987, *National Catholic Register*; available at www.catholiceducation.org/articles/apologetics/apo007.html, visited May 25, 2004.

13 Joseph Keating, *Christianity*, 2003, online edition of 1908 Catholic Encyclopedia; available at www.newadvent.org/cathen/03712a.html, visited May 25, 2004.
14 Ruether, *Faith and Fratricide*, p. 80.
15 A webpage by the Christian Scholars Group on Christian-Jewish Relations, for example, affirms and details the following principles, among others: "1. God's covenant with the Jewish people endures forever. 2. Jesus of Nazareth lived and died as a faithful Jew . . . 4. Judaism is a living faith, enriched by many centuries of development . . . 7. Christians should not target Jews for conversion." See Christian Scholars Group, *A Sacred Obligation: Rethinking Christian Faith in Relation to Judaism and the Jewish People*, 2002; available at www.bc.edu/research/cjl/meta-elements/sites/partners/csg/Sacred_Obligation.html, visited January 6, 2006.
16 Sander L. Gilman, *Difference and Pathology: Stereotypes of Sexuality, Race, and Madness* (Ithaca: Cornell University Press, 1985), p. 151.
17 Pellegrini similarly warns against making discontinuity between religious and racial prejudice the whole story of the history of anti-Judaism and antisemitism. See Pellegrini, *Performance Anxieties*, p. 20.
18 Raymond Williams, *Marxism and Literature* (New York: Oxford University Press, 1977), pp. 122ff.
19 Quentin Bell describes his and others' responses to *Three Guineas* in his biography: "What really seemed wrong with the book – and I am speaking here of my own reactions at the time – was the attempt to involve a discussion of women's rights with the far more agonising and immediate question of what we were to do in order to meet the ever-growing menace of Fascism and war . . . The book was pretty severely attacked." See Bell, *Virginia Woolf: A Biography*, p. 205.
20 Virginia Woolf, *Mrs. Dalloway* (New York: Harcourt Brace & Company, 1953), p. 37.
21 Virginia Woolf, *To the Lighthouse* (New York: Harcourt Brace & Company, 1989), pp. 62–63.
22 "Anyhow thats the end of six years floundering, striving, much agony, some ecstasy: lumping the Years and 3 Gs together as one book – as indeed they are" (*Diary* V, 148).
23 Loretta Stec, "Dystopian Modernism vs Utopian Feminism: Burdekin, Woolf, and West Respond to the Rise of Fascism," in Merry M. Pawlowski, ed., *Virginia Woolf and Fascism: Resisting the Dictators' Seduction* (New York: Palgrave, 2001), p. 188.
24 Jean Radford's *Dorothy Richardson* (London: Harvester Wheatsheaf, 1991) establishes important parallels in *Pilgrimage* to John Bunyan's *The Pilgrim's Progress* (1678).
25 Radford, *Dorothy Richardson*, p. 42.
26 Ibid.
27 In fact, there is a sense in which pilgrimage narratives in English generally do partake in supersessionist thought. The story of Paul's conversion on the road to

Damascus can be seen as a prototype. Beginning his journey a Jew, Paul travels along a road, experiences a blinding light/insight, and becomes a Christian, leaving his inadequate religion behind. Pilgrimage narratives similarly depict a person on a journey, surmounting impasses built of false belief to reach his or her destination transformed. Buried beneath the image of the road or pathway from darkness to light may be the image of a journey from Judaism to Christianity. Ruether summarizes how important Judaism is as a foil for Christianity's self-conception: Christianity defines itself as universal by dismissing Judaism as a paltry particularism, as transcendent by creating something to transcend (Ruether, *Faith and Fratricide*, pp. 239–240). Judaism is *the* point of origin for Christianity, and through the story of the transforming pilgrimage, Christianity continually leaves it behind.

28 As much as *Pilgrimage* views Jewishness as a flaw and an obstacle, it does not, in my opinion, enlist the discourse of contamination central to modern racial antisemitism. I disagree, that is, with Jane Garrity's claim that "[t]o the extent that Richardson produces deeply embedded stereotypes of the Jew, bound up with notions of degeneration and infection, she shares with several of her modernist contemporaries the fear of Semitic 'contamination.'" See Jane Garrity, *Step-Daughters of England: British Women Modernists and the National Imaginary* (New York: Manchester University Press, 2003), p. 109. Garrity's evidence for the trope of infection and contamination in the novel is thin: for example, when Miriam uses the word "contamination" in a café full of foreigners in *Interim* (1920), she is indeed in the company of the Jewish Mendizabal, but we do not learn if the other customers are Jews; moreover, she is thinking of what her "English friends" would say, "calling her back from a spectacle she could not witness without contamination" – even as Miriam herself is thrilled with the novelty of her café experience (*P* II, 394).

29 Radford, *Richardson*, p. 100.

30 Daniel Boyarin, *A Radical Jew: Paul and the Politics of Identity* (Berkeley: University of California Press, 1994), p. 7.

31 Gillian Hanscombe states that the final image "embodies Miriam's eventual acceptance of her own maternal longings . . . but the child is not her own." See Gillian Hanscombe, *The Art of Life: Dorothy Richardson and the Development of Feminist Consciousness* (Boston: Peter Owen, 1982), p. 159. Lynette Felber writes that although Miriam defines herself against Amabel, rejecting for herself "the dream of feminine fulfillment through marriage and motherhood," she nevertheless experiences them "vicariously through Amabel." See Lynette Felber, "A Manifesto for Feminine Modernism: Dorothy Richardson's *Pilgrimage*," in Lisa Rado, ed., *Rereading Modernism: New Directions in Feminist Criticism* (New York: Garland, 1994), p. 31.

32 Jean Radford, "The Woman and the Jew: Sex and Modernity," in Cheyette and Marcus, eds., *Modernity, Culture and "The Jew"*, p. 16.

33 Fromm, *Biography*, p. 371.

34 Ibid., p. 195.

35 This opposition is discussed in Boyarin, *A Radical Jew*, pp. 7 and 22ff.

3 Adding bathrooms, fomenting revolutions: modernity and Jewishness in Woolf and Warner

1 Zygmunt Bauman, *Modernity and the Holocaust* (Ithaca: Cornell University Press, 1989), p. 45.
2 Within the irrational strand of Western culture that was and is antisemitism, the perceived link between Jews and modernity easily coexisted with the incompatible view that Jews were relics of the ancient past, primitive and superseded. For analyses of the ways Jews were associated with modernity, see Zygmunt Bauman's *Modernity and the Holocaust*, Sander L. Gilman's *Difference and Pathology* and *The Jew's Body*, Daniel Boyarin and Jonathan Boyarin's *Jews and Other Differences*, and Jonathan Boyarin's *Storm from Paradise*. For literary critical readings of Jews as figures of the modern, see Bryan Cheyette and Laura Marcus's collection, *Modernity, Culture and "the Jew."*
3 Peter Gay, *Freud, Jews, and Other Germans: Masters and Victims in Modernist Culture* (New York: Oxford University Press, 1978), pp. 20–21. I am indebted to Marilyn Reizbaum for this quotation; see Reizbaum, *James Joyce's Judaic Other*, p. 17.
4 Todd Endelman, "Comparative Perspectives on Modern Anti-Semitism in the West," in David Berger, ed., *History and Hate: The Dimensions of Anti-Semitism* (Philadelphia: Jewish Publication Society, 1986), pp. 99–100.
5 Roberto Finzi, *Anti-Semitism: From Its European Roots to the Holocaust*, trans. Maud Jackson, The Windrush History of the 20th Century (Moreton-in-Marsh: Windrush Press, 1999), p. 64.
6 Reizbaum, *James Joyce's Judaic Other*, pp. 31, 62–63.
7 Michaels, *Our America*, p. 27.
8 Ibid., p. 26.
9 Ibid., pp. 72–74.
10 Mary Butts, *The Taverner Novels* (Kingston, NY: McPherson & Company, 1992), pp. 177, 241.
11 Ibid., p. 249.
12 Ibid., pp. 246, 302.
13 Kadish, *Bolsheviks and British Jews*, pp. 46–48.
14 Virginia Woolf, *Between the Acts*, ed. Susan Dick and Mary S. Millar (London: Blackwell, 2002), p. xxxiii.
15 Michelle Pridmore-Brown, "1939–1940: Of Virginia Woolf, Gramophones, and Fascism," *PMLA* 113.3 (1998), 408–421.
16 Ibid., 414.
17 Merry Pawlowski, too, discusses the relationship between Miss La Trobe and her audience in terms of the herd instinct and antifascism. See Merry M. Pawlowski, "Toward a Feminist Theory of the State: Virginia Woolf and Wyndham Lewis on Art, Gender, and Politics," in Pawlowski, ed., *Virginia Woolf and Fascism: Resisting the Dictators' Seduction* (New York: Palgrave, 2001), pp. 47–48.

18 Jed Esty, *A Shrinking Island: Modernism and National Culture in England* (Princeton: Princeton University Press, 2004), p. 104.
19 Ibid., p. 92.
20 On June 9, 1940, Woolf had written in her diary: "It struck me that one curious feeling is, that the writing 'I' has vanished. No audience. No echo. Thats part of one's death. Not altogether serious, for I correct Roger: send finally I hope tomorrow: & could finish P.H. But it is a fact – this disparition of an echo" (*Diary* V, 293). On July 24, 1940 she again wrote that "There's no standard to write for: no public to echo back" and then noted in the margin "a repetition I see" (*Diary* V, 304). She included the same sentiment in a letter to Elizabeth Robins on March 13, 1941: "Two nights ago they dropped incendiaries, in a row, like street lamps, all along the downs . . . Its difficult, I find, to write. No audience. No private stimulus, only this outer roar" (*Letters* VI, 479). For these additional references I am indebted to Dick and Millar's edition of *Between the Acts*. Ten years earlier, Woolf had Bernard use the same phrase in *The Waves*, describing a feeling of "complete desertion" when his self refuses to answer his call: "No fin breaks the waste of this immeasurable sea. Life has destroyed me. No echo comes when I speak, no varied words." See Virginia Woolf, *The Waves* (New York: Harcourt Brace Jovanovich, 1959), p. 284.
21 Bart Oliver appears to have heard a different story of the jewels' origins: that they were "dug up, so people said, by thin Ralph Manresa in his ragamuffin days" (*BTA* 202). It is also possible that this is a discrepancy Woolf would have corrected had she lived to revise the novel to her satisfaction. One reason to think that Bart's understanding may be left over from the earlier portrayal of Ralph – when he was present at the pageant and not definitively Jewish – is that Ralph is called "thin Ralph Manresa" both here and in the draft version in which he is first mentioned. See Mitchell A. Leaska, ed., *Pointz Hall: The Earlier and Later Typescripts of "Between the Acts"* (New York: New York University Press, 1983), p. 115.
22 Virginia Woolf, *Mrs. Dalloway* (New York: Harcourt Brace & Company, 1953), p.8.
23 The phrase "tons of money" echoes Woolf's phrase "millions of money" in the letter where she admitted it was snobbish to hate marrying a Jew (*Letters* IV, 195–196).
24 Leaska, ed., *Pointz Hall*, p. 64.
25 Ibid., p. 286.
26 Ibid., p. 115. In the published scene there is no reference at this point to Ralph Manresa; instead, it focuses on the similarities between Giles Oliver and Mr. Pisent (*BTA* 108).
27 Ibid., p. 286.
28 The word "twisted" is also used to describe William Dodge's face (*BTA* 37), subtly associating the Jew and the homosexual in ways congruent with Dodge's role as stand-in companion for Mrs. Manresa, and also with the homosexual Nicholas Pomjalovsky's former identity as Sara Pargiter's

Jewish lover in *The Years*. See Maren Linett, "The Jew in the Bath: Imperiled Imagination in Woolf's *The Years*," *Modern Fiction Studies* 42.2 (2002).
29 Willa Cather, *The Professor's House* (New York: Random House, 1990), pp. 67, 62.
30 Woolf, *Between the Acts*, ed. Dick and Millar, p.137.
31 Ibid.
32 The scars, the rape's metaphoric aspects, and the relation of the snake to the war are discussed by Patricia Laurence in "The Facts and Fugue of War: From *Three Guineas* to *Between the Acts*," in Mark Hussey, ed., *Virginia Woolf and War: Fiction, Reality, and Myth* (Syracuse: Syracuse University Press, 1991), p. 241.
33 In Cather's *The Professor's House*, the Jewish character, Louie Marsellus, is also having a new house built. "'He's doing us a Norwegian manor house, very harmonious with its setting, just the right thing for rugged pine woods and high headlands'" (Cather, *The Professor's House*, p. 28). But the text's emphasis on racial "stock" and on the opposition between American and foreign makes readers skeptical about his claim that the house could be "harmonious" in the American Midwest, and dubious that this Jew has any more right to a Norwegian manor house than he has to the money resulting from Tom Outland's discovery. Marsellus's description of the house introduces a standard of authenticity that Marsellus himself repeatedly fails to meet.
34 Leaska, ed., *Pointz Hall*, p. 162. In the published version the glasses are said not to comment on the accusation: "Liars most of us. Thieves too. (The glasses made no comment on that)" (*BTA* 187).
35 Sharf, *The British Press*, pp. 155, 167ff.
36 Ibid., p. 173.
37 Judith Greenberg, "'When Ears are Deaf and the Heart is Dry': Traumatic Reverberations in *Between the Acts*," *Woolf Studies Annual* 7 (2001), 53.
38 Natania Rosenfeld, "Monstrous Conjugations: Images of Dictatorship in the Anti-Fascist Writings of Virginia and Leonard Woolf," in Pawlowski, ed., *Virginia Woolf and Fascism* p. 124.
39 Ibid., p. 124. Rosenfeld is quoting Woolf's *Diary* IV, 346.
40 Leaska, ed., *Pointz Hall*, p. 128.
41 Laurence, "Facts and Fugue," p. 245.
42 Brustein, *Roots of Hate*, p. 266.
43 Arnold Rattenbury, "Plain Heart, Light Tether," *PN Review 23* 8.3 (1978), 47.
44 Geoffrey Ellis, "The Revolution of 1848–1849 in France," in R. J. W. Evans and Hartmut Pogge von Strandmann, eds., *The Revolutions in Europe, 1848–1849: From Reform to Reaction* (New York: Oxford University Press, 2000), p. 41.
45 Ibid., p. 34.
46 Ibid., p. 43.
47 Ibid., p. 42.
48 Harman, *Sylvia Townsend Warner*, p. 141.

49 Samuel Hynes addresses the middle-class character of the generation he is studying in his preface, and refers throughout to the writers' negotiations with class. See Hynes, *The Auden Generation*.
50 Barbara Brothers, "Through the Pantry Window: Sylvia Townsend Warner and the Spanish Civil War," in Frieda S. Brown et al., eds., *Rewriting the Good Fight: Critical Essays on the Literature of the Spanish Civil War* (East Lansing: Michigan State University Press, 1989), p. 162.
51 Sachar, *Modern Jewish History*, p. 110.
52 Robert Caserio, "Celibate Sisters-in-Revolution: Towards Reading Sylvia Townsend Warner," in Joseph A. Boone and Michael Cadden, eds., *Engendering Men: The Question of Male Feminist Criticism* (New York: Routledge, 1990), p. 265.
53 Julie Abraham, *Are Girls Necessary? Lesbian Writing and Modern Histories* (New York: Routledge, 1996), p. 6.
54 Gay Wachman, *Lesbian Empire: Radical Crosswriting in the Twenties* (New Brunswick: Rutgers University Press, 2001), p. 179.
55 Ibid., p. 214.
56 In her diary Warner wrote: "My last day [before she was to leave for a visit to London], and our first. It was a bridal of earth and sky." See Claire Harman, ed., *The Diaries of Sylvia Townsend Warner* (London: Virago, 1995), p. 70. Harman describes a day when the two women affirmed their deep commitment to each other: "The next morning Valentine said that it had been a marriage-night . . . From then on they . . . kept 12 January as a wedding anniversary, the most solemn of the many festive days of their private year" (Harman, *Sylvia Townsend Warner*, p. 111).
57 Wendy Mulford, *This Narrow Place: Sylvia Townsend Warner and Valentine Ackland: Life, Letters and Politics, 1930–1951* (London: Pandora Press, 1988), p. 120.
58 Ibid., pp. 121–122.
59 Ibid., p. 120.
60 I refer here to Michael André Bernstein, *Foregone Conclusions: Against Apocalyptic History* (Berkeley: University of California Press, 1994).
61 It is not clear whether Caserio ultimately accepts it either; he ends his essay by complicating the argument I describe here, asserting that the novel's ending both endorses Marxism and criticizes it "for the way it cannot come to theoretical terms with the unclassed – especially with the unclassed who are women and who passionately love women" (Caserio, "Celibate Sisters," p. 269).
62 W. H. Auden, *New Year Letter* (London: Faber and Faber, 1941).
63 Ibid., p. 265.
64 Ibid., p. 268.
65 "Sylvia Townsend Warner in Conversation," 35.
66 Wachman, *Lesbian Empire*, p. 214.
67 Hackett, *Sapphic Primitivism*, p. 119.
68 This argument is partially informed by Wendy Mulford's discussion of Warner's use of the pogrom. Although Mulford does not elaborate on what

"instabilities" she means, she writes suggestively that Warner "also uses [the pogrom] implicitly to point up the curious alliance of motives and classes which heralded the 1848 Commune in Paris, and to suggest from the outset some of the inherent instabilities that would contribute to its eventual downfall" (Mulford, *This Narrow Place*, p. 113).
69 Harman, ed., *Diaries*, p. 95.
70 Hynes, *The Auden Generation*, p. 162.
71 Ibid., p. 12.
72 H. Gustav Klaus, "Socialist Fiction in the 1930s: Some Preliminary Observations," in John Lucas, ed., *The 1930s: A Challenge to Orthodoxy* (Sussex: Harvester Press, 1978), pp. 18–19. Warner and Ackland attended the Second International Congress of Writers in Defence of Culture in Spain in 1937 and the Third International in New York in 1938.
73 Susanna Pinney, ed., *I'll Stand By You: The Letters of Sylvia Townsend Warner and Valentine Ackland* (London: Pimlico, 1998), p. 123.

4 The race must go on: gender, Jewishness, and racial continuity in Barnes and Richardson

1 Ruether, *Faith and Fratricide*, p. 37.
2 Ibid.
3 Ibid., p. 95.
4 Daniel Boyarin, *Carnal Israel: Reading Sex in Talmudic Culture* (Berkeley: University of California Press, 1993), p. 2.
5 Ibid., p. 5.
6 Matthew Arnold, *Culture and Anarchy* (New Haven: Yale University Press, 1994), pp. 143, 147, 145.
7 "The Jew in Europe."
8 Gilman, *The Jew's Body*, p. 38.
9 "Socialism and Judaism," *Times Literary Supplement*, September 23, 1926.
10 Gilman, *Difference and Pathology*, pp. 154–159.
11 Joyce, *Ulysses*, p. 497.
12 Ibid., p. 277.
13 Ibid., p. 403.
14 Biberman, *Masculinity, Anti-Semitism*, pp. 1–3.
15 Ibid., pp. 32–33.
16 Judith Halberstam, *Skin Shows: Gothic Horror and the Technology of Monsters* (Durham: Duke University Press, 1995), pp. 88ff.
17 Carlston, *Thinking Fascism*, p. 52.
18 The alternating names of the men in this family – Guido, Felix, Guido – replicate the names of the Jewish men in *Ulysses* – Lipoti/Leopold, Rudolph, Leopold, Rudy. This compounds both novels' emphasis on masculine continuity.
19 Judith Lee, "*Nightwood*: 'The Sweetest Lie,' " in Broe, ed., *Silence and Power*, p. 210.

20 Jacqueline Rose, "Dorothy Richardson and the Jew," in Cheyette, ed., *Between "Race" and Culture*, p. 122.
21 Otto Weininger, *Sex and Character* (New York: G. P. Putnam's Sons, 1906), p. 329.
22 Ragussis, *Figures of Conversion*, pp. 38–39.
23 Sylvia Townsend Warner, *Lolly Willowes or The Loving Huntsman* (London: Virago Press, 1993), p. 150.
24 Garrity, *Step-Daughters*, p. 112.
25 Joanne Winning discusses Richardson's familiarity with and use of sexology in *The Pilgrimage of Dorothy Richardson* (Madison: University of Wisconsin Press, 2000), pp. 39–68.
26 Garrity, *Step-Daughters*, p. 121.
27 Judith Butler, *Gender Trouble* (New York: Routledge, 1999), p. 143.
28 Garrity, *Step-Daughters*, p. 124.
29 Winning, *Pilgrimage*, pp. 144–171.
30 Josef Kastein, *Jews in Germany*, trans. Dorothy Richardson (London: Cresset Press, 1934), pp. xix–xx.
31 Sander L. Gilman devotes a chapter, entitled "The Jewish Voice," to this phenomenon in *The Jew's Body* and outlines the theme more fully in *Jewish Self-Hatred: Anti-Semitism and the Hidden Language of the Jews* (1986).
32 I am afraid that Natascha Würzbach's response to Michael is not anomalous in its assumptions that Michael's Jewishness *is* in fact responsible for his chauvinism and that Miriam rejects him simply because of that chauvinism. She writes that Miriam's "initial fascination with his Russo-Jewish strangeness also gives way to the sober recognition that his chauvinistic claims on women are actually founded on this." See Natascha Wurzbach, "Subjective Presentation of Characters from the Perspective of Miriam's Experience in Dorothy Richardson's Novel *Pilgrimage*," in Reingard M. Nischik and Barbara Korte, eds., *Modes of Narrative: Approaches to American, Canadian and British Fiction* (Würzburg: Königshausen and Neumann, 1990), p. 287. Elisabeth Bronfen similarly endorses Miriam's prejudices. She quotes Miriam's statement that she "'can't bear Jewesses'" without commenting on its misogyny or antisemitism, instead linking it to the privileging of "groups over individuals, an integral feature of Michael's Zionist world [which] also involves commitment to a one-sided and exclusive vision of reality." See Elisabeth Bronfen, *Dorothy Richardson's Art of Memory: Space Identity, Text*, trans. Victoria Appelbe (Manchester: Manchester University Press, 1999), p. 138. And Deborah Parsons, in her otherwise interesting discussion of Richardson and Amy Levy, joins these scholars in uncritically replicating Miriam's views. Although she calls Miriam's feelings about Michael's "racial identity" "[p]artly xenophobia," she nevertheless states that "Judaism is a religion that prioritizes the male and, hence, Miriam rejects it, unable 'to breathe always the atmosphere of the Jewish religious and social oblivion of women' (224)." See Deborah L. Parsons, *Streetwalking the Metropolis: Women, the City, and Modernity* (New

York: Oxford University Press, 2000), pp. 107–108. Parsons thus distances herself from Miriam's racial distaste but validates her religious prejudice.
33 Louis Golding, "Lotus and Manna," *Fortnightly Review* (1927), 366.
34 "The Defence of the West," *Times Literary Supplement* September 8, 1927.

5 The "No time region": time, trauma and Jewishness in Barnes and Rhys

1 Joy Castro helpfully suggests that trauma studies might do much to explain Rhys's characters' repeated victimization. See Joy Castro, "Jean Rhys," *Review of Contemporary Fiction* 20.2 (Summer 2000), 8.
2 Cathy Caruth, ed., *Trauma: Explorations in Memory* (Baltimore: Johns Hopkins University Press, 1995), p. 153.
3 Bessel van der Kolk and Onno van der Hart, "The Intrusive Past: The Flexibility of Memory and the Engraving of Trauma," in ibid, p. 172.
4 Catherine Whitley, "Nations and the Night: Excremental History in James Joyce's *Finnegans Wake* and Djuna Barnes' *Nightwood*," *Journal of Modern Literature* 24.1 (2000), 85.
5 Francis Wyndham and Diana Melly, eds., *Jean Rhys: Letters 1931–1966* (New York: Penguin, 1985), p. 138.
6 Ibid., p. 24.
7 Lynne Layton, "Trauma, Gender Identity and Sexuality: Discourses of Fragmentation," *American Imago* 52.1 (1995), 109.
8 Philip Herring discusses the evidence for an incestuous relationship between Zadel Barnes and her granddaughter in *Djuna*, pp. 52–59. He unaccountably denies that this relationship would have been traumatic, hesitating even to call it incest, instead referring to it – if it existed outside of the sexually explicit letters that Zadel wrote to Djuna – as "a rather droll, untraumatic, innocent variety of entertainment" (ibid. p. 57). He also notes that Barnes told George Barker that her father raped her when she was a young girl, but told others that she was raped at sixteen by an older man with her father's consent (ibid. p. 53). In "My Art Belongs to Daddy," Mary Lynn Broe vacillates between describing the relationship with Zadel as a violation and, implausibly, as protection against patriarchal violations. See Broe, "My Art Belongs to Daddy: Incest as Exile, The Textual Economics of Hayford Hall," in Mary Lynn Broe and Angela Ingram, eds., *Women's Writing in Exile* (Chapel Hill: University of North Carolina Press, 1989). Bonnie Kime Scott quotes a letter from Emily Coleman about Wald Barnes trying "to make love to" Djuna (Scott, *Refiguring Modernism*, p. 17). See also Lynda Curry, "'Tom, Take Mercy': Djuna Barnes' Drafts of *The Antiphon*," in Broe, ed., *Silence and Power*, and Louise A. DeSalvo, "'To Make Her Mutton at Sixteen': Rape, Incest, and Child Abuse in *The Antiphon*," in ibid.
9 Rhys's biographer Carole Angier describes this incident in Angier, *Jean Rhys*, pp. 26–29. Rhys wrote about it in a notebook referred to as the *Black Exercise*

Book, part of the Jean Rhys Papers, held in the Special Collections of the McFarlin Library at the University of Tulsa.
10 Joyce, *Ulysses*, p. 28.
11 Stocking, "The Turn-of-the-Century Concept of Race," 14.
12 For a sociological discussion of the ways Jews were seen as liminal and indeterminate in modern European culture, see Bauman, *Modernity and the Holocaust*.
13 Meryl Altman, "A Book of Repulsive Jews? Rereading *Nightwood*," *Review of Contemporary Fiction* 13.3 (1993), 164.
14 Victoria L. Smith, "A Story Beside(s) Itself: The Language of Loss in Djuna Barnes's *Nightwood*," *PMLA* 114.2 (1999), 196.
15 Pellegrini discusses these incompatible accusations as well, citing conversations with Daniel Boyarin, in *Performance Anxieties*, p. 21.
16 For a sense of how much Barnes was influenced by Joyce, I am indebted to Annette Gilson (personal communication); Herring, *Djuna*; Marilyn Reizbaum, "A 'Modernism of Marginality': The Link between James Joyce and Djuna Barnes," in Bonnie Kime Scott, ed., *New Alliances in Joyce Studies* (Newark: University of Delaware Press, 1998); Bonnie Kime Scott, "'The Look in the Throat of a Stricken Animal': Joyce as Met by Djuna Barnes," *Joyce Studies Annual* 2 (1991); and Whitley, "Nations and the Night."
17 Reizbaum, *James Joyce's Judaic Other*, p. 106.
18 Gilman, *Difference and Pathology*, p. 157.
19 Trubowitz, "In Search of the Jew," 315–316.
20 Barnes wrote to Emily Coleman that she had "wedded Robin to Felix to rebut the received opinion that lesbians would be heterosexuals if they had men to love" (Herring, *Djuna*, p. 209). Coleman, though, found Felix's story a "distraction" and thought Barnes should cut it back (Trubowitz, "In Search of the Jew," 311).
21 Jane Marcus, "Laughing at Leviticus: *Nightwood* as Woman's Circus Epic," in Broe, ed., *Silence and Power*, p. 223. Marcus has done a great deal of important political work on a variety of women modernists. The argument of this article, though, rests on a few troubling assumptions. It engages in what Michael André Bernstein calls "backshadowing" in its use of the Holocaust to legitimate and purport to explain Barnes's linkage of Jews, blacks, homosexuals, and circus performers. It also labels "purity" as "Jewish" because of the proscriptions in Leviticus. Worse, Marcus goes so far as to link the purity of Leviticus with Hitler's brand, as if the types of purity Leviticus prescribes would inevitably lead to the idea of racial superiority and further, to mass murder.
22 Julie Abraham, "'Woman, Remember You': Djuna Barnes and History," in Broe, ed., *Silence and Power*, p. 256.
23 Ibid., p. 255.
24 Ibid., p. 258.
25 Mairéad Hanrahan, "Djuna Barnes's *Nightwood*: The Cruci-Fiction of the Jew," *Paragraph* 24.1 (2001), 32.

26 James B. Scott, *Djuna Barnes* (Boston: Twayne, 1976), p. 110.
27 Other critics discuss the association between Robin and Nora's grandmother. See, for example, Karen Kaivola, *All Contraries Confounded: The Lyrical Fiction of Virginia Woolf, Djuna Barnes, and Marguerite Duras* (Iowa City: University of Iowa Press, 1991), pp. 89ff, and Mary Lynn Broe, "My Art Belongs to Daddy," pp. 70ff.
28 Kaivola, *All Contraries Confounded*, p. 90.
29 Herring, *Djuna*, p. 269, and Broe, "My Art Belongs to Daddy," p. 43.
30 Broe, "My Art Belongs to Daddy," p. 43.
31 Herring, *Djuna*, p. 208.
32 Hanrahan, "Djuna Barnes's *Nightwood*," 32–33.
33 Kaivola discusses the power Barnes gives Robin by associating her with the "primitive." See Karen Kaivola, "The Beast Turning Human': Constructions of the Primitive in *Nightwood*," *Review of Contemporary Fiction* 13.3 (1993), 172–185.
34 Tyrus Miller, *Late Modernism: Politics, Fiction, and the Arts Between the World Wars* (Berkeley: University of California Press, 1999), p. 24.
35 Djuna Barnes, *The Antiphon: A Play* (Los Angeles: Green Integer, 2000), p. 119.
36 Ibid., p. 52, and DeSalvo, "'To Make Her Mutton at Sixteen,'" p. 304.
37 Felix has a monocle "which shone, a round blind eye in the sun" (*N* 8); and we learn that his blind eye kept him out of the army (*N* 9). Felix himself links Robin to blindness, as he seeks for a way to understand her chronic forgetting: "'She has the touch of the blind who, because they see more with their fingers, forget more in their minds'" (*N* 42).
38 In a recent Lacanian reading of *Good Morning, Midnight*, Anne B. Simpson analyzes the traumatic subtext of the novel in ways similar to my readings here and in my article "'New Words, New Everything': Trauma and Fragmentation in Jean Rhys," *Twentieth-Century Literature* 51.4 (2005), 437–466. Both Simpson and I see Sasha as traumatized, trapped in dynamics of dissociation, and experiencing the repetition of trauma in her encounter with the *commis voyageur*. Simpson, however, reads Sasha as having been molested by her father, a claim for which I see little evidence. See Anne B. Simpson, *Territories of the Psyche: The Fiction of Jean Rhys* (New York: Palgrave, 2005), pp. 87–110.
39 Van der Kolk and van der Hart write that "[p]reviously traumatized people are vulnerable to experience current stress as a return of the trauma." See Van der Kolk and van der Hart, "The Intrusive Past," p. 174.
40 Sasha continually uses images of drowning and being rescued. For example, she describes herself as "[s]aved, rescued, fished-up, half-drowned, out of the deep, dark river, dry clothes, hair shampooed and set. Nobody would know I had ever been in it. Except, of course, that there always remains something" (*GM, M* 10). Rhys never makes clear whether this imagery is metaphoric or literal. But if Sasha did actually attempt to drown herself in a river, it would explain her references to an "old devil" who asked her, when she returned to

London "that famous winter five years ago," "'Why didn't you drown yourself . . . in the Seine?'" (*GM, M* 41).
41 Judith Herman, *Trauma and Recovery* (New York: Basic Books, 1997), pp. 42–43.
42 Rhys, *Smile Please*, p. 95.
43 Coral Ann Howells also discusses Sasha's fragmentation within her relationship with René in *Jean Rhys* (New York: St. Martin's Press, 1991), pp. 94–103.
44 Some critics, surprisingly, read René as entirely sympathetic. Angier, for example, writes that "René was Sasha's last chance of love, and she threw it away. That is unambiguously bad and sad" (Angier, *Jean Rhys*, p. 382). Howells, too, fails to hold René responsible for his brutality when she describes Sasha "putting her arm up over her face to ward off the blows which she expects from René, though it is she who is doing the wounding." See Howells, *Jean Rhys* p. 96.
45 Cathy Caruth, *Unclaimed Experience: Trauma, Narrative, and History* (Baltimore: Johns Hopkins University Press, 1996), pp. 1–2.
46 Herman, *Trauma and Recovery*, p. 37.
47 Caruth, *Unclaimed Experience*, p. 4.
48 Angier notes the resemblance of this passage to the events Rhys remembered around this time (see her *Jean Rhys*, p. 29).
49 This episode is contained in the *Black Exercise Book*. I am indebted to Mary Lou Emery and Laurie Teal for their transcriptions, also held at the University of Tulsa. Insightful accounts of this narrative can be found in Leah Rosenberg, "'The Rope, Of Course, Being Covered with Flowers': Metropolitan Discourses and the Construction of Creole Identity in Jean Rhys's 'Black Exercise Book'," *Jean Rhys Review* 11.1 (1999) and Sue Thomas, "'Grilled Sole' and an Experience of 'Mental' Seduction," *The Worlding of Jean Rhys* (Westport, CT: Greenwood Press, 1999).
50 Jean Rhys, *Black Exercise Book*, Rhys papers, Special Collections, McFarlin Library, University of Tulsa, pp. 68, 70.
51 Ibid., pp. 63, 74, 57.
52 Ibid., p. 14.
53 Ibid., p. 52.
54 Ibid., p. 62.
55 "Cruelty submission utter submission that was the story – I see now that he might have made it alot worse this rare and curious story. – After all Id been whipped alot I was used to the idea –" (Rhys, *Black Exercise Book*, p. 64). Rhys also introduces the story of Mr. Howard with a description of her first time resisting her mother's beatings (ibid., Emery notes, p. 7). And finally, she writes about wanting to tell her father what was wrong, but being unable to explain that she was being whipped "too often and much too severely, teased too much, thrust back on myself and given a kink that would last for the rest of my life" (ibid., Emery notes, p. 8).

56 Scott, ed., *The Gender of Modernism*, p. 384.
57 Ibid.
58 In fact, as Carl is given in *Voyage in the Dark*, he would be unlikely to force Anna if she told him to stop; we are therefore left with no hints as to the identity of the man in Ethel's flat. But in the earliest draft, *Triple Sec*, the character of Carl was much more exploitative than he is in *Voyage*, being both physically violent and emotionally brutal. In neither version, however, are we given reason to think he might worry about his heart or use the French phrase.
59 Herman, *Trauma and Recovery*, p. 1. In an article on Barnes, Frances M. Doughty describes her in terms startlingly similar to Herman's description of this dynamic: "To tell, not to tell, to tell in disguise? A central tension in Barnes' work is her effort to transform, to tell her story while keeping it secret. It is as if Barnes were stuck, able neither to let go of the effort nor to complete it. The telling is hidden and encoded, buried under a heavy brocade of style, never finished, never forthright." See Frances. M. Doughty, "Gilt on Cardboard: Djuna Barnes as Illustrator of Her Life and Work," in Broe, ed., *Silence and Power*, p. 137.
60 Mary Lou Emery discusses this scene briefly, noting that the referent for "it" might be Rhys's own experience of molestation as a child but that within the text it "refers to something that cannot be said, that must be deferred by the pronoun." See Mary Lou Emery, *Jean Rhys at World's End* (Austin: University of Texas Press, 1990), p. 90.
61 Wyndham and Melly, eds., *Jean Rhys: Letters*, pp. 71, 70.
62 Another hint of sexual trauma in Anna's past is presented through her thoughts of a "house servant" whom she saw on "an old slave-list" at Constance Estate, where she grew up. First, she tells Walter about having seen the slave-list and thinks: "Maillotte Boyd, aged 18, mulatto, house servant. The sins of the fathers Hester said are visited upon the children unto the third and fourth generation – don't talk such nonsense to the child Father said – a myth don't get tangled up in myths he said to me" (*V* 53). Anna remembers this young woman again when she is lying in bed with Walter, thinking of being dead one day: "Lying down with your arms by your sides and your eyes shut. 'Walter, will you put the light out? I don't like it in my eyes.' *Maillotte Boyd, aged 18. Maillotte Boyd, aged 18 . . . But I like it like this. I don't want it any other way but this*" (*V* 56). Angier, too, notes the link between Rhys's own sexual trauma and Anna's thoughts of Maillotte Boyd (Angier, *Jean Rhys*, p. 29).
63 Caruth, *Unclaimed Experience*, p. 62.
64 Angier, *Jean Rhys*, p. 112, and Rhys, *Smile Please*, p. 119.
65 In "'New Words, New Everything,'" I present my hypothesis that Sasha's dream about a man with a wound in his forehead is actually about her dead baby.
66 But we can also read Carl's name as a trace of his violence in *Triple Sec* – the "red" may suggest metaphoric blood on his hands. In the discarded ending of *Voyage in the Dark*, Anna thinks about being "sick because his hands had

such a lot of hair on them" (Scott, ed., *Gender of Modernism*, p. 387), and Rhys gives no referent for the memory. But the earlier *Triple Sec* version emphasizes Carl Stahl's hairy, brutal hands. We might link the name Stahl, German for steel, with the menacing steel hands in the nightmare and final vision of a machine in *Good Morning, Midnight*.
67 Emery, *Jean Rhys at World's End*, pp. 158–159.
68 Carol Angier points out that Sasha continually fears being looked at, and is happiest when she is the one looking at Serge and René (Angier, *Jean Rhys*, pp. 380–381).
69 Ibid., p. 365.
70 Wyndham and Melly, eds., *Jean Rhys: Letters*, pp. 137–138. Wyndham and Melly give the letter in the original French. This translation was rendered for me by Elizabeth Yellen.
71 Mary Lou Emery describes *ekphrasis* as that which (like Sasha's dreams), expresses what the narrative cannot quite say in her "Refiguring the Postcolonial Imagination: Tropes of Visuality in Writing by Rhys, Kincaid, and Cliff," *Tulsa Studies in Women's Literature* 16.2 (1997), 264.
72 Ibid.
73 Thomas, *The Worlding of Jean Rhys*, p. 139.
74 Veronica Marie Gregg describes this ending as Sasha "accepting her responsibility to the reviled Other, getting rid of her scorn, of that which is considered repulsive and less than human." See Gregg, *Jean Rhys's Historical Imagination*, p. 157. This reading might be possible if *Good Morning, Midnight* were a different, more optimistic novel. Gregg's argument, however, is far more sensible than Peter Wolfe's claim that the novel ends "like a conventional love story." See Wolfe, *Jean Rhys* (Boston: Twayne, 1980), p. 135. Kate Holden offers the most credible of this group of interpretations. She treats the ending as defiance in the sense that Sasha chooses human connection over the fascist "machine" world of late 1930s Europe. See Holden, "Formations of Discipline and Manliness: Culture, Politics and 1930s Women's Writing," *Journal of Gender Studies* 8.2 (1999), 152. But I cannot quite associate the *commis voyageur* with humanity as opposed to fascist conformity. In spite of Sasha's reference to him as a "poor devil of a human being," the *commis* remains ghostlike, has "mean eyes," and reminds her of a priest, a role within a hierarchical system not totally unlike the machine Sasha imagines. Furthermore, he is a "nightmare" figure and so is the figure with the steel hand. In the context of fascism, I would be inclined to see Sasha's acceptance of the *commis* as akin to her sudden desire to go to the Exhibition, with its Nazi pavilion, after wanting to avoid it all week: as giving up her attempt to keep the particular nightmare of fascism at bay.
75 Rhys, *Black Exercise Book*, p. 52.
76 Ibid., p. 64.
77 Bonnie Kime Scott discusses the implications of the scaffold as a metaphor in the introduction to *Refiguring Modernism*.

6 Metatextual Jewishness: shaping feminist modernism

1 While Rhys's portrait of Serge is both sympathetic and metatextually positive, her life was not without its antisemitic moments. In 1950, when she had a conflict with a Jewish tenant, she referred to him – to the police – as a "dirty stinking Jew"; when she was turned out of the police station for being irrational and enraged, she "stood outside the station, shouting 'You can't get justice. This country is run by rotten stinking Jews.'" See Angier, *Jean Rhys*, p. 453.
2 Trubowitz, "In Search of the Jew," 319.
3 Ibid., 325.
4 Hanrahan, "Djuna Barnes's *Nightwood*," p. 33.
5 Andrea L. Harris, *Other Sexes: Rewriting Difference from Woolf to Winterson* (Albany: State University of New York Press, 2000), p. 66.
6 Cheryl J. Plumb, *Fancy's Craft: Art and Identity in the Early Works of Djuna Barnes* (Selinsgrove: Susquehanna University Press, 1986), p. 14.
7 Ibid.
8 Felber, "A Manifesto for Feminine Modernism," p. 25.
9 Radford, *Dorothy Richardson*, p. 18.
10 Ibid., pp. 18–19.
11 John Rosenberg, *Dorothy Richardson, The Genius They Forgot: A Critical Biography* (London: Duckworth, 1973), p. 25.
12 Gillian Hanscombe, "Introduction," *Pilgrimage*, 4 vols. (London: Virago, 1979), I, p. 7.
13 Rose, "Dorothy Richardson and the Jew," p. 126.
14 Esty, *A Shrinking Island*, p. 86.
15 She also writes to Margaret Llewelyn Davies, "We have got a letter from Prince Bismarck in our pockets, as people say we might be unpopular as we are Jews" (*Letters* V, 388).
16 Alex Zwerdling, *Virginia Woolf and the Real World* (Berkeley: University of California Press, 1986), pp. 273, 274.
17 Lee, *Virginia Woolf*, p. 668.
18 Whittier-Ferguson, *Framing Pieces*, p. 90.
19 In this sense *Three Guineas* served as both a concession to arguments that all English people must involve themselves in fighting fascism, and a rebuttal: an argument that the best way to resist fascism was to resist all "unreal loyalties," including support of military organizations.
20 Linett, "The Jew in the Bath," pp. 354–357.
21 Virginia Woolf, *Carlyle's House and Other Sketches*, ed. David Bradshaw (London: Hesperus Press, 2003), p. 14.
22 Ibid.
23 As I mention above, Barnes, too, connects the word "florid" to Jews in the image of the "flowers brought to a pitch of florid ecstasy" which she links to the "sum total of what is the Jew." And Warner uses the word in her

description of Minna as Sophia first studies her: "A discordant face . . . for the features with their Jewish baroque, the hooked nose, the crescent eyebrows and heavy eyelids, the large full-lipped mouth, are florid, or should be" (*SWS* 124).

24 Hermione Lee notes that "a reluctance to eat and severe weight loss was one of the most extreme of these physical manifestations" of her "madness" (Lee, *Virginia Woolf,* p. 171).

25 Amy Levy, *Reuben Sachs* (London: Persephone Books, 2001), p. 2.

26 Schröder, "Tales of Abjection," 303.

27 A scrap of a letter written in 1932 also brings together Jews, bath accoutrements, and obstacles to writing – but this time the Jew is Leonard himself. From a hotel in Greece, Woolf writes to John Lehmann, "The truth is its almost impossible to put pen to paper. Here am I balanced on the side of a hotel bed with Marjorie and Roger popping in and out to suggest excursions, and Leonard ranging the sponge bags with a view to packing" (*Letters* V, 62). With the detail of the sponge bags, Woolf connects Leonard both to bathrooms and to interruptions that prevent her from writing. While this may represent an innocent coincidence, it may also be a trace of the same anxiety about how her physical proximity to Leonard opposes her creative energies.

28 Anthony Julius, *T. S. Eliot, Anti-Semitism, and Literary Form* (New York: Cambridge University Press, 1995), p. 29.

29 On Pound, see Robert Casillo, *The Genealogy of Demons: Anti-Semitism, Fascism, and the Myths of Ezra Pound* (Evanston, IL: Northwestern University Press, 1988). On Lewis, see Andrea Freud Lowenstein, *Loathsome Jews and Engulfing Women: Metaphors of Projection in the Works of Wyndham Lewis, Charles Williams, and Graham Greene* (New York: New York University Press, 1993).

Works cited

"About Zionism: Speeches and Letters by Professor Albert Einstein." Book review. *Times Literary Supplement*, November 27, 1930, p. 1003.
Abraham, Julie. *Are Girls Necessary? Lesbian Writing and Modern Histories*. New York: Routledge, 1996.
"'Woman, Remember You': Djuna Barnes and History." *Silence and Power: A Reevaluation of Djuna Barnes*. Ed. Mary Lynn Broe. Carbondale: Southern Illinois University Press, 1991.
Altman, Meryl. "A Book of Repulsive Jews? Rereading *Nightwood*." *Review of Contemporary Fiction* 13.3 (1993), 160–171.
Angier, Carol. *Jean Rhys: Life and Work*. Boston: Little, Brown, & Co., 1990.
Arnold, Matthew. *Culture and Anarchy*. New Haven: Yale University Press, 1994.
Auden, W. H. *New Year Letter*. London: Faber and Faber, 1941.
Barnes, Djuna. *The Antiphon: A Play*. Los Angeles: Green Integer, 2000.
Ladies Almanack. Normal, IL: Dalkey Archive Press, 1992.
Nightwood. New York: New Directions, 1961.
Bauman, Zygmunt. "Allosemitism: Premodern, Modern, Postmodern." *Modernity, Culture and "the Jew"*. Ed. Bryan Cheyette and Laura Marcus. Stanford: Stanford University Press, 1998.
Modernity and the Holocaust. Ithaca: Cornell University Press, 1989.
Bell, Quentin. *Virginia Woolf: A Biography*. New York: Harcourt Brace Jovanovich, 1972.
Bernstein, Michael André. *Foregone Conclusions: Against Apocalyptic History*. Berkeley: University of California Press, 1994.
Biale, David, Michael Galchinsky, and Susan Heschel, eds. *Insider/Outsider: American Jews and Multiculturalism*. Berkeley: University of California Press, 1998.
Biberman, Matthew. *Masculinity, Anti-Semitism, and Early Modern English Literature*. Burlington, VT: Ashgate, 2004.
Bishop, Clair Huchet. *How Catholics Look at Jews: An Inquiry into Spanish, French, and Italian Teaching Materials*. New York: Paulist Press, 1974.
Bowen, Elizabeth. *The House in Paris*. 1935. New York: Anchor Books, 2002.
Boyarin, Daniel. *Carnal Israel: Reading Sex in Talmudic Culture*. Berkeley: University of California Press, 1993.

A Radical Jew: Paul and the Politics of Identity. Berkeley: University of California Press, 1994.

Unheroic Conduct: The Rise of Heterosexuality and the Invention of the Jewish Man. Berkeley: University of California Press, 1997.

Boyarin, Daniel and Jonathan Boyarin, eds. *Jews and Other Differences: The New Jewish Cultural Studies*. Minneapolis: University of Minnesota Press, 1997.

Boyarin, Jonathan. *Storm from Paradise: The Politics of Jewish Memory*. Minneapolis: University of Minnesota Press, 1992.

Bradshaw, David. "Hyams Place: The Years, the Jews and the British Union of Fascists." *Women Writers of the 1930s: Gender, Politics and History*. Ed. Maroula Joannou. Edinburgh: Edinburgh University Press, 1999.

Broe, Mary Lynn. "*My Art Belongs to Daddy*: Incest as Exile, The Textual Economics of Hayford Hall." *Women's Writing in Exile*. Ed. Mary Lynn Broe and Angela Ingram. Chapel Hill: University of North Carolina Press, 1989.

Broe, Mary Lynn, ed. *Silence and Power: A Reevaluation of Djuna Barnes*. Carbondale: Southern Illinois University Press, 1991.

Bronfen, Elisabeth. *Dorothy Richardson's Art of Memory: Space Identity, Text*. Trans. Victoria Appelbe. Manchester: Manchester University Press, 1999.

Brothers, Barbara. "Through the Pantry Window: Sylvia Townsend Warner and the Spanish Civil War." *Rewriting the Good Fight: Critical Essays on the Literature of the Spanish Civil War*. Ed. Frieda S. Brown et al. East Lansing: Michigan State University Press, 1989.

Brustein, William I. *Roots of Hate: Anti-Semitism in Europe before the Holocaust*. New York: Cambridge University Press, 2003.

Bunzl, Matti. "Jews, Queers, and Other Symptoms." *GLQ: A Journal of Lesbian and Gay Studies* 6.2 (2000).

Symptoms of Modernity: Jews and Queers in Late 20th-Century Vienna. Berkeley: University of California Press, 2004.

Burke, Carolyn. "'Accidental Aloofness': Barnes, Loy, and Modernism." *Silence and Power: A Reevaluation of Djuna Barnes*. Ed. Mary Lynn Broe. Carbondale: Southern Illinois University Press, 1991.

Butler, Judith. *Gender Trouble*. New York: Routledge, 1999.

Butts, Mary. *The Taverner Novels*. Kingston, NY: McPherson & Company, 1992.

Camarasana, Linda. Exhibitions and Repetitions: Jean Rhys's "Good Morning, Midnight" and the World of Paris, 1937. Unpublished manuscript, 2002.

Carlston, Erin. *Thinking Fascism: Sapphic Modernism and Fascist Modernity*. Stanford: Stanford University Press, 1998.

Caruth, Cathy, ed. *Trauma: Explorations in Memory*. Baltimore: Johns Hopkins University Press, 1995.

Unclaimed Experience: Trauma, Narrative, and History. Baltimore: Johns Hopkins University Press, 1996.

Caserio, Robert. "Celibate Sisters-in-Revolution: Towards Reading Sylvia Townsend Warner." *Engendering Men: The Question of Male Feminist Criticism*. Ed. Joseph A. Boone and Michael Cadden. New York: Routledge, 1990.

Casillo, Robert. *The Genealogy of Demons: Anti-Semitism, Fascism, and the Myths of Ezra Pound*. Evanston, IL: Northwestern University Press, 1988.

Castle, Terry. *The Apparitional Lesbian: Female Homosexuality and Modern Culture*. New York: Columbia University Press, 1993.

Castro, Joy. "Jean Rhys." *Review of Contemporary Fiction* 20.2 (Summer 2000), 8.

Cather, Willa. *The Professor's House*. New York: Random House, 1990.

"The Challenge to Jewry: A Paradox of Persecution." *Times Literary Supplement*, June 13, 1936.

Cheyette, Bryan. *Constructions of 'the Jew' in English Literature and Society: Racial Representations 1875–1945*. New York: Cambridge University Press, 1993.

Cheyette, Bryan, ed. *Between "Race and Culture": Representations of "the Jew" in English and American Literature*. Stanford: Stanford University Press, 1996.

Cheyette, Bryan and Laura Marcus, eds. *Modernity, Culture and "the Jew."* Stanford: Stanford University Press, 1998.

Christian Scholars Group. *A Sacred Obligation: Rethinking Christian Faith in Relation to Judaism and the Jewish People*. Boston, 2002. www.bc.edu/research/cjl/meta-elements/sites/partners/csg/Sacred_Obligation.html. Visited January 6, 2006.

Cohen, Stuart. *English Zionists and British Jews: The Communal Politics of Anglo-Jewry, 1895–1920*. Princeton: Princeton University Press, 1982.

"Complete Translation of *Mein Kampf*: Bases of Hitler's Power-Politics." Book review. *Times Literary Supplement*, March 25, 1939.

Comstock, Margaret. "The Loudspeaker and the Human Voice: Politics and the Form of *The Years*." *Bulletin of the New York Public Library* 80 (1977).

Curry, Lynda. "'Tom, Take Mercy': Djuna Barnes' Drafts of *The Antiphon*." *Silence and Power: A Reevaluation of Djuna Barnes*. Ed. Mary Lynn Broe. Carbondale: Southern Illinois University Press, 1991.

Curtis, Jan. "The Room and the Black Background: A Re-Interpretation of Jean Rhys's *Good Morning, Midnight*." *World Literature Written in English* 25.2 (1985).

Davison, Neil. *James Joyce, "Ulysses," and the Construction of Jewish Identity*. New York: Cambridge University Press, 1996.

"The Defence of the West." *Times Literary Supplement* September 8, 1927.

Delany, Paul. *Literature, Money and the Market: From Trollope to Amis*. New York: Palgrave, 2002.

DeSalvo, Louise A. "'To Make Her Mutton at Sixteen': Rape, Incest, and Child Abuse in *The Antiphon*." *Silence and Power: A Reevaluation of Djuna Barnes*. Ed. Mary Lynn Broe. Carbondale: Southern Illinois University Press, 1991.

Dettmar, Kevin and Stephen Myers Watt, eds. *Marketing Modernisms: Self-Promotion, Canonization, Rereading*. Ann Arbor: University of Michigan Press, 1996.

Doughty, Frances. M. "Gilt on Cardboard: Djuna Barnes as Illustrator of Her Life and Work." *Silence and Power: A Reevaluation of Djuna Barnes*. Ed. Mary Lynn Broe. Carbondale: Southern Illinois University Press, 1991.

Efron, John. *Defenders of the Race: Jewish Doctors and Race Science in Fin-de-Siècle Europe*. New Haven: Yale University Press, 1994.
Ellis, Geoffrey. "The Revolution of 1848–1849 in France." *The Revolutions in Europe, 1848–1849: From Reform to Reaction*. Ed. R. J. W. Evans and Hartmut Pogge von Strandmann. New York: Oxford University Press, 2000.
Ellmann, Maud. "The Imaginary Jew: T. S. Eliot and Ezra Pound." *Between "Race" and Culture: Representations of "the Jew" in English and American Literature*. Ed. Bryan Cheyette. Stanford: Stanford University Press, 1996.
Emery, Mary Lou. *Jean Rhys at World's End*. Austin: University of Texas Press, 1990.
   "Refiguring the Postcolonial Imagination: Tropes of Visuality in Writing by Rhys, Kincaid, and Cliff." *Tulsa Studies in Women's Literature* 16.2 (1997).
Endelman, Todd. "Comparative Perspectives on Modern Anti-Semitism in the West." *History and Hate: The Dimensions of Anti-Semitism*. Ed. David Berger. Philadelphia: Jewish Publication Society, 1986.
   The Jews of Britain, 1656 to 2000. Berkeley: University of California Press, 2002.
   Radical Assimilation in English Jewish History 1656–1945. Bloomington: Indiana University Press, 1990.
Esty, Jed. *A Shrinking Island: Modernism and National Culture in England*. Princeton: Princeton University Press, 2004.
Felber, Lynette. "A Manifesto for Feminine Modernism: Dorothy Richardson's *Pilgrimage*." *Rereading Modernism: New Directions in Feminist Criticism*. Ed. Lisa Rado. New York: Garland, 1994.
Feldman, David. *Englishmen and Jews: Social Relations and Political Culture, 1840–1914*. New Haven: Yale University Press, 1994.
Finkielkraut, Alain. *The Imaginary Jew*. Trans. Kevin O'Neill and David Suchoff. Lincoln, NE: Bison Books, 1997.
Finzi, Roberto. *Anti-Semitism: From Its European Roots to the Holocaust*. Trans. Maud Jackson. Moreton-in-Marsh: Windrush Press, 1999.
Freedman, Jonathan. *The Temple of Culture: Assimilation and Anti-Semitism in Literary Anglo-America*. New York: Oxford University Press, 2000.
Fromm, Gloria. *Dorothy Richardson: A Biography*. Urbana: University of Illinois Press, 1977.
Gallagher, Catherine. "George Eliot and *Daniel Deronda*: The Prostitute and the Jewish Question." *Sex, Politics, and Science in the Nineteenth-Century Novel*. Ed. Ruth Yeazell. Baltimore: Johns Hopkins University Press, 1986.
Garrity, Jane. *Step-Daughters of England: British Women Modernists and the National Imaginary*. New York: Manchester University Press, 2003.
Gay, Peter. *Freud, Jews, and Other Germans: Masters and Victims in Modernist Culture*. New York: Oxford University Press, 1978.
Gentry, Kenneth, Jr. *Reformed Anti-Semitism or Dispensational Absurdity? A Consideration of Dispensational Charges Related to the Role of Israel in the Plan of God*. www.cmfnow.com/articles/pt567.html. Visited May 24, 2004.

Gilman, Sander L. *Difference and Pathology: Stereotypes of Sexuality, Race, and Madness*. Ithaca: Cornell University Press, 1985.
Jewish Self-Hatred: Anti-Semitism and the Hidden Language of the Jews. Baltimore: Johns Hopkins University Press, 1986.
The Jew's Body. New York: Routledge, 1991.
Golding, Louis. "Lotus and Manna." *Fortnightly Review* (1927).
Greenberg, Judith. "'When Ears Are Deaf and the Heart Is Dry': Traumatic Reverberations in *Between the Acts*." *Woolf Studies Annual* 7 (2001).
Gregg, Veronica Marie. *Jean Rhys's Historical Imagination: Reading and Writing the Creole*. Chapel Hill: University of North Carolina Press, 1995.
Hackett, Robin. *Sapphic Primitivism: Productions of Race, Class, and Sexuality in Key Works of Modern Fiction*. New Brunswick: Rutgers University Press, 2004.
Halberstam, Judith. *Skin Shows: Gothic Horror and the Technology of Monsters*. Durham: Duke University Press, 1995.
Hanrahan, Mairéad. "Djuna Barnes's *Nightwood*: The Cruci-Fiction of the Jew." *Paragraph* 24.1 (2001).
Hanscombe, Gillian. *The Art of Life: Dorothy Richardson and the Development of Feminist Consciousness*. Boston: Peter Owen, 1982.
"Introduction." *Pilgrimage*. 4 Vols. Vol. I. London: Virago, 1979.
Harman, Claire. *Sylvia Townsend Warner: A Biography*. London: Minerva, 1989.
Harman, Claire, ed. *The Diaries of Sylvia Townsend Warner*. London: Virago, 1995.
Harris, Andrea L. *Other Sexes: Rewriting Difference from Woolf to Winterson*. Suny Series in Feminist Criticism and Theory. Ed. Michelle A. Masse. Albany: State University of New York Press, 2000.
Hasan-Rokem, Galit and Alan Dundes, eds. *The Wandering Jew: Essays in the Interpretation of a Christian Legend*. Bloomington: Indiana University Press, 1986.
Hemingway, Ernest. *The Sun Also Rises*. New York: Scribner, 1970.
Herman, Judith. *Trauma and Recovery*. New York: Basic Books, 1997.
Herring, Phillip. *Djuna: The Life and Work of Djuna Barnes*. New York: Viking, 1995.
Hite, Molly. *The Other Side of the Story: Structures and Strategies of Contemporary Feminist Narrative*. Ithaca: Cornell University Press, 1989.
Holden, Kate. "Formations of Discipline and Manliness: Culture, Politics and 1930s Women's Writing." *Journal of Gender Studies* 8.2 (1999).
Howells, Coral Ann. *Jean Rhys*. New York: St. Martin's Press, 1991.
Hynes, Samuel. *The Auden Generation*. New York: Viking, 1977.
"In Defence of the Jews." Book review. *Times Literary Supplement*, March 25, 1939.
"The Jew in Europe." Book review. *Times Literary Supplement*, November 17, 1927.
"Jews in Babylonia." Book review. *Times Literary Supplement*, July 20, 1933.
"The Jews and Minority Rights." Book review. *Times Literary Supplement*, September 14, 1933.

Joyce, James. *Ulysses.* Ed. Hans Walter Gabler. New York: Random House, 1986.
Julius, Anthony. *T. S. Eliot, Anti-Semitism, and Literary Form: with a preface and responce to the critics.* New York: Cambridge University Press, 1995. London: Thames and Hudson, 2003.
Kadish, Sharman. *Bolsheviks and British Jews: The Anglo-Jewish Community, Britain, and the Russian Revolution.* London: Frank Cass Press, 1992.
Kaivola, Karen. *All Contraries Confounded: The Lyrical Fiction of Virginia Woolf, Djuna Barnes, and Marguerite Duras.* Iowa City: University of Iowa Press, 1991.
"The 'Beast Turning Human': Constructions of the Primitive in *Nightwood*." *Review of Contemporary Fiction* 13.3 (1993).
Kastein, Josef. *Jews in Germany.* Trans. Dorothy Richardson. London: Cresset Press, 1934.
Keating, Joseph. *Christianity.* 2003. Online edition of 1908 Catholic Encyclopedia. www.newadvent.org/cathen/03712a.html. Visited May 25, 2004.
Klaus, H. Gustav. "Socialist Fiction in the 1930s: Some Preliminary Observations." *The 1930s: A Challenge to Orthodoxy.* Ed. John Lucas. Sussex: Harvester Press, 1978.
Kreeft, Peter. *Comparing Christianity and Judaism.* May 1987. National Catholic Register. www.catholiceducation.org/articles/apologetics/apo007.html. Visited May 25, 2004.
Latham, Sean. *Am I a Snob? Modernism and the Novel.* Ithaca: Cornell University Press, 2003.
Laurence, Patricia. "The Facts and Fugue of War: From *Three Guineas* to *Between the Acts*." *Virginia Woolf and War: Fiction, Reality, and Myth.* Ed. Mark Hussey. Syracuse: Syracuse University Press, 1991.
Lawrence D. H. *Women in Love.* New York: The Modern Library, 2002.
Layton, Lynne. "Trauma, Gender Identity and Sexuality: Discourses of Fragmentation." *American Imago* 52.1 (1995).
Leaska, Mitchell A., ed. *Pointz Hall: The Earlier and Later Typescripts of "Between the Acts."* New York: New York University Press, 1983.
Lee, Hermione. *Virginia Woolf.* New York: Vintage Books, 1999.
Lee, Judith. "*Nightwood*: 'The Sweetest Lie.'" *Silence and Power: A Reevaluation of Djuna Barnes.* Ed. Mary Lynn Broe. Carbondale: Southern Illinois University Press, 1991.
Levine, Gary Martin. *The Merchant of Modernism: The Economic Jew in Anglo-American Literature, 1864–1939.* New York: Routledge, 2003.
Levy, Amy. *Reuben Sachs.* 1888. London: Persephone Books, 2001.
Lewis, Wyndham. *Hitler.* London: Chatto & Windus, 1931.
Time and Western Man. New York: Harcourt, Brace and Co., 1928.
Linett, Maren. "The Jew in the Bath: Imperiled Imagination in Woolf's *The Years*." *Modern Fiction Studies* 42.2 (2002).
"'New Words, New Everything': Trauma and Fragmentation in Jean Rhys." *Twentieth-Century Literature* 51.4 (2005).

Lowenstein, Andrea Freud. *Loathsome Jews and Engulfing Women: Metaphors of Projection in the Works of Wyndham Lewis, Charles Williams, and Graham Greene*. New York: New York University Press, 1993.

Marcus, Jane. "Laughing at Leviticus: *Nightwood* as Woman's Circus Epic." *Silence and Power: A Reevaluation of Djuna Barnes*. Ed. Mary Lynn Broe. Carbondale: Southern Illinois University Press, 1991.

——— *Virginia Woolf and the Languages of Patriarchy*. Bloomington: University of Indiana Press, 1987.

Michaels, Walter Benn. *Our America: Nativism, Modernism, and Pluralism*. Durham: Duke University Press, 1995.

Miller, Tyrus. *Late Modernism: Politics, Fiction, and the Arts Between the World Wars*. Berkeley: University of California Press, 1999.

Montefiore, Janet. "Listening to Minna: Realism, Feminism, and the Politics of Reading." *Paragraph* 14.1 (November 1991).

Morrison, Mark. *The Public Face of Modernism: Little Magazines, Audiences, and Reception, 1905–1920*. Madison: University of Wisconsin Press, 2001.

Mosse, George. *Nationalism and Sexuality: Middle-Class Morality and Sexual Norms in Modern Europe*. Madison: University of Wisonsin Press, 1985.

Mulford, Wendy. *This Narrow Place: Sylvia Townsend Warner and Valentine Ackland: Life, Letters and Politics, 1930–1951*. London: Pandora Press, 1988.

Parsons, Deborah L. *Streetwalking the Metropolis: Women, the City, and Modernity*. New York: Oxford University Press, 2000.

Pawlowski, Merry M. "Toward a Feminist Theory of the State: Virginia Woolf and Wyndham Lewis on Art, Gender, and Politics." *Virginia Woolf and Fascism: Resisting the Dictators' Seduction*. Ed. Merry M. Pawlowski. New York: Palgrave, 2001.

Pellegrini, Ann. *Performance Anxieties: Staging Psychoanalysis, Staging Race*. New York: Routledge, 1996.

Pinney, Susanna, ed. *I'll Stand by You: The Letters of Sylvia Townsend Warner and Valentine Ackland*. London: Pimlico, 1998.

Plumb, Cheryl J. *Fancy's Craft: Art and Identity in the Early Works of Djuna Barnes*. Selinsgrove: Susquehanna University Press, 1986.

Pound, Ezra. *The Cantos*. New York: New Directions, 1986.

Pridmore-Brown, Michelle. "1939–1940: Of Virginia Woolf, Gramophones, and Fascism." *PMLA* 113.3 (1998).

Radford, Jean. *Dorothy Richardson*. London: Harvester Wheatsheaf, 1991.

——— "The Woman and the Jew: Sex and Modernity." *Modernity, Culture and "the Jew."* Ed. Bryan Cheyette and Laura Marcus. Stanford: Stanford University Press, 1998.

Radin, Grace. *Virginia Woolf's "The Years": The Evolution of a Novel*. Knoxville: University of Tennessee Press, 1981.

Ragussis, Michael. *Figures of Conversion: "The Jewish Question" and English National Identity*. Durham: Duke University Press, 1995.

Rainey, Lawrence. *Institutions of Modernism: Literary Elites and Public Culture*. New Haven: Yale University Press, 1999.

Raitt, Suzanne. *Vita and Virginia: The Work and Friendship of Vita Sackville-West and Virginia Woolf.* New York: Oxford University Press, 1993.
Rattenbury, Arnold. "Plain Heart, Light Tether." *PN Review 23* 8.3 (1978).
Reizbaum, Marilyn. "A 'Modernism of Marginality': The Link between James Joyce and Djuna Barnes." *New Alliances in Joyce Studies.* Ed. Bonnie Kime Scott. Newark: University of Delaware Press, 1998.
James Joyce's Judaic Other. Stanford: Stanford University Press, 1999.
Rhys, Jean. *Black Exercise Book.* Rhys Papers, Special Collections, McFarlin Library, University of Tulsa.
Good Morning, Midnight. New York: W. W. Norton, 2000.
Jean Rhys: Letters 1931–1966. Ed. Francis Wyndham and Diana Melly. New York: Penguin, 1985.
Smile Please: An Unfinished Autobiography. New York: Harper & Row, 1979.
Voyage in the Dark. New York: W. W. Norton, 1982.
Wide Sargasso Sea. New York: W. W. Norton, 1966.
Richardson, Dorothy. *Pilgrimage.* 4 vols. J. M. Dent & Sons, 1967.
Windows on Modernism: Selected Letters of Dorothy Richardson. Ed. Gloria Fromm. Athens: University of Georgia Press, 1995.
Robertson, Ritchie. "Historicizing Weininger: The Nineteenth-Century German Image of the Feminized Jew." *Modernity, Culture And "The Jew".* Ed. Bryan Cheyette and Laura Marcus. Stanford: Stanford University Press, 1998.
Rose, Jacqueline. "Dorothy Richardson and the Jew." *Between "Race" and Culture.* Ed. Bryan Cheyette. Stanford: Stanford University Press, 1996.
Rosenberg, John. *Dorothy Richardson, The Genius They Forgot: A Critical Biography.* London: Duckworth, 1973.
Rosenberg, Leah. "'The Rope, Of Course, Being Covered With Flowers': Metropolitan Discourses and the Construction of Creole Identity in Jean Rhys's 'Black Exercise Book.'" *Jean Rhys Review* 11.1 (1999).
Rosenfeld, Natania. "Monstrous Conjugations: Images of Dictatorship in the Anti-Fascist Writings of Virginia and Leonard Woolf." *Virginia Woolf and Fascism: Resisting the Dictators' Seduction.* Ed. Merry M. Pawlowski. New York: Palgrave, 2001.
Ruether, Rosemary Radford. *Faith and Fratricide: The Theological Roots of Anti-Semitism.* New York: Seabury Press, 1974.
Sachar, Howard. *The Course of Modern Jewish History.* New York: Random House, 1990.
Samuel, Maurice. *Blood Accusation: The Strange History of the Beiliss Case.* New York: Alfred A. Knopf, 1966.
Samuels, Diane. *Kindertransport.* New York: Theatre Communications Group, 2000.
Schröder, Leena Kore. "Tales of Abjection and Miscegenation: Virginia Woolf's and Leonard Woolf's 'Jewish' Stories." *Twentieth Century Literature* 49.3 (2003).
Scott, Bonnie Kime. *Refiguring Modernism.* 2 vols. *Volume I: The Women of 1928.* Bloomington: Indiana University Press, 1995.

"'The Look in the Throat of a Stricken Animal': Joyce as Met by Djuna Barnes." *Joyce Studies Annual* 2 (1991).
Scott, Bonnie Kime, ed. *The Gender of Modernism*. Bloomington: Indiana University Press, 1990.
Scott, James B. *Djuna Barnes*. Boston: Twayne, 1976.
Sedgwick, Eve Kosofsky. *Between Men: English Literature and Male Homosocial Desire*. New York: Columbia University Press, 1985.
  Epistemology of the Closet. Berkeley: University of California Press, 1990.
Sharf, Andrew. *The British Press and Jews Under Nazi Rule*. New York: Oxford University Press, 1964.
Simpson, Anne B. *Territories of the Psyche: The Fiction of Jean Rhys*. New York: Palgrave, 2005.
Smith, Patricia Juliana. *Lesbian Panic: Homoeroticism in Modern British Women's Fiction*. New York: Columbia University Press, 1997.
Smith, Victoria L. "A Story Beside(s) Itself: The Language of Loss in Djuna Barnes's *Nightwood*." *PMLA* 114.2 (1999).
"Socialism and Judaism." *Times Literary Supplement*, September 23, 1926, p. 622.
Stec, Loretta. "Dystopian Modernism vs Utopian Feminism: Burdekin, Woolf, and West Respond to the Rise of Fascism." *Virginia Woolf and Fascism: Resisting the Dictators' Seduction*. Ed. Merry M. Pawlowski. New York: Palgrave, 2001.
Stocking, George. "The Turn-of-the-Century Concept of Race." *Modernism/Modernity* 1.1 (January 1994).
Surette, Leon. *Pound in Purgatory: From Economic Radicalism to Anti-Semitism*. Champaign: University of Illinois Press, 1999.
"Sylvia Townsend Warner in Conversation. An Interview with Warner Conducted by Val Warner and Michael Schmidt in 1975." *PN Review* 23 8.3 (1978).
Thomas, Sue. *The Worlding of Jean Rhys*. Westport, CT: Greenwood Press, 1999.
Tratner, Michael. *Modernism and Mass Politics: Joyce, Woolf, Eliot*. Stanford: Stanford University Press, 1995.
Trubowitz, Lara. "In Search of the Jew in Djuna Barnes's *Nightwood*: Jewishness, Antisemitism, Structure, and Style." *Modern Fiction Studies* 51.2 (2005).
Turner, Catherine. *Marketing Modernism Between the Two World Wars*. Amherst: University of Massachusetts Press, 2003.
Van der Kolk, Bessel and Onno van der Hart. "The Intrusive Past: The Flexibility of Memory and the Engraving of Trauma." *Trauma: Explorations in Memory*. Ed. Cathy Caruth. Baltimore: Johns Hopkins University Press, 1995.
Vaughan, Catherine. "The Money Pit: Filling the Blank Spaces in Jean Rhys's *Good Morning, Midnight*." Unpublished manuscript, 2003.
Vincent, John. *Disraeli*. New York: Oxford University Press, 1990.
Wachman, Gay. *Lesbian Empire: Radical Crosswriting in the Twenties*. New Brunswick: Rutgers University Press, 2001.

Walkowitz, Judith. *City of Dreadful Delight: Narratives of Sexual Danger in Late Victorian London.* Chicago: University of Chicago Press, 1992.
Warner, Sylvia Townsend. *Lolly Willowes or The Loving Huntsman.* London: Virago Press, 1993.
Summer Will Show. London: Virago Press, 1994.
Weininger, Otto. *Sex and Character.* New York: G. P. Putnam's Sons, 1906.
Whitley, Catherine. "Nations and the Night: Excremental History in James Joyce's *Finnegans Wake* and Djuna Barnes' *Nightwood*." *Journal of Modern Literature* 24.1 (2000).
Whittier-Ferguson, John. *Framing Pieces: Designs of the Gloss in Joyce, Woolf, and Pound.* New York: Oxford University Press, 1996.
Williams, Raymond. *Marxism and Literature.* New York: Oxford University Press, 1977.
Wilson, Jean Moorcroft. *Virginia Woolf and Anti-Semitism.* London: Cecil Woolf, 1995.
Winning, Joanne. *The Pilgrimage of Dorothy Richardson.* Madison: University of Wisconsin Press, 2000.
Wolfe, Peter. *Jean Rhys.* Boston: Twayne, 1980.
Woolf, Virginia. *A Room of One's Own.* New York: Harcourt Brace Jovanovich, 1981.
Between the Acts. New York: Harcourt Brace & Company, 1969.
Between the Acts. Ed. Susan Dick and Mary S. Millar. London: Blackwell, 2002.
Carlyle's House and Other Sketches. Ed. David Bradshaw. London: Hesperus Press, 2003.
The Common Reader: First Series. London: The Hogarth Press, 1951.
The Diary of Virginia Woolf. Ed. Anne Olivier Bell. 5 vols. New York: Harcourt Brace Jovanovich, 1977.
The Essays of Virginia Woolf. Ed. Andrew McNeillie. 3 vols. San Diego: Harcourt Brace Jovanovich, 1988.
"The Leaning Tower." *The Moment and Other Essays.* New York: Harcourt, Brace, Jovanovich, 1948.
The Letters of Virginia Woolf. Ed. Nigel Nicolson and Joanne Trautmann. 7 vols. New York: Harcourt Brace Jovanovich, 1978.
Moments of Being. New York: Harcourt Brace & Company, 1985.
Mrs. Dalloway. New York: Harcourt Brace & Company, 1953.
The Pargiters. The Virginia Woolf Manuscripts from the Henry W. and Albert A. Berg Collections of the New York Public Library, Woodbridge, CT, 1993.
Three Guineas. New York: Harcourt Brace & Company, 1966.
To the Lighthouse. New York: Harcourt Brace & Company, 1989.
The Waves. New York: Harcourt Brace Jovanovich, 1959.
Women and Writing. Ed. Michele Barrett. New York: Harcourt Brace Jovanovich, 1979.
The Years. New York: Harcourt Brace & Company, 1965.

Wurzbach, Natascha. "Subjective Presentation of Characters from the Perspective of Miriam's Experience in Dorothy Richardson's Novel *Pilgrimage.*" *Modes of Narrative: Approaches to American, Canadian and British Fiction.* Ed. Reingard M. Nischik and Barbara Korte. Würzburg: Königshausen and Neumann, 1990.

Žižek, Slavoj. "'I Hear You with My Eyes'; or, The Invisible Master." *Gaze and Voice as Love Objects.* Ed. Renata Salecl and Slavoj Žižek. Durham: Duke University Press, 1996.

Zwerdling, Alex. *Virginia Woolf and the Real World.* Berkeley: University of California Press, 1986.

Index

Abraham, Julie 102, 103, 145
Aliens Act, 1905 23
allosemitism 3
Altman, Meryl 143
antisemitism, feminist 74–75, 122–123
Arnold, Matthew 112
Auden, W. H. 99, 104, 109

Barnes, Djuna 11, 16, 20, 173, 174–176, 190
   The Antiphon 152
   Ladies Almanack 20
   Nightwood 30, 116–119, 124–125, 126, 128–129, 132, 139, 140–153, 172, 174–176
   personal history 141–142
Bauman, Zygmunt 3, 80
Beiliss, Mendel (trial) 23–24
Bell, Quentin 11, 52, 200
Bennett, Arnold 60, 61
Biberman, Matthew 7, 115
Bible, Christian
   Corinthians 78
   Galatians 78, *see also* Paul of Tarsus
   Matthew 62–63
   Romans 70, 78 *see also* Paul of Tarsus
Bolshevism 24–25
Bowen, Elizabeth 6–7
Boyarin, Daniel 7, 74, 78, 112
Boyarin, Jonathan 6
Bradshaw, David 53–55
British Union of Fascists 27, 54, 100
Broe, Mary Lynn 148, 208
Bronfen, Elisabeth 207
Brustein, William 32, 97
Bryher 133, 134
Bunyan, John 61, 200
Bunzl, Matti 28
Butler, Judith 130
Butts, Mary 82–83, 91, 195

Camarasana, Linda 45
Carlston, Erin 10, 117–118
Caruth, Cathy 140, 156–157, 161
Caserio, Robert 102, 104–105, 205
Castle, Terry 38, 197
Cather, Willa 90, 204
Catholic Encyclopedia 64
Cheyette, Bryan 9
Christian anti-Judaism 5–6, 80–81, 111–112 *see also* supersessionism
Comstock, Margaret 53
Conscription Act 24

Dick, Susan 84, 91
Disraeli, Benjamin 23
Doughty, Frances M. 212
Dreyfus Affair 23
DuMaurier, George 196–197

ekphrasis 168–169
Eliot, T. S. 4, 9, 153, 189
Ellis, Geoffrey 99
Emery, Mary Lou 168
Endelman, Todd 81
Esty, Jed 87, 180

Finkielkraut, Alain 2
Fitzgerald, F. Scott 81–82
Freedman, Jonathan 35–36, 59
Freud, Sigmund 7, 80, 95, 151
Fromm, Gloria 77

Gallagher, Catherine 35–36
Galsworthy, John 61,
Garrity, Jane 125–126, 130, 201
Gay, Peter 80
Gilman, Sander L. 7, 64, 113, 114, 144
Gordon, Mary 22
Grad, Benjamin 8, 78

Greenberg, Judith 94
Gregg, Veronica Marie 197, 213

Hackett, Robin 107, 196–197
Halberstam, Judith 115
Hall, Radclyffe 102
Hanrahan, Mairéad 146, 150, 174–175
Harman, Claire 99, 101, 205
Harris, Andrea L. 175
Hemingway, Ernest 10, 22, 33, 35, 81–82, 114, 189
Herman, Judith 154, 155, 157
Herring, Phillip 148, 149, 208
Hobson, J. A. 32,
Holden, Kate 213
Hynes, Samuel 109, 196, 205

incest 144, 145, 147–153

James, Henry 9
Jews
    alienation of 22–23
    metafictional uses of 31
    as mirrors 22
    stereotypes
        ancientness 5–6, 62, 75–76, 136–138
        artistry 33–34, 37, 42
        femininity (in men) 6–9, 30, 115, 124–139
        gluttony 185
        greed 5, 29, 32–59, 92–93
        literary outsiders 21–22, 134–135
        modernity 6, 29–30, 80–110
        obsession with procreation 111–139, 115–116,
        ostentation/vulgarity 1, 90–91, 184–185
        parvenu 90
        timelessness 30, 142–172
        vitality 185–186
Joyce, James 4–5, 9, 10, 22, 35, 60, 61
    A Portrait of the Artist as a Young Man 16
    Ulysses 8, 24, 33–34, 35, 81, 114–115, 116, 142, 171, 189, 206
Julius, Anthony 189

Kadish, Sharman 24–25, 83,
Kaivola, Karen 148
Kastein, Josef 134–135
Kautsky, Karl 113–114
Klaus, H. Gustav 109
Koteliansky, S. S. 135

Latham, Sean 59
Laurence, Patricia 96–97
Lawrence, D. H. 10, 33, 34, 35, 83, 189

Layton, Lynne 141
Lee, Hermione 51–52, 181
Lee, Judith 119
lesbian panic 28, 102, 131, 132
Levine, Gary Martin 196
Levy, Amy 186
Lewis, Wyndham 4–5, 6, 26, 189

MacCarthy, Desmond 21
Marcus, Jane 52–53, 145, 209
Michaels, Walter Benn 81–82
Millar, Mary 84, 91
Miller, Tyrus 151
Morrison, Mark 34, 195
Mosse, George 6
Mulford, Wendy 103–104, 205–206

Nazism 26, 27, 65, 66, 67, 79, 86, 94, 109, 133–134, 180

Parsons, Deborah 207–208
Paul of Tarsus 62, 70, 73, 74, 78, 112, 116, 120
Pawlowski, Merry 202
Pellegrini, Ann 8, 200
pilgrimage narratives 200–201
Plumb, Cheryl J. 175–176
Pound, Ezra 4, 9, 189
Pridmore-Brown, Michelle 86, 87, 96
Protocols of the Elders of Zion 24, 81, 97
Proust, Marcel 61
Publishing
    mass market 34
    women's 10–16, 35–36, 58

race science 6, 23, 64–65, 113–114, 136, 142, 144, 165
Radford, Jean 71, 72, 77, 177, 200
Radin, Grace 197–198
Ragussis, Michael 122, 195
Rattenbury, Arnold 98
Reizbaum, Marilyn 81, 144
Revolutions of 1848 98–100, 109
Rhys, Jean 11, 12–13, 17–18, 141, 142, 153–172, 173–174, 214
    After Leaving Mr. Mackenzie 168
    Black Exercise Book 171, 211
    Good Morning, Midnight 22, 29, 30, 36, 43–49, 141, 154, 155–158, 161–162, 164–172, 173–174
    personal history 8, 158, 161, 167–168, 171, 214
    Smile Please 12–13, 22, 155
    Triple Sec 212–213
    Voyage in the Dark 17–18, 30, 141, 154, 159–161, 162–164
    Wide Sargasso Sea 18

Index

Richardson, Dorothy 8, 14–16, 19–20, 29, 133–139, 173, 178
   Clear Horizon 123, 133–139
   Dawn's Left Hand 129–130, 176
   Deadlock 74, 94, 119–122, 123, 179
   Dimple Hill 70–79, 123, 179
   Interim 178
   March Moonlight 70–79, 123–124, 130–132, 177
   Pilgrimage, general discussion 29, 30, 119–124, 125–126, 126–132, 173, 176–179
   Pointed Roofs 14, 133
   Revolving Lights 74, 127–128
   The Trap 127
Robertson, Ritchie 7
Rose, Jacqueline 120, 179
Rosenfeld, Natania 95
Ruether, Rosemary 63, 111–112
Russian Revolution 24

Sachar, Howard 100
Samuels, Diane 62
Sandauer, Artur 3
Schröder, Leena Kore 57–58, 186–187
Scott, Bonnie Kime 10
Scott, James B. 147
Segal, Simon 8, 167–168
Shakespeare, William
   Shylock (*Merchant of Venice*) 32, 115
Sharf, Andrew 27, 94
Simpson, Anne B. 210
Smith, Victoria L. 144
Stoker, Bram 115
Supersessionism 29, 60–79, 113
   disavowed by Church 62
   see also Christian anti-Judaism

Thomas, Sue 169
Times Literary Supplement 25–26, 113, 136
trauma 30, 140–172 *see also* incest
Trubowitz, Lara 144–145, 174

Van der Hart, Onno 140
Van der Kolk, Bessel 140
Vaughan, Catherine 44, 45, 46

Wachman, Gay 102, 103, 107
Walkowitz, Judith 6
Warner, Sylvia Townsend 11, 13–14, 18–19, 173–174
   Communism 36, 42, 97–98, 99, 102, 104–109, 109–110,
   Lolly Willowes 123
   Summer Will Show 8, 29, 30, 36–43, 83, 97–110, 173–174,
Weininger, Otto 6, 7, 120, 144
Wells, H. G. 19, 61, 133,
Wharton, Edith 5, 32, 90, 114
Whittier-Ferguson, John 192
Williams, Raymond 65
Wilson, Jean Moorcroft 198,
Winning, Joanne 132
women modernists, political views 9–10, 114
Woolf, Virginia 11, 29, 173, 179–188
   "A Sketch of the Past" 62
   "The Duchess and the Jeweller" 54, 57
   "Jews" 184
   Between the Acts 5, 29, 83–97, 110, 117
   "Women and Fiction" 17
   letters and diaries 183–184, 184–188
   marriage 8, 50–52, 180–181, 182–183
   "Modern Fiction" 61
   "Mr. Bennett and Mrs. Brown" 17, 61
   Mrs. Dalloway 68, 88
   "Professions for Women" 17
   A Room of One's Own 11–12, 17, 18, 22, 59, 65–66, 74–75, 85, 96
   Three Guineas 22, 29, 36, 52–53, 55, 57, 58, 65–70, 86, 108, 180
   To the Lighthouse 68, 182
   The Waves 182, 203,
   "The Leaning Tower" 99
   The Years 1, 29, 36, 49–59, 67, 68–69, 180–183
Würzbach, Natascha 207

xenophobia 4

Zionism 25
Žižek, Slavoj 3–4
Zwerdling, Alex 181